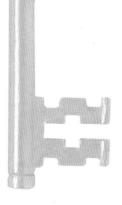

Key Ingredients

OPENING DOORS TO HOURS OF HAPPINESS

Le Bonheur Club, Inc.
Memphis, Tennessee

Key Ingredients

OPENING DOORS TO HOURS OF HAPPINESS

The Le Bonheur Club is an organization of women engaged in the promotion of volunteer service and charitable work for the operation of the Le Bonheur Children's Medical Center in Memphis, Tennessee. This book is dedicated to all the patients, physicians and associates of Le Bonheur. Profits realized from the sale of *Key Ingredients* will be used to further support the Le Bonheur Children's Medical Center.

Coordinating Board

Chairman
Arlene Wade

Vice Chairman
Elizabeth Mednikow

Recipe Collection and Index Coordinator
Debbi Freeburg

Chapter Coordinator
Kim Pitts

Testing and Tasting Coordinators
Judy Burkett
Linda Mynatt

Our heartfelt thanks and love must go to the wonderful families of
the above individuals for all of their endless sacrifices and constant support
and encouragement for this seemingly neverending labor of love.

Carmen Bond
Creative Director

"Woody" Woodliff Photography, Inc.
Photography

Jeff Lehr
Food Stylist

Cookbook Committee

Chapter Chairs

Appetizers/Game
Jamie McDonnell

Poultry
Nancy Barnett

Brunch/Breads/Beverages/Salads/Soups
Quinn Scott

Pasta/Vegetables
Paula Brown

Meats
Melinda Russell/Anne Krieg

Desserts
Martha Podesta

Seafood
Debbie Florendo

Kids
Jean Tuggle

Committees

Treasurer
Jill Crocker

Editorial Editor
Laurie Monypeny

Marketing Coordinator
Cynthia McElhaney

Promotions
Lauren Hendrix, Chair
Carol Ann Hendrix
Alyce Waller

Proofing
Mary Lawrence Flinn, Chair
Claudia Efird
Patty Johnson
Laurie Monypeny
Donna Rhodes
Glenda Shorb
Mimi Vestal

Key Ingredients Sponsors

Key Ingredients would not have been possible without the financial support of individuals and businesses. We are grateful for these immeasurable gifts.

Diamond Level
International Paper

Morrison Management Specialists – A Member of the Compass Group

Platinum Level
First Tennessee Bank

Elizabeth and Jay Mednikow

Gold Level
The Memphis Flyer

Carmen and Matt Bond

Silver Level

Lipscomb and Pitts, Insurance

Methodist-Le Bonheur Foundation

Judy and Charles Burkett

Debbie and Ken Edmundson

Ann and Frank Gusmus, Jr.

Nancy and John Kelley, Jr.

Patron Level

EWR, Inc.

Summerfield Packaging, Inc.

Libby and John Aaron

Lindley and Charles Buchas, Jr.

Jill and Joe Crocker

Sue Dodd

Debra Flanary

Jane Griffin

Carolyn Grizzard

Denise and Bob Henning

Ila and Thomas Johnson

Gail and Noah Kimball

Pat Klinke

Fini and Dennis Koerner

Melinda and Phil Russell

Missy and Todd Stockstill

Acknowledgements

Special thanks to these individuals and businesses who helped in the creation of *Key Ingredients* by lending us their beautiful personal possessions to use as props for the photographs. Their abounding generosity helped elevate this book to a higher level.

Linda Felts Interiors

Shawn Swetmon

Alan's Oriental Rugs

Woody Woodliff Photography

Kroger Florist

Carmen Bond

Debbi Freeburg

Jamie McDonnell

Elizabeth Mednikow

Penny and Joe Tice

Arlene Wade

The Keys To Life

*I*n 1923 sixteen women joined together to sew for the children of Leath Orphanage. Because they sewed for one hour, they chose the name Le Bonheur, meaning Hour of Happiness, for their group. Little did they know the impact these humble beginnings would have on our community, for out of their concern for children, a world-class pediatric medical center would emerge.

During the early years, the Le Bonheur Club grew in its desire to help children. Working closely with the Children's Bureau and other volunteer agencies, the Club sent children to summer camp, drove children to the dentist and doctor, and became Big Sisters to teenage girls. Although Le Bonheur Club's volunteer service earned many community awards it became apparent that the Club would be able to help more children through fundraising efforts. To this end, the Le Bonheur Club participated in a wide variety of money-making efforts, including horse shows, a national tennis tournament, and the grand opening of the roof of the Hotel Peabody. Even with all the fundraising projects, club members never lessened their commitment to volunteer work, continuing clinic work at the Children's Bureau, opening a shelter home for wards of the Children's Bureau, and establishing two medical clinics for children.

In 1944, the Pediatric Society contacted the Le Bonheur Club for help with funding much-needed hospital beds for children. The idea of a children's hospital was born, and the Le Bonheur Club readily undertook the challenge. A hospital committee was formed, and conferences were held with the University of Tennessee. On June 15, 1952, the Club's dream was realized with the opening of an 89 bed, $2.5 million hospital. The keys to Le Bonheur Children's Hospital were tied to balloons and released into the air, signifying the doors would always be open to all sick children.

Since that day, the Le Bonheur Club has worked closely with the hospital, helping it become one of the premier children's hospitals in the country. In the beginning, Club members spent many hours sewing hospital gowns and crib sheets, stocking a Bunny Room with toys for patients, and serving coffee to weary parents. They also continued their fundraising efforts with the famous Children's Fund Drive, the U.S. Indoor Tennis Tournament, the Memphis Hunter-Jumper Classic, and many galas and fashion shows. As the years passed, both Le Bonheur Children's Hospital and the Le Bonheur Club changed. The hospital has become Le Bonheur Children's Medical Center, a pediatric medical facility known nationwide for its cutting edge technology and commitment to children's health. The Club has changed also, adapting to the needs of the hospital and the children who come through its doors.

By purchasing this cookbook, you have helped to open the door to the future for a sick child. For this, we thank you!

6

Key Courses

Appetizers

1953

*I*n the fall of 1953, I was a six year-old second grader from Covington, Tennessee, and had just attended my first Mid-South Fair. Shortly thereafter, I became very ill. Running a high fever, headachy and very nauseated, I was diagnosed by our local physician as "having a virus." After two weeks in a local clinic, I slipped into a coma for three days and was getting progressively worse. My parents immediately took me to Memphis.

Upon seeing a pediatrician, I was admitted to Le Bonheur Children's Hospital where I was placed in isolation and diagnosed with the fear of all parents, "paralytic poliomyelitis." By this time, I could not lift my head off the pillow, hold a spoon in my hand or stand on my legs, but I could breathe on my own.

Le Bonheur was barely a year old in October 1953, but was caring for polio patients on the entire second floor. This was the last major epidemic of polio in the Mid-South. Le Bonheur became home for my mother and me for the next 13 weeks. In the eyes of a child, that is a very long time. The fact that the staff allowed parents to stay with their children, even in isolation, was a new concept. The building was unconventional with rooms showcasing full glass windows that looked over a landscaped lawn. The rooms were bright and decorated for children with child-size fixtures.

The atmosphere of the hospital was special. Le Bonheur Club volunteers were working everywhere: reading to children in the playroom, working in the gift shop and drug store and bringing around little Golden Books for us to read.

Approximately five years later I returned to Le Bonheur to have corrective surgery on my leg. I visited the famous "Bunny Room," where children were allowed to pick any toy before surgery. This special toy would be waiting for me in my room after surgery. Of course, the Le Bonheur Club volunteers kept the Bunny Room stocked to the brim.

By the grace of God and His guidance to the doctors, wonderful staff and volunteers at Le Bonheur almost 50 years ago, I am now a wife, mother and grandmother. Le Bonheur holds many memories for me, and in recent years, I have witnessed during our grandchild's visits that it is still an outstanding hospital.

Mushroom and Thyme Palmiers

1 pound fresh mushrooms
1½ medium onions, peeled
6 tablespoons butter
2 tablespoons all-purpose flour
1½ teaspoons lemon juice
1½ teaspoons dried thyme

⅛ teaspoon cayenne pepper
Salt and freshly ground pepper
3 sheets frozen puff pastry, thawed
2 eggs
2 teaspoons water

When determining amounts to prepare for your dinner party, plan on twelve hors d'oeuvres per person.

In a food processor, finely chop mushrooms and onions in separate batches. Melt butter in a large skillet over medium heat. Add mushrooms and onions to skillet and cook, stirring occasionally, for about 10 minutes or until juice evaporates. Add flour, lemon juice, thyme and cayenne. Season with salt and pepper. Reduce heat to low and cook about 2 minutes. Set aside to cool.

Place unfolded pastry sheets on a flat surface. Spread one third of vegetable mixture on each pastry sheet and roll up from both edges to the center. Press the two rolled sides together. Wrap each roll tightly in separate sheets of plastic wrap and freeze for at least one hour. If frozen for a long period of time, allow to thaw slightly before slicing.

Use a serrated knife to cut rolls into ¼ inch slices. Place slices on parchment paper and allow to thaw before baking. Whisk together eggs and water. Brush egg mixture over tops of palmiers. Bake at 400 degrees for 18 to 20 minutes.

Yield: 4 to 5 dozen

Tomato-Feta Appetizers

1 frozen puff pastry sheet, thawed

1 cup mozzarella cheese, shredded

1 (4 ounce) package crumbled feta cheese

¼ cup Vidalia or other sweet onion, minced

1 clove garlic, minced

2 tablespoons fresh basil, finely chopped

1 tablespoon fresh thyme or oregano, finely chopped

1 tablespoon fresh chives, finely chopped

4 Roma tomatoes, thinly sliced

1 tablespoon virgin olive oil

Roll puff pastry into a square on a lightly floured surface. Transfer to an ungreased baking sheet. Bake at 400 degrees for 10 minutes or until golden brown. Carefully transfer to a wire rack to cool.

When cool, return sheet to baking sheet. Sprinkle with cheeses, onions and garlic. Top with basil, thyme, and chives. Arrange tomato slices in a single layer on top and drizzle with oil. Bake at 400 degrees for 15 minutes or until cheese melts. Cut into squares with 1 tomato slice in each square.

Yield: about 2 dozen

Red Pepper Pastry Pockets

1 tablespoon margarine

2 tablespoons onion, finely chopped

1 clove garlic, minced

1 (7 ounce) jar roasted sweet red peppers, drained and chopped to equal ⅓ cup

½ (8 ounce) package reduced-fat cream cheese, softened

2 tablespoons Parmesan cheese, grated

1 heaping teaspoon dried Italian seasoning

1 (17 ounce) package frozen puff pastry, thawed

Milk

Freshly grated Parmesan cheese

Heat margarine in a small skillet. Add onions and garlic and sauté about 3 minutes or until onions are tender. Remove from heat. Stir red peppers, cream cheese, Parmesan cheese and Italian seasoning into skillet. Set aside.

Unfold pastry sheets on a lightly floured surface. Roll each sheet into a 10 inch square. Cut each sheet into sixteen (2½ inch) squares. Brush edges of each square with milk. Spoon about 1 teaspoon of cream cheese filling onto the center of each pastry square. Fold each square in half over the filling, forming a rectangle. Seal edges with a fork and cut tiny slits into the top of each pastry. Brush with milk and sprinkle with freshly grated Parmesan cheese. Arrange pastries on an ungreased baking sheet. Bake at 400 degrees for 20 minutes or until golden. Remove from oven and cool on a wire rack for about 5 minutes. Serve warm.

Yield: 32 pastry pockets

These may be made ahead and frozen, unbaked, in a zip-top bag for up to 1 month. To serve, thaw pastries for 10 minutes and bake as directed above.

Mini Chicken Cups

1½ pounds boneless, skinless chicken breast halves

1 cup Ranch salad dressing

¼ teaspoon salt

¼ teaspoon cumin

2 cups shredded Mexican blend cheese

2 tablespoons chili seasoning

½ cup red bell pepper, finely chopped

½ cup green bell pepper, finely chopped

1 package wonton wrappers

Cook chicken in boiling water for about 20 minutes or until cooked through. Cool and cut into small pieces. In a bowl, combine chicken, dressing, salt, cumin, cheese, chili seasoning and bell peppers.

Spray mini muffin pans with non-stick cooking spray. Place and form 1 wonton wrapper in each muffin cup. Bake wrappers at 350 degrees for 5 minutes or until light brown. Transfer baked wrapper cups to a foil-lined baking sheet. Spoon a generous tablespoon of chicken mixture into each wonton cup. Return to oven and bake 10 minutes longer. If desired, serve with salsa and sour cream.

Yield: 45 cups

Chicken mixture can be made ahead and refrigerated until ready to use.

Feta Date Phyllo Triangles

1 (8 ounce) package cream cheese,
    softened

1 (8 ounce) package crumbled feta
    cheese

2 teaspoons freshly grated nutmeg,
    or to taste

1 (16 ounce) package frozen phyllo
    dough, thawed

1 stick butter, melted

1 (8 ounce) can whole pitted dates,
    halved

Cream together cream cheese, feta cheese and nutmeg. Set aside. Lay 1 sheet of phyllo dough on a flat surface and brush with butter. Repeat dough and butter layers twice for a stack of 3 phyllo sheets. Cut stack lengthwise into 1 inch strips. Place 1 tablespoon of cheese mixture on each strip, 1½ inches from an edge. Press a date half into each mound of cheese mixture. Fold over the short end of phyllo at an angle to make a seal over the cheese. Fold remaining length of phyllo strip in alternating triangles. Seal end with butter. Place each triangle on parchment paper on a baking sheet. Bake at 350 degrees for 15 to 18 minutes or until golden.

Yield: 60 triangles

Triangles can be frozen prior to baking.

Texas Firecrackers

2 boneless, skinless chicken breast
    halves
24 pepperoncini salad peppers

6 ounces Monterey Jack pepper
    cheese, cut into 24 strips
12 frozen phyllo sheets, thawed
1 stick butter, melted

Cook chicken in boiling water until done. Drain, cool and cut into 24 (2½ inch) strips. Cut top from peppers and remove seeds. Stuff each pepper with a chicken strip and a cheese strip. Divide phyllo sheets into stacks of three sheets each, brushing each sheet with butter before adding the next. Cut stack crosswise into thirds, then cut in half lengthwise. Place a stuffed pepper 1 inch from the edge of each stack. Roll up and twist ends to seal. Place on baking sheets. Bake at 375 degrees for 20 to 25 minutes.

Yield: 24 firecrackers

Cover phyllo with a damp towel to keep moist while working with it.

Gruyère Onion Tarts

1½ tablespoons butter
2 cups onions, thinly sliced
2 cloves garlic, chopped
¼ teaspoon salt
¼ teaspoon black pepper
¼ teaspoon dried sage
¼ teaspoon dried thyme

⅛ teaspoon dried rosemary
¾ cup Gruyère cheese, shredded
¼ cup heavy cream
24 mini phyllo pastry shells
4 thick slices bacon, cooked crisp,
    drained and finely chopped
Chopped parsley for garnish

Melt butter in a large skillet. Add onions, garlic, salt, pepper, sage, thyme and rosemary. Cook, stirring occasionally, 15 to 20 minutes or until lightly browned. Remove from heat and stir in cheese and cream.

Place phyllo shells on a baking sheet. Spoon onion mixture into shells. Sprinkle bacon and parsley on top. Bake at 350 degrees for 9 to 11 minutes. Serve immediately.

Yield: 24 tarts

Spinach and Artichokes in Puff Pastry

1 (10 ounce) package frozen chopped spinach, thawed and squeezed dry

1 (14-ounce) can artichoke hearts, drained and chopped

½ cup mayonnaise

¾ cup Parmesan cheese, grated

1 teaspoon garlic powder, or more to taste

2 teaspoons lemon juice

Dash of Tabasco sauce

Salt and pepper to taste

2 (17 ounce) packages frozen puff pastry, thawed 30 minutes

Combine spinach, artichoke, mayonnaise, cheese, garlic powder, lemon juice and Tabasco. Salt and pepper to taste. Unfold pastry sheet and place on a lightly floured surface. Spread half of spinach mixture evenly over pastry sheet. Roll up jelly roll fashion, pressing to seal seam. Wrap in plastic wrap. Repeat using remaining pastry sheet and spinach mixture. Freeze rolls 30 minutes. Cut rolls into ½ inch thick slices and place on a baking sheet. Bake at 400 degrees for 20 minutes.

Yield: 4 dozen

Uncut rolls can be frozen up to 3 months. Allow logs to thaw slightly before slicing.

Key Notes

Jazzy Shrimp

2 tablespoons butter

1 tablespoon olive oil

1 cup onion, finely chopped

¾ cup chili sauce

¼ cup water

3 tablespoons Worcestershire sauce

3 tablespoons firmly packed light
    brown sugar

1 tablespoon distilled white vinegar

1 tablespoon tomato paste

¼ teaspoon dried mustard

⅛ teaspoon hot pepper sauce

40 medium shrimp, peeled and
    deveined

40 strips bacon

Melt butter and oil in a large skillet. Add onions and sauté until transparent. Add chili sauce, water, Worcestershire sauce, sugar, vinegar, tomato paste, mustard and pepper sauce. Bring to a boil. Reduce heat and simmer 20 to 25 minutes or until thickened. Remove from heat. Wrap each shrimp with a strip of bacon and secure with a toothpick. Place shrimp in sauce and let soak for 5 to 10 minutes. Transfer shrimp to a broiler tray, placing shrimp 2 inches apart. Broil 4 inches from heat source for 3 to 4 minutes on each side.

Yield: 40 shrimp

Serve this dish over rice for a great main course for 4.

Smoked Salmon Roulade

1 (8 ounce) package cream cheese, softened
1 teaspoon fresh chives, minced
½ teaspoon fresh dill, chopped
Salt and pepper to taste
4 (9 inch) prepared crêpes
1 pound smoked salmon, thinly sliced
1 ounce caviar (optional)

Beat cream cheese, chives, dill, salt and pepper until smooth. Spread mixture evenly over crêpes with a spatula. Divide salmon evenly over crêpes. Roll up each crêpe jelly roll fashion and wrap tightly in plastic. Refrigerate 2 hours.

To serve, cut rolls diagonally into ½ inch thick slices. Serve with a dollop of caviar on each slice.

Yield: 5 dozen

Prepared crêpes can be found in the produce section of the grocery store.

Crab Salad in Endive

½ cup mayonnaise
½ cup celery, finely diced
1 tablespoon capers, drained
1½ teaspoons fresh dill, minced
1 teaspoon chives, minced
2 teaspoons tarragon vinegar
Pinch of kosher salt
Pinch of black pepper
1 pound lump crabmeat
4 heads Belgian endive

Combine mayonnaise, celery, capers, dill, chives, vinegar, salt and pepper in a bowl. Gently stir in crabmeat.

Cut off base of each head of endive and separate the leaves. Spoon a teaspoon of crabmeat filling into the end of each endive leaf. Arrange filled leaves of a platter and serve.

Yield: 25 spears

Capered Shrimp, Artichokes and Mushrooms

4 pounds cooked shrimp, peeled and deveined

2 (14 ounce) cans artichoke hearts, drained and quartered

1 (3¼ ounce) jar capers, drained

2 pounds fresh small mushrooms

1 cup tarragon vinegar

½ cup vegetable oil

1 teaspoon garlic, minced

2 tablespoons Worcestershire sauce

½ cup Catalina dressing

½ cup sugar, dissolved in ½ cup water

1 teaspoon salt

1 tablespoon curry powder

2 tablespoons lemon juice

Combine shrimp, artichoke hearts, capers and mushrooms in a large bowl. Set aside. In a separate bowl, combine vinegar, oil, garlic, Worcestershire sauce, dressing, sugar water, salt, curry powder and lemon juice. Pour mixture over shrimp. Cover and refrigerate several hours or overnight. Drain well before serving.

Yield: 15 to 20 servings

Recipe could also be served over a bed of lettuce for an elegant first course.

Baked Oysters

Also makes an ideal first course for dinner.

36 oysters (about 1 pint), well
    drained
1½ sticks butter, softened
1 cup parsley, chopped
1 tablespoon Worcestershire sauce
Dash of Tabasco sauce (optional)
1 teaspoon lemon juice, or to taste

1 teaspoon salt
½ teaspoon black pepper
8 saltine crackers, crushed
1 (8 ounce) can sliced mushrooms
6 small lemon wedges for garnish
French bread

Combine oysters, butter, parsley, Worcestershire sauce, Tabasco,
lemon juice, salt, pepper, cracker crumbs and mushrooms in a large bowl.
Divide mixture evenly among 6 ramekins. Top the center of each ramekin
with a lemon wedge and place ramekins on a baking dish. Bake at 350
degrees for about 20 minutes. Serve hot with thin slices of French bread.

Yield: 6 servings

**This dish can be prepared in advance and refrigerated until ready
to bake.**

Oysters

Winter is a better
time to eat oysters
because that's when the
waters are coldest and
the oysters' flavor is the
best. After purchasing,
keep oysters flat on ice
or in a refrigerator.
Make sure that the
oyster shells are tightly
closed. Raw oysters on
the half shell will always
taste better if shucked
just before serving.
When the oysters are
to be cooked, it's fine to
buy shucked, vacuum-
packed oysters.

Classic Pork Tenders with Chipotle Spread

A must for cocktail buffets.

Pork

¼ cup soy sauce

¼ cup bourbon or apple juice

2 tablespoons brown sugar

1½ pounds pork tenderloin

Chipotle Spread

2 cans chipotle chile peppers in adobo sauce

1 shallot, coarsely chopped

1 egg

Dash of kosher salt

1½ cups peanut oil

Juice of 1 to 2 limes

Cocktail dinner rolls

Pork

Combine soy sauce, bourbon and sugar in a shallow dish or a zip-top bag. Prick pork several times with a fork and place in marinade. Turn to coat and cover or seal. Refrigerate 8 hours.

When ready to cook, remove pork and discard marinade. Grill, covered, over medium-high heat for 12 minutes on each side or until internal temperature of pork reaches 160 degrees. Thinly slice pork and serve on cocktail dinner rolls with chipotle spread.

Chipotle Spread

Puree peppers and shallot in a food processor until smooth. Blend in egg and salt. With food processor running, add oil in a slow, steady stream until blended. Stir in lime juice.

Yield: 8 to 10 servings

Pork Satay with Peanut Dipping Sauce

Pork

2 pounds pork tenderloin	1 teaspoon ground ginger
2 cloves garlic, minced	1 tablespoon lemon juice
1 tablespoon canola oil	1/4 cup strong coffee
2 teaspoons chili powder	24 (10 inch) wooden skewers

Peanut Sauce

1 tablespoon canola oil	2 tablespoons soy sauce
1 onion, chopped	3 tablespoons brown sugar
2 cloves garlic, minced	1 tablespoon lemon juice
1 cup chunky peanut butter	1 tablespoon lime juice
1 cup coconut milk	1/4 teaspoon cinnamon
1/2 cup milk	Cayenne pepper to taste

Pork

Slice pork into strips 1/4 inch thick and 1 inch wide. Combine garlic, oil, chili powder, ginger, lemon juice and coffee in a glass dish. Add pork to marinade and refrigerate several hours or overnight. To serve, thread pork strips onto skewers. Grill to desired degree of doneness. Serve with Peanut Sauce.

Peanut Sauce

Heat oil in a large saucepan. Add onion and garlic and sauté until softened. Stir in peanut butter, coconut milk, milk, soy sauce, sugar, juices, cinnamon and cayenne until blended. Bring to a simmer and cook 5 minutes. Cool and refrigerate or freeze until ready to use.

Yield: 24 skewers

Chicken or beef may be substituted for the pork.

Chili and Bacon Breadsticks

16 slices bacon, chilled
½ cup brown sugar

2 tablespoons chili powder
32 very thin breadsticks

Cut bacon in half lengthwise using a sharp serrated knife. Combine sugar and chili powder in a large plastic bag. Place a couple of pieces of bacon at a time in seasoning bag and shake to coat. Gently wrap one bacon slice around each breadstick and place on a greased broiler pan. Bake at 350 degrees for 16 minutes. Gently loosen breadsticks from pan and cool 15 minutes. Serve at room temperature.

Yield: 32 breadsticks

As an alternative, dredge bacon in Parmesan cheese instead of chili mixture.

Duck Wrapped Jalapeño Bites

Surprise the guests at your next cocktail party with these spicy bites.

4 to 6 duck breasts
1 cup Italian dressing
1 box rounded toothpicks

1 pound bacon
¼ cup sliced jalapeño peppers
1 (8 ounce) can whole water
   chestnuts, drained and halved

Cut duck into 1 inch strips; then cut strips in half lengthwise. Marinate duck pieces in Italian dressing for 6 hours or preferably overnight.

Soak toothpicks in water for 15 minutes. Cut bacon slices in half crosswise. To assemble, lay one piece of duck on a slice of bacon. Top with a pepper slice and water chestnut. Roll bacon around filling and secure with a toothpick. Repeat with remaining ingredients. Grill over medium heat, turning often, for 10 minutes or until bacon is crisp. Serve immediately.

Yield: about 40 to 60 pieces

Grilled Sausage with Honey Plum Dip

My husband loves to eat this hot off the grill. I have to move quickly to get my share!

1 (16 ounce) package smoked
   sausage
1 (7 ounce) jar Asian plum sauce

1 tablespoon fresh lime juice
2 teaspoons honey
2 teaspoons Chinese hot mustard

Grill sausage over medium-high heat for 8 to 10 minutes. Cut sausage on the diagonal into 1 inch pieces. Serve sausage with dip.

To make dip, whisk together plum sauce, lime juice, honey and mustard. If preparing ahead, refrigerate dip for up to several days. Serve dip at room temperature.

Yield: 4 to 6 servings

Asian Chicken Drummies

¼ cup soy sauce
¼ cup peanut oil
3 tablespoons honey
½ cup hoisin sauce
Zest of 1 large orange
Juice of 1 large orange
4 cloves garlic, minced

2½ tablespoons fresh ginger, minced
1 tablespoon Chinese hot mustard or
   hot Dijon mustard
Salt and freshly ground black pepper
⅛ teaspoon Chinese five-spice
   powder
16 to 24 chicken wing drumettes

Combine soy sauce, oil, honey, hoisin sauce, orange zest and juice, garlic, ginger, mustard, salt, pepper and five spice powder in a large bowl. Add chicken and toss to coat well. Cover and marinate in refrigerator for 4 hours or overnight.

When ready to cook, drain chicken, reserving marinade. Arrange chicken on a flat wire rack in a large foil-lined roasting pan. Bake at 375 degrees for 16 minutes. Increase oven temperature to 450 degrees. Baste chicken with reserved marinade and bake 10 minutes longer or until brown.

Yield: 24 pieces

Shiitake and Goat Cheese Tart

Crust

1½ cups all-purpose flour

¼ teaspoon salt

¾ cup unsalted butter, chilled and cut into pieces

¼ cup ice cold water

Filling

1½ cups heavy cream

5 large cloves garlic, peeled

1 egg

¼ teaspoon salt

2 tablespoons extra virgin olive oil

8 ounces fresh shiitake mushroom caps, sliced, some reserved for garnish

4 ounces soft fresh goat cheese, softened

Kosher salt and freshly ground pepper to taste

Crust

Blend flour and salt in a food processor. Add butter and process until mixture resembles coarse meal. Add water and process until moist clumps form. Gather the dough into a ball and flatten into a disk. Wrap dough in plastic and chill at least 30 minutes. Can be made ahead up to this point. If necessary, soften dough slightly before rolling out. Roll out dough on a floured surface to a 15 inch circle. Transfer to a 9 inch round tart pan with a removable bottom. Trim off excess dough. Freeze 30 minutes. Remove from freezer and line crust with foil. Fill with pie weights or dried beans. Bake at 375 degrees for about 20 minutes or until sides are set. Remove weights and foil. Return crust to oven and bake 15 minutes or until pale golden. If bubbles form while baking, pierce with a toothpick. Cool.

Filling

Bring cream and garlic to a boil in a heavy saucepan. Reduce heat to medium and simmer, whisking occasionally, for 15 minutes or until cream is reduced to 1 cup. Cool mixture and puree in a food processor or blender. Add egg and salt. In a heavy skillet, heat oil over medium-high heat. Add mushrooms and sauté 5 minutes or until tender. Season with salt and pepper. Cool.

Spread cheese over cooled crust. Add cream mixture and sprinkle mushrooms on top. Bake at 375 degrees for 20 minutes or until filling is set. Cool on a wire rack.

Yield: 8 servings

For a time-saver, use refrigerated pie crust. Roll out dough to fit a 9 inch tart pan and bake as directed on package.

For a colorful option, top with sun-dried tomatoes.

Belgian Endive Appetizer

2 tablespoons butter
½ pound walnuts, coarsely chopped
2 tablespoons brown sugar
4-5 heads Belgian endive, separated
    into spears

½ pound Gorgonzola bleu cheese, or
    to taste
½ red bell pepper, finely diced
½ yellow bell pepper, finely diced
2 tablespoons balsamic vinegar
2 tablespoons Italian dressing

Melt butter in a skillet. Add walnuts and toss to coat. Add sugar and cook and stir until walnuts are coated in caramelized brown sugar. Remove from heat and cool.

Arrange endive on a platter. Sprinkle with walnuts, then cheese. Top with bell peppers. Combine vinegar and Italian dressing and drizzle over top.

Yield: about 30 spears

To partially prepare ahead, prepare endive the day before but only top with caramelized walnuts and cheese. Refrigerate. Marinate bell peppers in vinegar dressing overnight. To serve, top endive with bell peppers and dressing.

Roasted Stuffed Mushrooms

Filling

1 tablespoon olive oil

1 cup onion, chopped

8 ounces prosciutto, chopped

1 (10 ounce) package frozen
chopped spinach, thawed and
squeezed dry

4 ounces crumbled goat cheese with
roasted red peppers and basil

½ (8 ounce) package cream cheese,
softened

¼ teaspoon dried crushed red
pepper flakes

Salt and pepper to taste

Mushrooms

2¾ pounds baby portobella
mushrooms, about 1½ inch
diameter, stemmed

¼ cup olive oil

Filling

Heat oil in a heavy medium skillet over medium heat. Add onions and sauté 5 minutes or until tender. Add prosciutto and sauté 5 minutes longer or until brown. Remove from heat and mix in spinach, goat cheese, cream cheese and pepper flakes. Season with salt and pepper.

Mushrooms

Line 2 rimmed large baking sheets with foil. Toss mushrooms with olive oil. Place mushrooms, rounded side down, in a single layer on 2 large foil-lined baking sheets. Bake at 375 degrees for 20 minutes or until centers fill with liquid. Turn mushrooms over and bake another 20 minutes or until brown.

Spoon 1 heaping teaspoon of filling into each mushroom cap. Bake 10 minutes or until heated through. Transfer to a platter and serve warm.

Yield: 4 to 6 servings

Filled mushrooms can be prepared up to 1 day ahead before baking.

Marvelous Mushrooms

2 pounds whole button mushrooms
1 green bell pepper, chopped
1 red bell pepper, chopped
1 large onion, chopped
1 stick butter

2 tablespoons Dijon mustard
2 tablespoons Worcestershire sauce
½ cup brown sugar
¾ cup red wine

Sauté mushrooms, bell peppers and onions in butter until onions are clear. Stir in mustard, Worcestershire sauce, sugar and wine. Cook, uncovered, over medium heat for 45 minutes or until most of liquid is absorbed. Serve in a chaffing dish on a buffet or on a plate for a first course.

Yield: 4 to 6 servings

These mushrooms can be prepared up to 1 day ahead. Reheat in microwave when ready to serve.

Chilled Asparagus with Sour Cream Sauce

2 pounds fresh asparagus
1 cup sour cream
¼ cup Parmesan cheese, grated

1 teaspoon freshly squeezed lemon juice
½ teaspoon salt
2 tablespoons toasted sesame seeds (optional)

Snap off and discard asparagus ends. Cook asparagus in a steamer or in lightly salted simmering water for 4 to 5 minutes or until crisp-tender. Refrigerate until cool. Combine sour cream, cheese, lemon juice and salt. Serve sour cream sauce in a hollowed out red or yellow bell pepper. Surround pepper with asparagus on a lettuce-lined serving tray. If serving as a vegetable, spoon sauce over each serving and sprinkle with sesame seeds.

Yield: 4 servings

Cleaning Fresh Mushrooms

Trim the stems but avoid washing the mushrooms because they absorb water like a sponge and water promotes decay. Instead, wipe them clean with damp cloth or scrape them gently with a paring knife.

Kosher Salt

This inexpensive coarse salt is evaporated from brine and contains no additives or added iodine. Kosher salt is popular among chefs because its coarse texture makes it easy to pinch between your fingers and sprinkle onto foods. Measure for measure, one teaspoon of kosher salt contains less salt than the same amount of iodized salt.

Dipping Asparagus

¾ cup sour cream

1 cup mayonnaise

3 tablespoons red onion, chopped

2 tablespoons lemon juice

1 tablespoon plus 1 teaspoon capers, drained and chopped

¼ teaspoon onion powder

¼ teaspoon garlic powder

2 teaspoons dried tarragon

½ teaspoon sugar

¼ teaspoon black pepper

2 bunches asparagus, cut into 4 inch lengths

3 cups ice

6 cups water

1½ teaspoons kosher salt

Whisk together sour cream, mayonnaise, onions, lemon juice, capers, onion powder, garlic powder, tarragon, sugar and pepper for a dipping sauce. Refrigerate 2 hours or until chilled. Dipping sauce can be refrigerated for up to 2 days.

Steam asparagus in boiling water for 3 to 5 minutes or until tender. Mix ice, water and salt in large bowl. Drain asparagus and plunge into ice water. Let stand until cold. Drain and transfer asparagus to a paper-lined plate until dry. Refrigerate. Serve asparagus chilled with dipping sauce.

Yield: 48 spears

Add lemon or orange zest to dipping sauce for some added flavor.

Marinated Cheese

½ cup olive oil

½ cup white wine vinegar

1 (2 ounce) jar diced pimiento

3 tablespoons fresh parsley, chopped

3 tablespoons green onion, minced

3 cloves garlic, minced

1 teaspoon sugar

¾ teaspoon dried basil

½ teaspoon salt

½ teaspoon black pepper

1 (8 ounce) 5½x2x1 inch block
    sharp Cheddar cheese, chilled

1 (8 ounce) 5½x2x1 inch block
    Monterey Jack cheese, chilled

Assorted crackers

Combine oil, vinegar, pimiento, parsley, onions, garlic, sugar, basil, salt and pepper in a jar. Cover tightly and shake. Set aside. Cut cheese blocks in half lengthwise, then cut crosswise into ¼ inch thick slices. Stack cheese slices in an alternating pattern and place stack on its side in a shallow serving dish. Pour marinade over cheese. Cover and refrigerate at least 8 hours. Serve with assorted crackers.

Yield: 16 servings

Fontina Fondue

1 pound fontina cheese, shredded

2½ tablespoons all-purpose flour

1 clove garlic, halved

2 cups dry white wine

2 tablespoons sherry

1 tablespoon lemon juice

¼ teaspoon nutmeg

1 loaf assorted breads, cut into
    1 inch cubes

In a medium bowl, toss cheese with flour. Rub garlic on the inside of a heavy saucepan and discard garlic. Add wine and sherry to saucepan. Bring to a simmer over medium heat. Add 1 cup of cheese to saucepan and stir until melted. Repeat with remaining cheese, a handful at a time. Add lemon juice and nutmeg. Cook and stir 2 minutes or until mixture begins to bubble. Transfer to a fondue pot and keep warm with a heat source. Serve with bread cubes.

Yield: 16 to 18 servings

Key Notes

Bleu cheese has a marvelous, sharp, tangy flavor that intensifies with age. Roquefort, the king of cheese, has a rich, creamy texture but a tingly taste. England's Stilton, first sold in the 18th century, is mellow with a pale yellow interior. Ultra-pungent Gorgonzola is one of Italy's greatest cheeses. Spain's Cabrales boasts a blend of cow, goat and sheep milk and Denmark's mild Danablu can be sliced, spread or crumbled. America's Maytag Bleu is a spicy, crumbly cheese that takes six months to mature. No matter how you look at it, the power of bleu cheese never ceases to delight!

Bleu Cheese and Walnut Spread

6 ounces bleu cheese
2 (8 ounce) packages cream cheese, softened
1 teaspoon Cognac

Salt and pepper to taste
⅓ cup walnuts, finely chopped
¼ cup fresh chives, finely chopped
Assorted crackers

Cream bleu cheese and cream cheese until well blended. Mix in cognac and season with salt and pepper. Add walnuts and chives and blend well. Serve chilled or at room temperature with assorted crackers.

Yield: 10 servings

Boursin Cheese Spread

2 cloves garlic, crushed
2 (8 ounce) packages cream cheese, softened
1 (8 ounce) package whipped sweet cream butter, softened
¼ to ½ teaspoon black pepper
½ teaspoon salt

½ teaspoon dried thyme
½ teaspoon basil
½ teaspoon oregano
½ teaspoon dill
½ teaspoon marjoram
Assorted crackers or bread

Combine garlic, cream cheese, butter, pepper, salt, thyme, basil, oregano, dill and marjoram in a food processor fitted with a steel blade. Process until well blended, soft and creamy. Refrigerate overnight or freeze up to 2 weeks. Serve cheese spread at room temperature with assorted crackers or bread.

Yield: 3 cups

For a unique presentation, pipe softened cheese spread onto Belgium endive or red pepper strips. Your guests will think you worked for hours.

Stacked Spinach and Cheese Wheel

First and Fourth Layers

3 cups Cheddar cheese, shredded

¾ cup mayonnaise

2 cups chopped walnuts

Second Layer

1 (10 ounce) package frozen chopped spinach, thawed and squeezed dry

1 (8 ounce) package cream cheese, softened

Third Layer

1 (8 ounce) package cream cheese, softened

⅓ cup chutney

½ teaspoon curry powder

First Layer

Combine Cheddar cheese, mayonnaise and walnuts. Spread half of mixture over the bottom of a greased 9 inch springform pan. Reserve remaining mixture for fourth layer.

Second Layer

Combine spinach and cream cheese and spread over first layer.

Third Layer

Mix together cream cheese, chutney and curry powder. Spread over spinach layer.

Fourth Layer

Spread reserved Cheddar cheese mixture over third layer. Refrigerate at least 1 hour before serving. Serve with crackers.

Yield: 24 servings

Cheese Kabobs

3 cloves garlic

1 cup extra virgin olive oil

¼ cup fresh basil, minced

6 pepperoncini, stems removed

8 ounces Monterey Jack cheese, cut into 1 inch cubes

8 ounces mozzarella cheese, cut into 1 inch cubes

1 loaf sourdough bread, cut into 1 inch cubes, crusts discarded

Bamboo skewers

Blend garlic, oil, basil and pepperoncini in a food processor until pureed. Transfer mixture to a shallow bowl. Add cheese cubes and mix until coated. Marinate at room temperature for at least 1 hour or preferably overnight. Soak bamboo skewers in water for at least 1 hour prior to grilling to prevent burning.

When ready to cook, skewer bread and cheese cubes, beginning and ending with bread. Brush bread with marinade. Grill 2 minutes or until bread toasts and cheese softens.

Yield: 10 to 15 servings

Substitute Monterey Jack or mozzarella cheese with Cheddar or Gruyère cheese. Salami or prosciutto can be added to the skewers.

The marinade is also good with poultry, beef or seafood. Marinade can be stored for up to 3 months in a refrigerator.

Bleu Cheese Flan

¾ cup buttery cracker crumbs

2 tablespoons margarine, melted

2 (8 ounce) packages cream cheese, softened

2 (4 ounce) packages bleu cheese, crumbled

⅔ cup sour cream

3 eggs, beaten

⅛ teaspoon black pepper

1 cup sour cream

½ cup sliced almonds

Assorted fresh fruit or French bread

Combine crumbs and margarine and press into the bottom of a 9 inch springform pan. Bake at 350 degrees for 10 minutes.

Blend together cream cheese and bleu cheese with an electric mixer at medium speed. Add ⅔ cup sour cream, eggs and pepper. Pour mixture over crust. Bake at 300 degrees for 45 minutes. Stir 1 cup sour cream and carefully spread over top of flan. Bake 10 minutes longer. Loosen flan from pan but cool before removing sides. Press almond slices into sides of flan. Serve chilled with assorted fresh fruit or French bread slices.

Yield: 16 servings

Crazy About Corn Dip

2 (8 ounce) packages cream cheese, softened

¼ cup lime juice

1 tablespoon ground cumin

½ teaspoon salt

Dash of black pepper

¼ cup vegetable oil

1 (16 ounce) can whole kernel corn, drained

1 cup chopped pecans

1 small white onion, finely chopped

Tortilla chips

Beat cream cheese, lime juice, cumin, salt, pepper and oil with an electric mixer until blended. Fold in corn, pecans and onions. Serve with tortilla chips. Store unused portion up to 1 week in refrigerator.

Yield: 10 to 12 servings

Roasted Garlic with Feta

½ cup olive oil

2 teaspoons ground oregano

1 teaspoon dried basil

4 small heads garlic

4 ounces feta cheese

½ (8 ounce) package cream cheese, softened

¾ teaspoon Greek seasoning

½ (4¼ ounce) can black olives, chopped

French bread

Divide oil, oregano and basil evenly among 4 muffin cups. Cut off top of garlic heads and place a head in each muffin cup, cut side down. Bake at 350 degrees for 20 to 30 minutes or until tender.

Meanwhile, mix feta cheese, cream cheese, Greek seasoning and black olives. Form mixture into a loaf or any other shape and place on a serving platter. Squeeze out pulp of garlic cloves and place pulp on cheese mixture. Serve with French bread slices or torn bread chunks. For individual appetizers, place a dollop of cheese mixture on garlic Melba rounds and top each with a clove of garlic.

Yield: 15 to 20 servings

White Bean Hummus

1 (15 ounce) can white beans, rinsed and drained

3 tablespoons fresh lemon juice

¼ teaspoon sesame oil

½ teaspoon ground cumin

½ teaspoon paprika

¼ teaspoon salt

2 cloves garlic

Combine beans, lemon juice, sesame oil, cumin, paprika, salt and garlic in a food processor and process until smooth. Store up to 1 week in refrigerator. Serve with cumin pita chips.

Yield: 1¼ cups

Vegetable Confetti
with Lemon Cumin Pita Crisps

Vegetable Confetti

2 large zucchini, ¼ inch diced

2 large summer squash, ¼ inch diced

3 medium cucumbers, peeled, seeded and ¼ inch diced

1¼ cups tarragon vinegar

2 medium red onions, ¼ inch diced

8 ripe medium tomatoes, ¼ inch diced

1 red bell pepper, ¼ inch diced

1 yellow bell pepper, ¼ inch diced

1 green bell pepper, ¼ inch diced

½ cup fresh cilantro, chopped

¾ cup olive oil

Salt and pepper to taste

Lemon Cumin Pita Crisps

6 pita bread

5 tablespoons butter, softened

2 teaspoons lemon pepper

2 teaspoons ground cumin

Vegetable Confetti

Combine zucchini, summer squash and cucumbers in a bowl. Add vinegar and toss to coat. Marinate 45 minutes at room temperature. In a separate bowl, combine onions, tomatoes, bell peppers and cilantro. Drain squash mixture and add to onion mixture. Toss. Drizzle with olive oil and season with salt and pepper. Add extra vinegar, if desired. Chill at least 2 hours before serving.

Lemon Cumin Pita Crisps

Separate each pita bread into 2 circles. Blend butter, lemon pepper and cumin. Spread mixture over pita halves. Cut each half into 8 triangles. Bake at 350 degrees for 8 to 12 minutes or until crisp.

Yield: 12 to 16 servings

Sun-Dried Tomato Torte

Pesto

1 cup fresh basil	½ teaspoon salt
2 large cloves garlic	¼ teaspoon black pepper
3 tablespoons olive oil	½ to ¾ cup Parmesan cheese, grated
¾ cup pine nuts or walnuts	

Torte

1 (8 ounce) package cream cheese, softened	15 sun-dried tomatoes packed in oil, drained and chopped
1 (6 to 8 ounce) package feta cheese with tomato and basil	¼ cup pine nuts, toasted
	Assorted crackers

Pesto

Process basil and garlic in a food processor. With processor running, add oil in a steady stream, 1 tablespoon at a time. Add nuts, salt, pepper and cheese. Process until well blended.

Torte

Combine cream and feta cheeses in a mixing bowl. Using about one third of cheese mixture, spread a circular layer over a serving plate. Top with one third each of pesto and tomatoes. Repeat layers two more times. Top with toasted nuts. Serve with assorted crackers.

Yield: 8 to 10 servings

Red Hot Pepper Party Dip

1 (4 ounce) jar roasted red peppers, drained

1 (4 ounce) jar sun-dried tomatoes packed in oil, drained and patted dry

1 clove garlic

2 teaspoons ground cumin

¼ cup fresh cilantro, chopped

¼ cup green onions, white part only, chopped

1 (8 ounce) package reduced-fat cream cheese

2 pickled jalapeño peppers, sliced

Dash of seasoning salt

Dash of cayenne pepper

Chips or pita crisps, see page 37 for recipe

Process red peppers, tomatoes, garlic, cumin, cilantro, onions, cream cheese, jalapeño peppers, seasoning salt and cayenne in a food processor until smooth. Refrigerate in an airtight container for at least 1 hour. Serve with chips or pita crisps.

Yield: 1½ cups

For a decorative serving dish, cut a red bell pepper in half and remove seeds. Spoon dip into pepper halves and serve.

For a festive presentation, serve this dip in a hollowed-out red or green bell pepper.

Summertime Salsa

This sweet and juicy salsa is a real crowd-pleaser. Add heat to sweet with a jalapeño pepper!

2 cups watermelon, seeded and chopped

2 tablespoons red onion, minced

2 tablespoons fresh cilantro, chopped

1 to 2 jalapeño peppers, minced

⅛ teaspoon ginger, grated

1 tablespoon fresh flat-leaf parsley, chopped

½ teaspoon salt

½ teaspoon black pepper

Combine watermelon, onions, cilantro, jalapeño peppers, ginger, parsley, salt and pepper, mixing gently. Allow salsa to stand at room temperature for 30 minutes for flavors to blend. Serve as a dip or over grilled fish.

Yield: 8 servings

A great way to serve this salsa is to hollow out the watermelon. Line it with foil and fill with Summertime Salsa. This is a fun and dramatic way to serve salsa to your guests.

Pepper and Olive Crostini

1 large green bell pepper

1 large yellow bell pepper

1 large red bell pepper

1 (5 ounce) jar stuffed green olives, drained and sliced

2 tablespoons red onion, minced

1 tablespoon capers, drained

2 tablespoons olive oil

1 tablespoon balsamic vinegar

4 tablespoons butter

¼ cup olive oil

1 clove garlic, minced

2 (2 inch diameter) loaves French bread, sliced ½ inch thick

To roast peppers, cut all bell peppers in half lengthwise and remove seeds and membranes. Place peppers, skin side up, on a baking sheet. Use a hand to flat peppers. Broil about 3 inches from heat source for 15 to 20 minutes or until blackened. Immediately transfer peppers to a plastic bag. Seal and allow peppers to steam for 10 to 15 minutes. Remove charred skin. Cut peppers into 2 inch long thin strips. Combine peppers, olives, onion, capers, 2 tablespoons oil and vinegar.

In a saucepan, heat butter, ¼ cup oil and garlic. Brush mixture over both sides of each bread slice and place on a baking sheet. Bake bread at 350 degrees for 10 to 12 minutes or until light golden and crisp. Spread pepper mixture over warm bread slices and serve immediately.

Yield: 20 to 25 servings

Crumbled feta cheese can be added to pepper mixture.

Emerald Coast Wraps

1 (8 ounce) package cream cheese, softened

½ cup chutney

2 tablespoons mayonnaise

8 (12 inch) diameter flour tortillas

1 pound thinly sliced turkey

1 bunch green onions, chopped

1 (10 ounce) bag fresh spinach

Combine cream cheese, chutney and mayonnaise. Spread mixture evenly over tortillas. Top with turkey, onions and spinach. Roll tortillas tightly. To serve, cut rolls in half or into 1 inch pieces.

Yield: 24 servings

Roasted Tomato and Basil Relish

For a simple bruschetta appetizer, spread this relish on pretoasted baguette slices from your local bakery.

1 pound plum tomatoes, seeded and very coarsely chopped

½ cup fresh basil, chopped

½ cup Parmesan cheese, grated

2 tablespoons olive oil

3 cloves garlic, minced

¼ teaspoon crushed red pepper flakes

Salt and pepper to taste

1 baguette, sliced

Combine tomatoes, basil, cheese, oil, garlic and pepper flakes in a 1 quart baking dish. Bake at 350 degrees for 30 minutes. Season with salt and pepper and cool to room temperature. Brush baguette slices with olive oil and lightly toast in the oven before serving.

Yield: 20 to 24 servings

Spiced Almonds

These almonds remind me of those warm roasted nuts one can enjoy while strolling the streets of New York City.

2 teaspoons salt

½ teaspoon ground cumin

2 teaspoons ground ginger

1 teaspoon crushed red pepper flakes

Pinch of cayenne pepper

¼ cup sesame seeds

¼ cup sugar

2 tablespoons vegetable oil

3 cups whole almonds or cashews

½ cup sugar

Combine salt, cumin, ginger, pepper flakes, cayenne, sesame seeds and ¼ cup sugar in a large bowl. Heat oil in a heavy skillet over medium heat. Add nuts and cook and stir continuously for 2 minutes or until fragrant. Sprinkle ½ cup sugar over nuts and shake pan occasionally to prevent burning. Stir only when sugar starts to melt and caramelize. Remove skillet from heat when nuts are dark golden brown.

Immediately add nuts to spice mixture and toss quickly to coat well. While still hot, spread nuts on a nonstick baking sheet and separate from one another. When cool, transfer to an airtight container and store up to 2 to 3 weeks.

Yield: 3 cups

Key Notes

Soups

Pumpkin Soup with a Thai Twist

1997

*W*hen I found out two years ago that my sister's unborn baby had a heart defect, I felt helpless to do anything about it. I knew nothing I could do or say would change the heartbreak the parents were facing. When their son underwent open heart surgery at just one-week old, we all hoped and prayed a lot but did not know what else we could do.

This child now is a happy, healthy 17-month old, thanks to Le Bonheur and its wonderful, talented doctors and staff. And I realize something now that I never realized before....There is something else we can do. We can show our love and concern by donating to Le Bonheur to help other children just as others have done for this child. Le Bonheur performs miracles every day and I want to be a part of that.

2001

*U*nfortunately, the staff at Le Bonheur sees countless accidents in a day. For most parents, this is the only time they will experience the wonderful care provided at Le Bonheur.

My daughter was a patient at Le Bonheur for a week. I was blessed with a healthy child since her birth until an evening in October. My daughter had an accident on her bicycle that left her with several head injuries. She was riding home on her bike and accidentally hit her front brakes, which flipped her onto the pavement hitting her skull. There was no other evidence of scrapes or bruises. After we realized she had an accident, she was sent by ambulance from Milan, Tennessee, (about 1 1/2 hours away) to Le Bonheur.

It is a very scary feeling when your child is not well. When you are faced with a nightmare experience like this, it is almost too much to bear. I can honestly say that I never felt alone while at Le Bonheur because of God's grace and the hospital's exceptional care. The doctors, nurses and staff were unbelievable in their professionalism and outstanding concern for our care. I cannot say enough about Le Bonheur. I was completely amazed how such a large hospital could employ so many wonderful people who touched our lives. They helped make an unbearable experience bearable.

Pumpkin Soup with a Thai Twist

2 (16 ounce) cans fat free chicken broth

1 (15 ounce) can pumpkin

1 (12 ounce) container mango nectar

¼ cup reduced fat chunky peanut butter

2 tablespoons rice vinegar

1½ tablespoons minced green onions

1 teaspoon fresh ginger, grated

¼ teaspoon dried red pepper flakes

½ teaspoon orange zest

1 clove garlic, crushed

Chopped fresh cilantro for garnish (optional)

Combine broth, pumpkin and mango nectar in a large pot and bring to a boil. Reduce heat and cover. Simmer 10 minutes.

In a blender, combine 1 cup of pumpkin mixture with peanut butter. Process until smooth and add mixture to pot. Stir in vinegar, onions, ginger, pepper flakes, orange zest and garlic. Cook 5 minutes or until thoroughly heated. Sprinkle cilantro on individual servings, if desired.

Yield: 6 servings

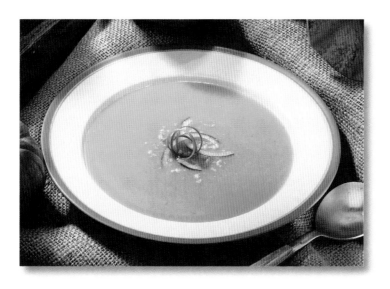

Yummy Brie Soup

4 tablespoons butter

½ cup yellow onions, chopped

½ cup celery, sliced

¼ cup all-purpose flour

2 cups milk

2 cups chicken broth

¾ pound Brie cheese, rind removed, cubed

Salt and pepper to taste

Chopped chives for garnish

Melt butter in a large pot. Add onions and celery and sauté until soft and transparent. Stir in flour and cook until bubbly. Remove from heat. Gradually stir in milk and broth. Return mixture to heat and stir until soup thickens. Add cheese and stir until melted. Season with salt and pepper. Garnish each serving with chives. Serve immediately.

Yield: 6 servings

Brie is a soft, creamy yellow lightly-rinded French cow's-milk cheese made in a section of Ile-de-France and neighboring Champagne. Dress up a wheel of Brie by spreading with honey, microwaving at 70% power for one minute. Sprinkle with toasted chopped walnuts. For a different taste, top with mango chutney, cook for one minute and sprinkle with chopped cooked bacon.

Spicy Red Pepper Soup

4 tablespoons butter

1 onion, sliced

1 shallot, sliced

1 tablespoon paprika

4 red bell peppers, seeded and sliced

¼ teaspoon cayenne pepper

½ teaspoon dried thyme

1 teaspoon dried basil

1 teaspoon dried oregano

¼ cup all-purpose flour

4½ cups chicken broth, heated

1 tablespoon tomato paste

2 tablespoons heavy cream

Salt and pepper to taste

Heat butter in a large saucepan. Add onions, shallots and paprika and sauté 5 minutes. Add bell peppers, cayenne, thyme, basil and oregano. Cook over low heat for 20 minutes, stirring occasionally. Mix in flour and cook 2 minutes. Blend in broth and increase heat to medium. Mix in tomato paste and cook 15 minutes longer. Puree mixture in a food processor. Stir in cream. Serve hot.

Yield: 4 servings

Sausage-Tortellini Soup

1 pound hot or mild Italian sausage,
  casings discarded

1 large onion, chopped

1 clove garlic, pressed

3 (14½ ounce) cans chicken or beef
  broth

2 (14½ ounce) cans diced tomatoes,
  undrained

1 (8 ounce) can tomato sauce

1 cup dry red wine

2 carrots, thinly sliced

1 tablespoon sugar

2 teaspoons Italian seasoning

2 small zucchini, sliced

1 (9 ounce) package refrigerated
  cheese tortellini

½ cup Parmesan cheese, shredded

Brown sausage, onions and garlic in a Dutch oven over medium-high heat; drain. Return mixture to pot and stir in broth, tomatoes, tomato sauce, wine, carrots, sugar and Italian seasoning. Bring to a boil. Reduce heat and simmer 30 minutes. Skim off fat. Stir in zucchini and tortellini. Simmer 10 minutes longer. Sprinkle individual servings with cheese.

Yield: 6 servings

The South is known for its genuine hospitality. This comforting soup is perfect to take to a family caring for a new baby, settling into a new home or feeling the loss of a loved one.

Good Deeds

"Do good for
the pure love of
doing good."

Make something
that will make
somebody's day a
little brighter.

Take warm soup
to a neighbor or
friend who
is sick.

Bake muffins, put
in a plastic bag and tie
with a pretty ribbon.

Minnesota Wild Rice Soup

2 tablespoons butter

½ cup onion, chopped

¼ cup celery, chopped

¼ cup carrot, chopped

1½ cups fresh mushrooms, sliced

¼ cup all-purpose flour

½ teaspoon salt

¼ teaspoon black pepper

2 cups beef broth

1 cup half-and-half

1 cup cooked wild rice

1 teaspoon dried tarragon

Melt butter in a saucepan. Add onions, celery and carrots and sauté 3 minutes. Reduce heat and add mushrooms. Cook 3 minutes longer. Stir in flour, salt and pepper. Add broth and half-and-half. Cook and stir until thick, smooth and bubbly. Add rice and tarragon.

Yield: 4 servings

Red Bell Pepper Bisque

1 cup onion, chopped

2 cloves garlic, minced

3 tablespoons butter

2 cups red bell pepper
    (about 3 peppers), chopped

½ teaspoon hot pepper sauce

3 tablespoons all-purpose flour

2 cups chicken broth

2 cups half-and-half

1 cup Swiss cheese, grated

In a 3 quart saucepan, sauté onions and garlic in butter for 5 to 8 minutes or until softened. Add bell peppers and sauté 5 minutes. Mix in hot pepper sauce and flour and cook 2 minutes. Whisk in broth and cook over medium heat until mixture slightly thickens. Transfer to a food processor and puree until smooth. At this point, mixture can be refrigerated for up to 1 day.

When ready to serve, return mixture to saucepan. Whisk in half-and-half. Heat to serving temperature and stir in cheese until melted.

Yield: 6 servings

Roasted Tomato Soup

For a light and healthy meal, try this comforting soup with grilled vegetables on foccacia. See page 85 for the roasted vegetable recipe.

3 pounds tomatoes, halved and seeded

2 onions, sliced into rings

2 serrano chili peppers, halved and seeded

¼ cup olive oil

2 tablespoons balsamic vinegar

Salt and pepper to taste

6 cloves garlic, thinly sliced

3 cups chicken broth

½ cup dry white wine

Fresh basil for garnish

Combine tomatoes, onions and peppers in a mixing bowl. Add oil, vinegar, salt and pepper. Toss vegetables to mix and coat. Drain vegetables, reserving liquid. Grill vegetables over white-hot coals or broil. Cook until vegetable skins blacken and blister. Remove from heat and remove blackened skins. Chop coarsely and set aside.

Heat reserved liquid in a large stockpot over medium heat. Add garlic and sauté until tender. Add broth, wine and chopped vegetables. Bring to a boil. Reduce heat and simmer 7 to 10 minutes. Garnish each serving with basil.

Yield: 4 servings

Sun Valley Potato Soup

2 (14½ ounce) cans chicken broth

6 medium-size red potatoes, peeled and diced

1 medium onion, chopped

½ teaspoon ground nutmeg

1 teaspoon salt

1 teaspoon black pepper

2½ cups half-and-half

2 (10½ ounce) cans cut asparagus, drained

2 (5 ounce) jars processed pimiento cheese spread

Combine broth, potatoes, onions, nutmeg, salt and pepper in a Dutch oven. Bring to a boil. Reduce heat, cover and simmer 5 minutes or until potatoes are softened. Stir in half-and-half, asparagus and cheese spread. Simmer, uncovered, stirring frequently until thoroughly heated; do not bring to a boil.

Yield: 12 cups, 6 servings

Tomato Dill Soup

3 tablespoons butter

2 cups onion, diced

3 cloves garlic, minced

2 (28 ounce) cans whole tomatoes, drained, seeded and coarsely chopped, juice reserved

3½ tablespoons all-purpose flour

3 tablespoons tomato paste

2 cups chicken broth

3 cups chicken broth

1 cup half-and-half

¼ teaspoon white pepper

3 tablespoons fresh dill, finely chopped

½ cup sour cream

Fresh dill sprigs for garnish (optional)

Melt butter in a large stockpot over medium heat. Add onions and garlic and cook 10 to 20 minutes or until golden and translucent. Add drained tomatoes and cook over high heat for 4 minutes, stirring constantly. Remove from heat and stir in flour until well blended. Add tomato paste. Gradually whisk in 2 cups broth until smooth. Bring to a boil, stirring constantly. Reduce heat, cover and simmer 10 minutes.

Transfer mixture to a blender and process until pureed. Return to pot and stir in 3 cups broth, half-and-half, white pepper and chopped dill. Add reserved tomato juice and cook until heated through. Soup can be served at this point, or simmered several more hours to deepen the flavors. To serve, top individual servings with a 1 tablespoon sour cream and garnish with dill sprigs.

Yield: 8 servings

Boardwalk Seafood Bisque

4 tablespoons butter or olive oil

1 large onion, very finely chopped

½ cup celery, very finely chopped

2 cloves garlic, minced

2 tablespoons all-purpose flour

2 tablespoons tomato paste

3 cups half-and-half

2 cups chicken broth

1 bay leaf

1 teaspoon dried basil, or to taste

1 tablespoon Tabasco sauce

¼ teaspoon salt

1 teaspoon Creole seasoning

1 pound shrimp, peeled and deveined

½ pound scallops

½ pound crabmeat

¼ cup green onions, finely chopped

Melt butter in a large stockpot. Add onions, celery and garlic and sauté until tender. Stir in flour and tomato paste and cook 1 minute. Remove from heat and gradually stir in half-and-half and broth. Add bay leaf, basil, Tabasco, salt and Creole seasoning. Bring to a boil. Reduce heat and simmer 10 minutes. Add shrimp, scallops, crabmeat and green onions. Simmer 5 minutes or until shrimp are pink and scallops are opaque. Remove bay leaf. Serve with French bread.

Yield: 6 to 8 servings

Portobella Mushroom Soup

For thickening cream soups, one tablespoon flour to each cup of milk or cream is the usual proportion. Potato soups use less flour because potatoes are natural thickening agents.

4 tablespoons butter

5 leek bulbs, finely chopped

1 medium onion, finely chopped

10 ounces portobella mushrooms, coarsely chopped

¼ cup plus 2 tablespoons all-purpose flour

3 cups chicken broth

3 tablespoons dry sherry

2 cups half-and-half

¼ teaspoon cayenne pepper, or to taste

Kosher salt and freshly ground white pepper to taste

3 tablespoons dry sherry

1 ounce portobella mushrooms, coarsely chopped

1 tablespoon butter

Crumbled cheese straws for garnish

Melt 4 tablespoons butter in a large Dutch oven over medium heat. Add leeks and onions and sauté 10 minutes or until translucent and softened. Add 10 ounces mushrooms and sauté 5 minutes. Reduce heat to low and blend in flour. Cook, stirring occasionally, for 3 minutes or until thickened. Gradually stir in broth and 3 tablespoons sherry. Bring to a boil, stirring constantly. Reduce heat to a simmer. Cook, stirring constantly, for 10 minutes or until thickened. Add half-and-half, cayenne, salt, white pepper and 3 tablespoons sherry. Simmer 5 minutes.

Meanwhile, sauté 1 ounce mushrooms in 1 tablespoon butter. After soup has simmered, puree in a food processor. While hot, ladle pureed soup into bowls. Top with sautéed mushrooms and cheese straws.

Yield: 4 servings

Super Bowl Soup

You will score touchdowns with fanatical football fans with this soup version of a cheeseburger.

½ pound ground beef

¾ cup onion, chopped

¾ cup carrot, shredded

¾ cup celery, diced

1 teaspoon dried basil

1 teaspoon dried parsley

1 tablespoon margarine

1 (32 ounce) box chicken broth

4 cups potatoes, peeled and diced
  (about 1¾ pounds)

3 tablespoons margarine

¼ cup all-purpose flour

8 ounces processed cheese loaf, cubed

1½ cups milk

¾ teaspoon salt

¼ teaspoon black pepper

¼ cup sour cream

Brown meat, drain and set aside. In a large saucepan, sauté onions, carrots, celery, basil and parsley in 1 tablespoon margarine until tender. Add broth, potatoes and browned beef. Bring to a boil. Reduce heat, cover and simmer 10 to 12 minutes or until potatoes are tender.

Meanwhile, in a small saucepan, melt 3 tablespoons margarine. Stir in flour and cook and stir 3 to 4 minutes or until bubbly. Blend flour mixture into soup and bring to a boil. Cook and stir 2 minutes. Reduce heat to low. Stir in cheese, milk, salt and pepper until cheese melts. Remove from heat and blend in sour cream.

Yield: 6 servings

Potato Cheese Soup

3 medium potatoes, peeled and diced
1/3 cup onion, chopped
Milk
3 tablespoons butter, melted
2 tablespoons all-purpose flour
2 teaspoons dried parsley

3/4 teaspoon salt
1/2 teaspoon black pepper
1 cup Swiss cheese, shredded
Bacon, cooked and crumbled for
  garnish (optional)

Combine potatoes and onions with 1 cup water in a saucepan. Cook until potatoes are tender. Mash potatoes and onions in saucepan with a fork; do not drain. Measure potato mixture and add enough milk to equal 5 cups. Return to saucepan.

Blend butter, flour, parsley, salt and pepper in a bowl. Stir flour mixture into potato mixture until well blended. Cook over medium heat until thick and bubbly. Add cheese and cook until cheese is partially melted. Garnish with bacon and serve immediately.

Yield: 4 servings

White Chili

Chicken Broth

2 pounds boneless, skinless chicken breast halves

2 cups canned chicken broth

2 cups water

1 bay leaf

1 onion, quartered

2 carrots, halved

2 stalks celery

1 teaspoon cumin seed

Salt and pepper to taste

Chili

1 tablespoon olive oil

1 onion, chopped

6 cloves garlic, minced

2 (4 ounce) cans chopped green chiles

1 tablespoon ground cumin

2 teaspoons dried oregano, crushed

1/4 teaspoon ground cloves

1/4 to 1/2 teaspoon cayenne pepper, or to taste

1 pound dried great Northern beans, rinsed and soaked overnight

Shredded Monterey Jack cheese

Fresh cilantro

Chicken Broth

Combine chicken breasts, broth, water, bay leaf, onion, carrots, celery, cumin, salt and pepper in a large stockpot. Simmer 20 minutes or until chicken is tender. Remove chicken and strain broth. Add extra canned chicken broth to strained broth if needed to equal 6 cups. Cool chicken and shred, Refrigerate chicken and broth until needed.

Chili

Heat oil in same stockpot. Add onions and sauté until translucent. Add garlic, chiles, cumin, oregano, cloves and cayenne. Sauté 2 minutes. Drain and rinse beans and add to stockpot along with chicken broth. Bring to a boil. Reduce heat and simmer 2 to 3 hours or until beans are tender, stirring occasionally. Add shredded chicken and simmer at least 1 hour longer. If desired, further cooking over very low heat will intensify flavor. Ladle soup into bowls and garnish with cheese and cilantro.

Yield: 6 to 8 servings

Black Bean and Sweet Red Pepper Soup

A light, refreshing soup for black bean lovers.

1 cup dried black beans

8 cups chicken broth, divided

2 small bay leaves

¼ cup olive oil

1 large onion, coarsely chopped

1 small clove garlic, finely chopped

1 cup canned tomatoes, drained and chopped

2 tablespoons red wine

1 teaspoon sugar

¼ teaspoon black pepper

1½ cups dry elbow macaroni

2 large red bell peppers, roasted, peeled and chopped

Fresh parsley and green onion for garnish

Rinse beans and place in a stockpot. Add water to cover beans by 1 inch. Bring to a boil and cook 2 minutes. Remove from heat, cover and allow to stand for 1 hour.

Drain beans and return to pot. Add 3 cups of broth and bring to a boil. Reduce heat to simmer. Add bay leaves and simmer about 1 hour, 30 minutes or until beans begin to become tender.

Heat oil in a skillet and sauté onions 5 minutes or until wilted. Add garlic and cook 1 minute longer. Add onion and garlic mixture to pot along with tomatoes. Cook 1 hour longer or until beans are completely cooked. Add chicken broth as needed while cooking. Stir in wine, sugar, pepper and remaining broth.

Meanwhile, cook macaroni in boiling water for 6 minutes or until partially cooked. Drain and add macaroni and bell peppers to bean mixture. Simmer until macaroni is completely cooked. Remove from heat and let stand 5 minutes before serving. Garnish as desired with parsley and green onion.

Yield: 8 servings

Fireside Corn Chowder

½ cup salt pork, diced

1 red bell pepper, diced

1 cup onion, diced

1 cup celery, diced

3 tablespoons all-purpose flour

1 (14½ ounce) can chicken broth

1 cup water

1 cup potatoes, diced

¼ teaspoon dried thyme

1 teaspoon salt

½ teaspoon black pepper

1 (15 ounce) can whole kernel corn, drained

3 cups half-and-half

2 tablespoons parsley

Sauté salt pork in a large stockpot until dark brown. Remove pork and reserve. Add bell peppers, onions and celery to pork drippings and sauté until translucent. Blend in flour and cook, stirring constantly, for a few minutes. Add broth, water, potatoes, thyme, salt, pepper and corn. Simmer until potatoes are tender.

Meanwhile, in a saucepan, heat half-and-half over medium heat for 12 minutes or until tiny bubbles begin to form around the edge of pan. Do not boil. Add scalded half-and-half and parsley to stockpot. Add reserved pork and heat over low to medium heat.

Yield: 6 servings

White Bean Soup with Sun-Dried Tomatoes

1 tablespoon olive oil

1 large onion, chopped

1 large clove garlic, chopped

1 large carrot, chopped

¼ teaspoon dried red pepper flakes, or to taste

1 (15 ounce) can cannellini beans, drained

5 cups chicken broth

⅔ cup dry pasta shells or bow ties

⅓ cup sun-dried tomatoes, chopped

Salt and pepper to taste

Chopped fresh basil or thyme for garnish

Heat oil in a large saucepan. Add onion, garlic, carrots and pepper flakes and sauté until softened. Reduce heat, cover and cook 10 minutes. Add beans and broth and bring to a boil. Add pasta and tomatoes. Simmer 10 minutes or until pasta is tender. Season with salt and pepper. Sprinkle each serving with fresh herbs.

Yield: 4 servings

Chilled Squash Soup

2 cups yellow squash, sliced

2 tablespoons butter or margarine

½ cup chicken broth

¼ cup onion, finely chopped

½ teaspoon salt

3 to 4 drops hot pepper sauce

3½ cups chicken broth

1 (8 ounce) container sour cream

Parsley for garnish

Combine squash, butter and ½ cup chicken broth in a medium saucepan. Cover and cook 10 minutes or until squash is tender. Transfer to a blender. Add onions, salt, pepper sauce and 3½ cups chicken broth. Blend until smooth. Pour into a large bowl and chill several hours. Stir in sour cream just before serving. Garnish with parsley.

Yield: 4 servings

Smoky Pasta and Bean Soup

6 slices lean smoked bacon, diced

1 small onion, finely chopped

1 stalk celery, finely chopped

1 medium carrot, shredded

2 cloves garlic, crushed

⅛ teaspoon dried red pepper flakes

2 cups canned crushed tomatoes

Salt to taste

2½ cups canned white beans, drained

6 cups chicken broth

¾ cup dry macaroni or other small pasta

Freshly grated Parmesan cheese (optional)

Sauté bacon in a large saucepan until done. Add onions, celery, carrots, garlic and pepper flakes and sauté 10 minutes or until vegetables are softened. Stir in tomatoes and salt. Cook, stirring occasionally, for 10 minutes. Stir in beans. Add broth and bring to a gentle boil. Add macaroni and cook 15 minutes or until pasta is tender but still firm. Serve immediately with cheese or cover and refrigerate until ready to serve. Reheat gently to serving temperature.

Yield: 6 servings

Key Notes

Salads

Caribbean Chicken Salad

1997

"*T*hink of how many children are saved every year and go on to lead normal lives, thanks to Le Bonheur Children's Medical Center." The mother who said these words should know. Her three children were born with the same kidney defect. All three are doing well, thanks to the unique expertise and loving care they received at Le Bonheur.

The problem was ureteral reflux, where a misplaced and enlarged ureter stunts the normal growth of a kidney. "Everyone said the baby would never make it," said the mother. "Then we found a Le Bonheur pediatric urologist, who gave us hope." At the age of four months, the son had his first surgery. The daughter was tested for the same abnormality, and at almost the same time, the mother discovered she was carrying another daughter who shared the kidney defect.

The three tots underwent eight surgeries. Though no more surgery is expected, the mother never wants to be far away from Le Bonheur. For this family, Le Bonheur is something that "you just can't forget. Everyone remembers you and genuinely cares about your children. Memphis is fortunate to have a wonderful hospital like Le Bonheur."

Caribbean Chicken Salad with Cilantro-Lime Vinaigrette

Cilantro-Lime Vinaigrette

¼ cup fresh lime juice

¼ cup light olive oil

2 tablespoons rice wine vinegar

2 tablespoons sugar

1 teaspoon ground cumin

1 teaspoon chili powder

¼ teaspoon salt

¼ teaspoon cayenne pepper

1 clove garlic, minced

1 tablespoon fresh cilantro, chopped

Salad

2 cups grilled chicken, diced

1 cup jicama, peeled and finely diced

1 cup mango, peeled and diced

1 cup canned black beans, rinsed and drained (optional)

Cilantro-Lime Vinaigrette

1 head Bibb lettuce, torn

1 head radicchio, torn

1 star fruit, sliced for garnish

Cilantro-Lime Vinaigrette

Combine lime juice, olive oil, vinegar, sugar, cumin, chili powder, salt, cayenne, garlic and cilantro in a mixing bowl. Whisk together until blended.

Salad

Combine chicken, jicama, mango, beans and vinaigrette in a mixing bowl. Toss gently. Arrange greens on 4 serving plates. Spoon chicken mixture over greens. Garnish with star fruit.

Yield: 4 salad servings, ½ cup vinaigrette

Jicama

To peel jicama, cut off the two ends with a knife. Starting at either end, scrape the skin with the side of a teaspoon from end to end, following the curve and bumps. The thin, papery peel will strip away with very little pressure. Jicama also makes a great substitute for water chestnuts in stir-fries.

Starfruit

Ripe starfruit is bright yellow in color and tastes sweet.

Champagne

Champagne comes in many different styles. Which type you choose depends on your taste and how you plan to serve it. Brut and extra brut are very dry, with just a touch of sugar. These make wonderful apéritifs to serve with slightly salty appetizers. Extra dry champagnes are slightly sweeter than bruts and go well with mildly spicy foods. Sec and demi-sec refer to sweet champagnes and are served with dessert.

Champagne and Bleu Cheese Salad

Dressing

½ teaspoon salt

⅛ teaspoon freshly ground black
 pepper

¼ cup fresh lemon juice

½ teaspoon prepared mustard

¾ cup olive oil

3 tablespoons champagne

Salad

1 head red leaf and 1 head green
 leaf lettuce, torn

1 bunch green onions, diced

1 red bell pepper, cut into thin strips

1 yellow bell pepper, cut into thin
 strips

1 (11 ounce) can Mandarin oranges,
 drained

½ cup walnuts, chopped and toasted

½ cup pecans, chopped and toasted

Dressing

1 (4 ounce) package bleu cheese,
 crumbled

Dressing

Combine salt, pepper, lemon juice, mustard, oil and champagne in a jar. Seal tightly and shake well.

Salad

Place mixed greens in a bowl. Add onions and bell peppers. Pat dry oranges with a paper towel and arrange on top of salad. Sprinkle with walnuts and pecans. Drizzle with dressing and sprinkle cheese on top.

Yield: 6 servings

For a slightly different taste, substitute shredded Parmesan cheese for the bleu cheese.

Eclectic Salad

Dressing

½ cup sugar

2 tablespoons sesame seeds

1 tablespoon poppy seeds

1½ teaspoons Worcestershire sauce

¼ teaspoon paprika

½ cup canola oil

Salad

4 cups mixed greens

1 pint strawberries, sliced

½ cup sliced almonds, toasted

½ cup crumbled bleu cheese, crumbled

Dressing

Combine sugar, sesame seeds, poppy seeds, Worcestershire sauce, paprika and oil and mix well.

Salad

Combine greens, strawberries, almonds and cheese in a bowl. Drizzle with dressing and toss to mix.

Yield: 4 servings

Lettuce Equivalents

One medium
head of lettuce:

Bibb lettuce yields
4 cups leaves;

iceberg lettuce yields
10 cups leaves
or
8 cups shredded;

leaf lettuce yields
8 cups leaves;

romaine lettuce yields
8 cups leaves.

Watercress

An herb of European origin, the watercress has a mildly pungent flavor and is a favorite salad ingredient. It is quite perishable, so refrigerate immediately in a plastic bag. Use within a day or two of purchase. Wash just before using.

Radicchio, Watercress and Walnut Salad

Walnut Vinaigrette

¼ cup walnut oil

¼ cup vegetable oil

1 tablespoon red wine vinegar

2 teaspoons fresh lemon juice

¼ teaspoon Dijon mustard, coarse ground style

¼ teaspoon salt

1 clove garlic, minced

2 to 4 tablespoons walnuts, chopped and toasted

Salad

1 small head radicchio, trimmed

3 bunches watercress, stemmed

Walnut Vinaigrette

½ cup walnuts, preferably black walnuts, toasted

½ cup Parmesan cheese, shaved

Walnut Vinaigrette

Combine oils, vinegar, lemon juice, mustard and salt in a small jar. Seal tightly and shake well. Add garlic and walnuts and allow to stand at room temperature for 1 hour, shaking occasionally. Discard garlic. Shake well before using.

Salad

Carefully peel off radicchio leaves. Select the 4 best leaves and place a leaf on each serving plate. Shred remaining radicchio into ¼ inch wide strips. Combine shredded radicchio and watercress. Drizzle vinaigrette on top and toss. Divide mixture over radicchio leaves. Scatter walnuts and cheese over each serving. Serve immediately.

Yield: 4 servings

Goat Cheese and Apple Salad

Roasted Onions

2 red onions, thinly sliced

¼ cup balsamic vinegar

¼ cup hazelnut oil

Salt and pepper to taste

Cheese

11 ounces goat cheese

1 cup finely chopped hazelnuts, toasted

1 cup bread crumbs

2 egg yolks

¼ cup water

Dressing and Assembly

¼ cup balsamic vinegar

½ cup hazelnut oil

2 tablespoons lemon juice

1 tablespoon Dijon mustard

Salt and pepper to taste

Mixed greens, torn

3 red apples, thinly sliced

Hazelnuts, halved and toasted

Roasted Onions

Toss onions with vinegar and oil. Season with salt and pepper and arrange on a baking sheet. Bake at 350 degrees for 20 minutes. Cool to room temperature. Onions may be done ahead and refrigerated until ready to use. Bring to room temperature before serving.

Cheese

Slice goat cheese into eight (½ inch thick) slices. Mix chopped hazelnuts and bread crumbs in a shallow dish. Mix egg yolks and water in a separate dish. Dip cheese slices in egg wash and then into bread crumb mixture, pressing coating onto cheese to stick. Refrigerate cheese until chilled. Place on a baking sheet. Bake at 400 degrees for 10 minutes.

Dressing and Assembly

Whisk vinegar, oil, lemon juice and mustard. Season with salt and pepper.

To assemble salad, toss mixed greens and apple slices with dressing. Place roasted onions on top of greens. Add cheese slices and hazelnut halves.

Yield: 8 servings

Toasting Hazelnuts

Place hazelnuts on a baking sheet and toast at 350 degrees for 12 minutes, shaking the pan twice. While the nuts are still hot, place them on a clean towel and rub to remove the skin.

Mesclun with Pears, Asiago and Toasted Cashews

The usual proportion in salad dressings is one part vinegar with two to three parts oil. Always add herbs to vinegar then add oil, which coats the herbs and lessens the release of flavors. A dash of mustard or paprika will slow separation. Vinegar and salt in dressings wilt lettuce and impair vitamin content of salad ingredients so add immediately before serving.

Dressing

5 tablespoons olive oil

2 tablespoons balsamic vinegar

1 teaspoon honey

1 teaspoon Dijon mustard

1 tablespoon green onions, finely chopped

Salt and pepper to taste

Salad

4 cups mesclun greens

2 ripe pears, thinly sliced

2 ounces Asiago cheese, shaved with a vegetable peeler

½ cup unsalted cashews, toasted (2 ounces)

Dressing

Combine oil, vinegar, honey, mustard, onions, salt and pepper in a container with a lid. Seal tightly and shake well. Set aside. Dressing can be prepared up to a day in advance.

Salad

Toss greens with about two thirds of the dressing. Divide greens among individual salad plates. Arrange pear slices over greens in a spiral or other decorative pattern. Drizzle with additional dressing. Top with cheese and cashews.

Yield: 4 servings

Spinach Salad

Dressing

1 pound bacon

1 clove garlic, minced

½ small onion, diced

½ cup cider vinegar

1 tablespoon Dijon mustard

¼ cup honey

Pecans

4 tablespoons butter

½ cup packed brown sugar

1 cup pecans

Salad

8 cups baby spinach, washed and stemmed

2 small apples, diced

8 tablespoons bleu cheese, crumbled

Salt and pepper to taste

Dressing

Cook bacon in a skillet. Remove bacon and drain, reserving fat in skillet. Add garlic and onions to fat and sauté. Stir in vinegar, mustard and honey. Keep dressing warm but not hot.

Pecans

Melt butter in a saucepan. Add sugar and cook until sugar dissolves. Add pecans and toss to coat.

Salad

To assemble salads, toss spinach with some of dressing. Divide spinach among 8 salad plates. Top each with apples and a tablespoon of cheese. Season with salt and pepper. Divide pecans among plates. Serve with remaining dressing on the side.

Yield: 8 servings

Pecans can be prepared ahead and stored in an airtight container.

Spinach

Spinach was brought to the United States from Spain and is notorious for being gritty because it grows on short stems close to the ground. To quickly cook prewashed-bagged spinach, poke a hole in the bag with a sharp knife. Place the bag in the microwave oven, hole side up. Cook on high power until the spinach is wilted about three minutes. Season as desired.

Crunchy Salad Croutons

1 stick butter

Powdered garlic to taste

3 tablespoons Parmesan cheese, grated

4 slices stale bread

Melt butter in a 12 inch skillet over low heat. Season with garlic. Add cheese and stir to make a thin paste. Remove crusts from bread and cut bread slices into "crouton size" cubes. If bread is not very dry, place cubed bread in an oven on low heat for a few minutes to allow to dry out. Add bread cubes to butter mixture and stir gently until butter is absorbed. Transfer to a baking sheet. Bake at 250 to 300 degrees, turning occasionally, until golden brown. Cool before serving.

Be sure to make more than you need - people love snacking on them.

Spinach Salad with Feta and Bacon Dressing

Feta and Bacon Dressing

⅓ cup feta cheese, crumbled

1 tablespoon fresh lemon juice

2½ tablespoons water

1 tablespoon mayonnaise

2 tablespoons olive oil

Salad

4 slices bacon, chopped

1 bunch spinach, washed, dried, stemmed and torn

½ medium-size red onion, thinly sliced

Crumbled feta cheese for garnish

Feta and Bacon Dressing

Combine cheese, lemon juice, water and mayonnaise in a blender. Process until smooth. With motor running, add oil in a steady stream and blend until emulsified.

Salad

Cook bacon in a small skillet until crisp. Drain and toss with spinach, onions and dressing. If desired, garnish with feta cheese.

Yield: 2 servings

Fresh Spinach Maison

The flaming of the cognac in this salad will thrill your supper club.

2 bunches fresh spinach, washed, dried and stemmed

1 cup Canadian bacon or regular bacon, cubed

2 cloves garlic, minced (optional)

½ teaspoon dry English mustard

¼ cup Worcestershire sauce

2 dashes hot pepper sauce

5 tablespoons packed brown sugar

⅓ cup malt vinegar

Red onion, sliced into rings

¼ cup Cognac

Salt and pepper to taste

Place spinach in a large salad bowl. Cook bacon in a skillet until crisp. Remove bacon and drain, reserving fat in skillet. Add garlic, mustard, Worcestershire sauce, hot pepper sauce and sugar to skillet. Cook over medium heat, stirring with a wooden spoon until blended. Add vinegar and onion rings and cook and stir until dressing comes to a boil. Pour hot dressing over spinach and toss. Place spinach on warm salad plates. Add cognac and bacon to skillet and carefully flame. Allow flame to die completely. Sprinkle bacon over salad. Season with salt and pepper.

Yield: 6 to 8 servings

Key Notes

Avocado

The avocado, known as an alligator pear, is a tropical fruit that is ripened in a paper bag at room temperature. Sprinkle lemon juice on avocado slices to slow browning.

California Salad

Dressing

¼ cup orange juice

½ cup olive oil

2 tablespoons sugar

2 tablespoons red wine vinegar

1 tablespoon lemon juice

¼ teaspoon salt

½ teaspoon honey

¼ cup salted sunflower seeds

Salad

1 head red leaf lettuce, torn

1 head green leaf lettuce, torn

1 avocado, peeled and sliced

1 (11 ounce) can Mandarin oranges, drained

2 tablespoons green onions, chopped

Dressing

Place orange juice, oil, sugar, vinegar, lemon juice, salt, honey and sunflower seeds in a container with a lid. Seal and shake until mixed.

Salad

Combine lettuce, avocado, oranges and green onions in a bowl. Add dressing and toss.

Yield: 4 servings

Great salad for with fish or at a brunch.

South Florida Salad with Raspberry Vinaigrette

Raspberry Vinaigrette

⅓ cup olive oil

⅓ cup raspberry vinegar

3 tablespoons sugar

½ teaspoon hot pepper sauce

½ teaspoon salt

¼ teaspoon freshly ground black pepper

½ teaspoon cinnamon

Salad

3 cups mixed greens

4 cups baby spinach leaves

1 pound chicken tenders, fried or grilled

¼ cup sliced almonds, toasted

1 cup fresh strawberries, sliced

1 cup Mandarin oranges

2 tablespoons red onion, chopped

Raspberry Vinaigrette

Place oil, vinegar, sugar, pepper sauce, salt, pepper and cinnamon in a jar. Seal tightly and shake well. Allow to stand at room temperature for at least 2 hours. Shake well before serving.

Salad

Combine mixed greens and spinach in a bowl. Add chicken, almonds, strawberries, oranges and onions. Pour dressing over top.

Yield: 2 servings

Sesame seeds and raspberries can also be added to the salad.

This salad will remind you of relaxing under an umbrella with sand beneath your feet and the sea breeze on your face.

Marinated Greek Salad

Dressing

Reserved artichoke liquid from salad

¼ cup red wine vinegar

¼ teaspoon ground oregano

Salt and pepper to taste

¼ teaspoon dried basil

Salad

2 medium tomatoes, cut into wedges

1 medium zucchini, julienned

1 medium cucumber, sliced

1 cup pitted kalamata olives, sliced

1 medium-size red onion, thinly sliced

¾ cup feta cheese, crumbled

1 (16 ounce) jar marinated artichoke hearts in oil, drained, liquid reserved

1 head red leaf lettuce, leaves separated

Dressing

Combine reserved artichoke liquid, vinegar, oregano, salt, pepper and oregano and mix.

Salad

Toss together tomatoes, zucchini, cucumber, olives, onions and cheese in a bowl. Add artichoke hearts. Pour dressing over salad and toss. Refrigerate at least 8 hours. Drain salad and serve on a platter lined with lettuce leaves.

Yield: 6 servings

Salad Riviera

Dressing

3 tablespoons olive oil

3 tablespoons vegetable oil

3 tablespoons wine vinegar

1 tablespoon Dijon mustard

Salt and pepper to taste

Salad

1 (16 ounce) can hearts of palm, drained

1 (14 ounce) can artichoke hearts, drained

½ cup red bell pepper, chopped

½ cup green bell pepper, chopped

10 black olives, halved

Dressing

1 head Boston lettuce, torn

12 cherry tomatoes, halved

2 hard-cooked eggs, sliced (optional)

Dressing

Combine oils, vinegar, mustard, salt and pepper and mix well.

Salad

In a bowl, combine hearts of palm, artichoke hearts, bell peppers and olives. Add dressing and toss. Chill at least 1 hour. Serve mixture on a bed of lettuce. Garnish with cherry tomatoes and egg slices.

Yield: 4 to 6 servings

Cauliflower Salad

1 large head cauliflower, separated into small florets

½ pound bacon, cooked and crumbled

2 medium tomatoes, diced, or 1 cup cherry tomatoes, halved

1 bunch green onions, chopped

1 cup diced or shredded Cheddar cheese

½ cup pimiento stuffed olives, sliced

½ cup mayonnaise

Salt and pepper to taste

Combine cauliflower, bacon, tomatoes, green onions, cheese, olives and mayonnaise. Toss to mix. Season with salt and pepper. Serve chilled.

Yield: 10 to 12 servings

Perfect Hard-Boiled Eggs

Place eggs in a single layer in a saucepan and cover with cold water by 1 inch. Bring to boil over high heat. As soon as water boils, remove the pan from the heat, cover and let sit 15 minutes. Drain and run cold water over the eggs. When completely cooled, refrigerate in the shells for up to 1 week.

Grated Cheese

Cheddar cheese is easier to grate if it is placed in the freezer for ten to twenty minutes. One pound of hard cheese yields four to five cups grated cheese.

Beef, Broccoli and Asparagus Salad

This will take center stage at your picnic in the gardens, where real men eat salad!

1 cup soy sauce

3 tablespoons garlic, minced

6 tablespoons rice wine vinegar

1¼ cups sesame oil

3 tablespoons fresh ginger, grated

3 pounds center cut beef tenderloin

1 cup honey

1½ pounds fresh asparagus, cut into 2 to 3 inch lengths

2 bunches broccoli, cut into florets

1 red bell pepper, julienned

Combine soy sauce, garlic, vinegar, oil and ginger in a shallow dish or plastic zip-top bag. Add tenderloin and marinate 1 to 2 hours. Remove tenderloin, reserving marinade. Grill or roast tenderloin to desired degree of doneness; 140 degrees for rare, 145 degrees for medium rare, 150 degrees for medium. Slice tenderloin and place in a deep dish.

Meanwhile, pour reserved marinade into a saucepan. Bring to a boil and cook 2 minutes. Remove from heat and cool. Mix honey into marinade.

Blanch asparagus and broccoli in boiling water for 1 minute. Plunge into ice water until cooled; drain. Add asparagus, broccoli and bell peppers to tenderloin. Pour marinade over top and toss. Serve warm, at room temperature or chilled.

Yield: 8 to 10 servings

Grecian Scallop Salad with Balsamic Dressing

Balsamic Dressing

⅓ cup plus 1 tablespoon balsamic
   vinegar

1 tablespoon honey

½ teaspoon fresh ginger, grated

1 plum tomato, seeded and finely
   chopped

1 teaspoon garlic, minced

Salad

1 pound bay scallops

2 tablespoons lemon juice

3 tablespoons garlic, chopped

1 head or bag Romaine lettuce, torn

2 tomatoes, chopped

1 cucumber, chopped

1½ cups cooked rice

1 cup feta cheese, crumbled

Balsamic Dressing

Combine vinegar, honey, ginger, tomato and garlic in a small, heavy saucepan. Cook over medium heat for 12 minutes or until dressing is syrupy and has reduced to a scant ¼ cup. Cool to room temperature.

Salad

Sauté scallops in a large nonstick skillet coated with cooking spray over medium heat for 2 minutes. Add lemon juice and garlic. Cook 3 minutes or until scallops are thoroughly cooked. Set aside to cool.

In a large bowl, toss lettuce with tomatoes and cucumbers. Top with rice. Add scallops and sprinkle with feta cheese. Pour dressing over salad and toss.

Yield: 4 servings

The Scoop on Scallops

Bay Scallops are smaller and have a sweet, delicate flavor but can be easily overcooked. Sea Scallops are larger and easier to grill. Buy scallops the day you plan to serve them and keep them refrigerated until ready to cook.

Grilled Duck Salad

Whether topped with sliced duck or crisp bacon, this piquant salad is a winner!

Dressing

1 cup vegetable oil

½ cup sugar

½ cup red wine vinegar

3 tablespoons soy sauce

Salt and pepper to taste

Salad

4 duck breasts, grilled and sliced

¼ cup soy sauce

½ cup olive oil

1 (7 ounce) package spring salad mix

Dressing

1 cup craisins

4 ounces goat cheese, crumbled

Dressing

Combine oil, sugar, vinegar, soy sauce, salt and pepper and mix well.

Salad

Marinate duck breasts in soy sauce and oil overnight in the refrigerator. Grill breasts to desired degree of doneness. Cool and slice.

Place salad mix in a large bowl. Pour dressing over top. Add cranberries and cheese and toss. Divide salad among 4 salad plates. Top with sliced duck.

Yield: 4 servings

If duck is not available, substitute crumbled bacon.

Bombay Shrimp Salad

This is a yummy Asian twist for shrimp lovers.

Dressing

½ cup olive oil

½ cup sugar

1 tablespoon soy sauce

1 teaspoon curry powder

1 teaspoon salt

3 tablespoons cider vinegar

½ teaspoon celery salt

Salad

1 (10 ounce) package frozen peas, cooked and cooled

1 cup brown rice, cooked and cooled

1½ cups celery, chopped

¾ pound fresh shrimp, cooked, cooled and deveined

¼ cup onion, chopped

½ cup sliced almonds

Dressing

Combine oil, sugar, soy sauce, curry powder, salt, vinegar and celery salt and mix well.

Salad

Mix together peas, rice, celery, shrimp, onions and almonds in a large bowl. Pour dressing over salad and mix well. Refrigerate overnight.

Yield: 10 to 12 servings

Tuna Salad on the Wild Side

A far cry from the tuna salad you grew up eating.

1 (6 ounce) package long grain and wild rice mix

½ cup mayonnaise

¼ cup sour cream

½ cup celery, chopped

2 tablespoons onion, finely chopped

1 (12 ounce) can solid white tuna in water, drained and flaked

1 cup salted cashews

Lettuce leaves or mixed greens

Cook rice according directions on package; cool. In a bowl, combine mayonnaise, sour cream, celery, onions, tuna and cashews. Mix well. Stir in rice. Chill before serving. Serve on lettuce leaves or a bed or mixed greens.

Yield: 6 servings

Key Notes

The Notion of Nuts

If a recipe calls for
1 cup chopped nuts,
you chop the nuts first
then measure the 1 cup.
If the recipe calls for
1 cup nuts, chopped,
then you measure
1 cup whole nuts and
then chop.

Wild Rice and Chicken Salad

A colorful addition to your buffet table when served on a silver tray lined with Bibb lettuce and cherry tomatoes.

1 (6 ounce) box wild rice mix

1 cup mayonnaise

1 teaspoon sugar

1 teaspoon plus a dash curry powder

½ teaspoon salt

½ cup green onions, chopped

½ cup celery, chopped

4 ounces Mandarin oranges, drained

½ cup chopped pecans

1 pound chicken breast halves,
    cooked and chopped

Cook rice mix according to directions on package. Cool completely. Mix cooled rice with mayonnaise, sugar, curry powder and salt. Add green onions, celery, Mandarin oranges, pecans and cooked chicken. Gently toss until mixed.

Yield: 6 to 8 servings

Awesome Chicken Salad

Not your basic chicken salad. Truly awesome!

2 cups chicken broth

¼ teaspoon dried rosemary

½ teaspoon lemon pepper

1 teaspoon dried thyme

1 teaspoon salt

6 boneless, skinless chicken breast
    halves, shredded

1 (12 ounce) package fancy
    shredded Swiss cheese

½ cup green bell pepper, chopped

2 cups celery, chopped

2 cups pecans, chopped

2 (16 ounce) bottles poppy seed
    dressing

1 pound green grapes, halved

Combine broth, rosemary, lemon pepper, thyme and salt in a large skillet. Add chicken breasts. Cover and cook 20 minutes. Cool and shred chicken. Combine chicken with cheese, bell peppers, celery, pecans and dressing. Gently mix until thoroughly combined. Stir in grapes just before serving. This salad is best when made a day ahead.

Yield: 12 servings

Tennessee Tomato Salad

Tarragon Vinaigrette

¼ cup tarragon vinegar

¼ cup olive oil

1 tablespoon fresh basil, chopped

½ teaspoon lemon juice

½ teaspoon green onions, finely chopped

½ teaspoon honey

¼ teaspoon Dijon mustard

Salad

2 medium tomatoes, sliced

8 ounces fresh mozzarella cheese or goat cheese, thinly sliced

6 large fresh basil leaves, finely chopped

½ teaspoon black pepper

¼ cup Tarragon Vinaigrette

1 sweet onion, thinly sliced

1 medium cucumber, thinly sliced (optional)

¼ cup Tarragon Vinaigrette

Tarragon Vinaigrette

Combine vinegar, oil, basil, lemon juice, green onions, honey and mustard in a blender. Process until smooth.

Salad

Layer tomato and cheese slices in a shallow dish. Sprinkle with half the basil leaves and half the pepper. Drizzle with ¼ cup tarragon vinaigrette. Top with onions and cucumbers. Sprinkle with remaining basil and pepper. Drizzle remaining ¼ cup vinaigrette on top. Cover and chill 4 hours.

Yield: 4 to 6 servings, ½ cup vinaigrette

You know summer has arrived when the Farmer's Market is overflowing with red, ripe tomatoes from Ripley, Tennessee. This is a perfect way to enjoy tomatoes at their peak.

It is a real joke with my friends that I, the owner of two restaurants, rarely cook at home. I did, however, prepare this salad twice in one week and it was a hit with my friends both times. Now they think I am a great cook!

Marinated Mushroom Salad

¼ cup red wine vinegar

¼ cup olive oil

½ teaspoon sugar

2 tablespoons Greek seasoning

1 (8 ounce) package sliced fresh
   mushrooms

2 green onions, sliced

2 slices Swiss cheese, cut into small
   cubes

Fresh baby spinach or romaine lettuce

Combine vinegar, oil, sugar and Greek seasoning. Place mushrooms, green onions and cheese in a bowl. Pour dressing mixture over mushrooms. Allow to stand at least 1 hour. Serve over spinach or romaine lettuce.

Yield: 4 servings

For a mushroom appetizer, substitute small whole mushrooms and serve with toothpicks.

Summer Pasta Salad

1 pound shell or rotini pasta or
   other of choice

1 cup sugar

1 cup vinegar

½ cup vegetable oil

2 teaspoons prepared mustard

1 teaspoon salt

1 teaspoon black pepper

1 teaspoon garlic powder

½ cup red onion, chopped

1 cup cucumbers, chopped

¼ cup red bell pepper, chopped

¼ cup green bell pepper, chopped

1 tablespoon dried parsley

1 cup tomatoes, diced

Cook pasta until tender. Drain, rinse and cool. Meanwhile, mix together sugar, vinegar, oil, mustard, salt, pepper and garlic powder in a large bowl. Add onions, cucumbers, bell peppers and parsley. Mix in drained pasta. Chill several hours. Mix in tomatoes just before serving.

Yield: 10 to 12 servings

Chilled Tomato and Artichoke Salad

Save your best tomatoes for this cool, colorful, marinated delight!

Balsamic Vinaigrette

1 teaspoon Dijon mustard

2 tablespoons balsamic vinegar

¼ cup extra virgin olive oil

Salt and pepper to taste

Salad

4 large tomatoes, peeled and cut into wedges

½ medium-size red onion, thinly sliced into rings

2 (14 ounce) cans artichoke hearts, quartered

1 tablespoon parsley, chopped

Balsamic Vinaigrette

Whisk together mustard and vinegar in a bowl. Gradually whisk in oil. Season with salt and pepper.

Salad

Combine tomatoes, onions, artichokes and parsley in a bowl. Add vinaigrette and toss. Chill before serving.

Yield: 4 servings

Grape Luncheon Salad

Try this sweet and different salad to round out your next ladies luncheon.

2 pounds red seedless grapes

2 pounds green seedless grapes

1 cup sour cream

1 (8 ounce) package cream cheese, softened

1 teaspoon vanilla

1 cup packed dark brown sugar

1 pound walnuts, chopped and toasted

Remove grapes from stem and place in a large bowl. Mix together sour cream, cream cheese and vanilla. Add mixture to grapes and toss. Combine sugar and walnuts and spread over grapes. Refrigerate until ready to serve.

Yield: 10 to 12 servings

Our Favorite
Bleu Cheese Potato Salad

Key Notes

An old favorite with a slightly new twist.

3 pounds small red-skin potatoes, quartered

⅔ cup olive oil

½ cup apple cider vinegar

¼ cup minced shallots

1 tablespoon fresh parsley, chopped

1 tablespoon fresh chives, chopped

1 tablespoon coarse grain Dijon mustard

2 teaspoons honey

2 teaspoons lemon zest

Salt and pepper to taste

10 slices bacon

12 romaine lettuce leaves

⅔ cup crumbled bleu cheese

1 hard-boiled egg, grated (optional)

Chopped fresh chives for garnish

Cook potatoes in a large pot of boiling water for 8 minutes or until tender. Meanwhile, combine oil, vinegar, shallots, parsley, 1 tablespoon chives, mustard, honey and lemon zest in a large bowl. Whisk to mix and season with salt and pepper. When potatoes are done cooking, drain and add to bowl with dressing while still warm. Toss to combine and season with salt and pepper as needed. At this point, salad can be covered and refrigerated for up to 1 day.

Cook bacon over medium heat until crisp. Drain and crumble bacon. Arrange lettuce leaves around the edge of a serving container. Spoon salad into the center and sprinkle with bacon, bleu cheese and egg. Garnish with chopped fresh chives.

Yield: 8 servings

Roasted Vegetable Salad

1 ear corn
1 red bell pepper
1 tomato
1 tablespoon lime juice

1 tablespoon lemon juice
2 tablespoons white wine vinegar
¼ cup olive oil
Salt and pepper to taste

Roast corn, bell pepper and tomato on the grill. Cut corn kernels off cob and dice pepper and tomato. Combine vegetables with lime and lemon juices, vinegar and oil. Season with salt and pepper.

Yield: 2 servings

This spectacular combination is a great side dish for grilled chicken. Place your vegetables in a tortilla wrap for a fun alternative.

Layered Antipasto Salad

Show off this lovely layered salad in your Grandmother's vintage glass serving bowl.

1 head romaine lettuce
2 tomatoes, chopped
1 (10 ounce) jar marinated
    artichoke hearts, quartered
1 (6 ounce) package small pepperoni
    slices

4 ounces mozzarella cheese, shredded
1 (8 ounce) bottle Italian dressing
1 (5 ounce) can black olives
4 slices bacon, cooked and crumbled
Crunchy Salad Croutons,
    see page 70 for recipe

Layer salad ingredients in the following order in a salad bowl: one third of lettuce, half of tomatoes, artichokes, one third of lettuce, pepperoni, cheese, drizzle with dressing, remaining lettuce, remaining tomatoes, olives, bacon, drizzle with dressing. Refrigerate at least 3 hours before serving. Add croutons.

Yield: 8 to 10 servings

Breads, Brunch & Beverages

1960

*I*llness affects children at various ages and unexpected times. Whenever an sickness occurs, it is reassuring to know that Le Bonheur Children's Medical Center, with its dedicated team of caring professionals, is within our reach. I was hospitalized for pneumonia at Le Bonheur when I was six years old. Although it is vague, I remember being a patient there and the great care I received from the staff. One of the things I recall as I began to feel better was a Le Bonheur Club volunteer who would come around with a book cart, and I would select different books to read. My mother recalls the nurses placing ice packs on me to bring down the fever and assuring her that I would be fine.

In 1981, I returned to Le Bonheur again as one of their pharmacists working the midnight shift. It is a great feeling to be able to give back to the hospital that had once taken care of me.

1991

*W*hen a newborn baby has to spend long periods of time in the hospital, it is a very difficult time for the parents. In these cases, there is no better place for that child than at Le Bonheur, where concerned staff comfort and care for parents as well as the child.

My daughter spent the first 7 months of her life on a ventilator at Le Bonheur. Since that time, she has needed a ventilator on two separate occasions. I am grateful to report that, apart from a recent cold, she is quite well now. My husband and I are thankful to all the doctors, nurses and respiratory therapists who cared for her and became our friends. We consider our daughter a true miracle.

I think it is important for people in our area to be familiar with the many life-saving techniques that are available at Le Bonheur. Fortunately, both parents and children can benefit from this wonderful expertise. Of course, the majority of children never require invasive techniques for survival, but it is certainly a blessing to have this hospital close if a child needs care.

Onion Rosemary Rolls

The onion and rosemary aroma of these shiny, crusted dinner rolls says, "Lead me to the butter!"

2 cups onions, finely chopped

2 tablespoons olive oil

2 packages active dry yeast

½ cup warm water
(115 to 120 degrees)

2 cups warm milk
(115 to 120 degrees)

¼ cup vegetable shortening

¼ cup honey

2 teaspoons salt

5 to 6 cups unbleached flour

2 tablespoons fresh rosemary, chopped

1½ cups whole wheat flour

Olive oil (optional)

Sauté onions in olive oil until soft but not browned; set aside to cool. In a large bowl, stir yeast into water until softened. Add cooled onions, milk, shortening, honey, salt and 2 cups unbleached flour. Beat vigorously for 2 minutes. Blend in rosemary and whole wheat flour. Gradually add remaining unbleached flour, ¼ cup at a time, until dough pulls away from the side of the bowl. Turn dough onto a floured surface. Knead, adding flour a little at a time, until dough is smooth and elastic. Place dough in a greased bowl, turning to coat dough ball. Cover with a tightly woven towel and let rise 1 hour or until dough doubles in size. Turn out onto a greased surface and divide into 36 pieces. Shape each into an 8 inch strand and then tie in a knot. Place rolls 3 inches apart on parchment-lined baking sheets. Cover rolls with towel for 45 minutes or until dough doubles in size. Bake at 400 degrees for 15 minutes. Immediately remove rolls from baking sheets and place on cooling racks. For a shiny, soft crust, brush tops with olive oil.

Yield: 36 rolls

The secret to these fabulous dinner rolls is that the water should be warm as a baby's bath but not too hot to kill the yeast or scald the baby.

Dinner Rolls

2 packages active dry yeast
1 cup warm water (115 to 120 degrees)
1 cup vegetable shortening
¾ cup sugar

1½ teaspoons salt
1 cup boiling water
2 eggs, well beaten
6 cups all-purpose flour
Melted butter

Combine yeast and warm water in a small glass bowl; set aside. In a large mixing bowl, blend shortening, sugar and salt. Add boiling water and stir until cooled. Add eggs. Stir in dissolved yeast until mixed. Blend in flour, 2 cups at a time. Cover and refrigerate dough at least 4 hours or up to several days.

Roll dough out on a floured surface. Cut to desired size and shape into balls. Dip rolls completely in melted butter. Fold each roll over a dull knife to make a half-moon shape. Place rolls close together on an ungreased jelly-roll pan. Place pan in a cold oven with a bowl of hot water under the rack. Let dough rise 2 hours or until rolls nearly double in size. Remove rolls to preheat oven. Bake at 425 degrees for 10 to 12 minutes or until golden brown.

Yield: 36 rolls

These yummy rolls can be made ahead and frozen for 3 weeks.

Potato Rolls

1½ medium potatoes, peeled and
    quartered
1 cup whole milk
1 package active dry yeast
½ cup plus 1 teaspoon sugar

⅔ cup vegetable oil
1 large egg, beaten
2 teaspoons salt
6½ to 6¾ cups bread flour
Melted butter

Cook potatoes in boiling water for 20 minutes or until tender. Drain potatoes, reserving ½ cup of cooking water. In a large bowl, combine reserved water with milk and heat until just warm (105 to 115 degrees). Stir in yeast and sugar and let stand until dissolved. The yeast will rise some at this stage.

Mash potatoes. Measure 1 cup packed mashed potatoes and add to yeast mixture along with oil, egg and salt. Blend well. Add flour just until a stiff dough is formed. Turn dough onto a lightly floured surface. Knead 8 to 10 minutes by hand or about 6 minutes with a dough hook on an electric stand mixer. Add more flour as needed to prevent sticking while kneading. Place in a large greased bowl, turning dough over so top is greased. Cover with a warm, damp cloth and let rise in a warm place (80 degrees) for 1 hour and 30 minutes or until doubled in size. Punch down dough and divide into fourths. Divide each fourth into twelve 1½ inch balls. Arrange balls in four 8 or 9 inch greased round cake pans. Cover each pan with a warm, damp cloth and let rise in a warm place for 45 minutes or until doubled in size. Bake at 400 degrees for 10 to 15 minutes or until golden brown. Brush tops with melted butter immediately after removing from oven. Serve rolls warm.

Yield: 48 small rolls

This recipe can be used as a base for monkey bread. After rolls have risen a second time, dip each roll in melted butter and in cinnamon sugar and layer in a funnel pan. Bake as directed. Kids love this!

This recipe can be made well in advance. To do this, after the dough has risen for the first time, place in an airtight container and refrigerate up to 1 month. To bake, take out the amount of dough needed, roll into balls and place in cake pans to rise a second time. Bake as directed above. A great recipe for new moms!

Onion Cheese French Bread

4 tablespoons butter

¾ cup Cheddar cheese, shredded

½ cup mayonnaise

¼ cup green onions, chopped

1 (16 ounce) loaf French bread

Combine butter, cheese, mayonnaise and onions. Slice bread loaf in half lengthwise. Spread mixture over cut sides of bread. Place on a baking sheet, cut-side up. Broil 6 inches from heat source for 2 minutes or until bubbly.

Herb Biscuits

1 (8 ounce) package cream cheese, softened

1 stick butter, softened

1 cup self-rising flour

1 teaspoon dried basil

Beat cream cheese and butter with an electric mixer at medium speed for 2 minutes or until creamy. Gradually add flour and basil and mix just until blended. Spoon dough into ungreased miniature muffin cups, filling to the top. Bake at 400 degrees for 15 minutes or until golden.

Yield: 6 servings

Pumpkin Apple Muffins

Make this your favorite Fall treat.

1⅔ cups all-purpose flour

1 teaspoon baking soda

¼ teaspoon baking powder

¼ teaspoon salt

1 tablespoon pumpkin pie spice

1 cup sugar

1 cup canned pumpkin

1 stick butter, melted

2 eggs, lightly beaten

1 Granny Smith apple, peeled and finely chopped

3 tablespoons sugar

1 teaspoon pumpkin pie spice

Combine flour, baking soda, baking powder, salt, 1 tablespoon pumpkin pie spice and 1 cup sugar in a large bowl, making a well in the center of the mixture. In a separate bowl, combine pumpkin, butter and eggs and add to dry ingredients. Stir until mixture is just moistened. Fold in apples. Spoon dough into greased muffin cups, filling two-thirds full. Combine 3 tablespoons sugar and 1 teaspoon pumpkin pie spice and sprinkle over muffins. Bake at 350 degrees for 20 minutes. Remove from pans immediately and cool on wire racks.

Yield: 24 muffins

Cheddar-Jalapeño Corn Sticks

Add some zip to traditional corn sticks.

1 cup yellow cornmeal

1 teaspoon sugar

½ teaspoon baking soda

½ teaspoon salt

1 cup buttermilk, well shaken

1 egg

1 cup sharp Cheddar cheese,
  coarsely shredded

¼ cup green onions, finely chopped

1 to 2 tablespoons pickled jalapeño,
  drained and finely chopped

4 tablespoons unsalted butter,
  melted

Heat 2 well-seasoned cast iron corn stick pans, each with seven 5x½ inch molds, or a well-seasoned 9 inch cast iron skillet in the center of a 425 degree oven.

Blend cornmeal, sugar, baking soda and salt in a large bowl. In a separate bowl, whisk together buttermilk and egg. Add liquid to cornmeal mixture along with cheese, onions, jalapeño and 2 tablespoons butter. Stir until just combined.

Remove pans from oven and divide 2 tablespoons butter among molds. Quickly divide cornmeal batter among molds, about 3 tablespoons batter each. Bake at 425 degrees for 12 to 15 minutes or until tops are golden and a tester comes out clean. Cool corn sticks in molds for 3 to 5 minutes before removing from pans. Serve warm. If using a skillet, pour all of batter into skillet and bake 15 to 20 minutes.

Yield: 14 corn sticks

Key Notes

Not-So-Sweet Muffins

1 egg
½ cup milk
4 tablespoons margarine, melted

½ cup sugar
1½ cups self-rising flour

Combine egg, milk, margarine, sugar and flour and stir until moist but still lumpy. Spoon batter into greased mini muffin cups. Bake at 350 degrees for 20 minutes.

Yield: 24 mini muffins

Blueberry Muffins

3 cups all-purpose flour
1 tablespoon baking powder
½ teaspoon salt
½ teaspoon baking soda
1¼ sticks unsalted butter, softened
1 cup sugar
2 eggs

1½ cups plain low-fat yogurt
1½ cups blueberries
1 tablespoon all-purpose flour
Melted butter
½ cup sugar
2 teaspoons cinnamon

Combine 3 cups all-purpose flour, baking powder, salt and baking soda in a medium mixing bowl; set aside. In a large mixing bowl, cream unsalted butter and 1 cup sugar with an electric mixer on medium-high speed for 2 minutes or until fluffy. Add eggs, one at a time, beating well after each addition. Blend in dry ingredients and yogurt, alternately, in 3 batches. Toss blueberries with 1 tablespoon flour and fold into batter. Spoon batter into muffin cups coated with nonstick cooking spray. Bake at 375 degrees for 25 to 30 minutes or until golden. Cool in pan on a wire rack for 5 minutes. Remove muffins and brush tops while warm with melted butter, then dip in a mixture of ½ cup sugar and cinnamon. Serve warm.

Yield: 12 muffins

For a chocolate treat, substitute 1½ cups chocolate chips for the blueberries.

Grate orange, lemon and lime peels before discarding. Store the zest in an airtight container in the refrigerator. It will be ready for use in flavoring breads and cakes.

Orange Pecan Muffins

1 cup sugar

1 stick butter, softened

2 eggs

1 teaspoon baking soda

Zest of 1 orange

2 cups all-purpose flour

1 cup buttermilk

¾ cup pecans, finely chopped

⅓ cup orange juice, fresh preferred

1 tablespoon sugar

Cream 1 cup sugar and butter. Add eggs, 1 at a time, beating well after each addition. Stir in baking soda and orange zest. Add half the flour and half the buttermilk. Stir slightly. Add remaining flour and buttermilk. Fold in pecans. Spoon batter into paper-lined or greased muffin cups. Bake at 375 degrees for 20 to 25 minutes. Drizzle orange juice over hot muffins and sprinkle with 1 tablespoon sugar. Cool before removing from muffin pan.

Yield: 12 regular or 48 mini muffins

Bourbon Pecan Quick Bread

3 cups all-purpose flour

1 cup sugar

4 teaspoons baking powder

1½ teaspoons salt

4 tablespoons butter or margarine

2 teaspoons orange zest

1¼ cups chopped pecans

1 egg

1 cup milk

½ cup bourbon

2 tablespoons bourbon (optional)

Combine flour, sugar, baking powder and salt in a mixing bowl. Cut in butter to resemble coarse crumbs. Add orange zest and pecans. In a small bowl, mix egg, milk and ½ cup bourbon together. Add mixture to dry ingredients and stir until just moistened. Spoon batter into a greased and floured 9x5 inch loaf pan. Bake at 350 degrees for 60 to 70 minutes. When done, sprinkle with 2 tablespoons bourbon, if desired. Cool in pans 10 minutes before transferring to a wire rack to cool completely.

Yield: 1 loaf

Maple Pecan Muffins

2 cups self-rising flour
¼ cup packed light brown sugar
1 egg
½ cup maple syrup
1 cup milk

5 tablespoons butter, melted
1 teaspoon vanilla
1 cup chopped pecans
1 tablespoon granulated sugar
⅛ teaspoon cinnamon

Combine flour and brown sugar in a bowl. Stir in egg, syrup, milk, butter and vanilla until just moistened. Stir in pecans. Spoon batter into greased mini muffin cups. Mix granulated sugar and cinnamon and sprinkle over tops. Bake at 400 degrees for 12 to 15 minutes.

Yield: 36 mini muffins

Blueberry Lime Bread

Great for breakfast or brunch. This bread will surely open the door to a new neighbor's heart.

1 cup sugar
6 tablespoons butter, softened
2 eggs
½ cup milk
1 teaspoon baking powder
½ teaspoon salt

1½ cups flour
Zest of 1 lime
½ cup fresh blueberries
½ cup sugar
Juice of 1 lime

Cream 1 cup sugar and butter until light. Beat in eggs. Mix in ½ cup milk. In a separate bowl, sift together baking powder, salt and flour. Add dry ingredients to creamed mixture and beat until smooth. Fold in lime zest and blueberries. Pour batter into a greased 5x9 inch loaf pan. Bake at 350 degrees for 1 hour or until a toothpick inserted in the center comes out clean. Combine ½ cup sugar and lime juice and mix until sugar dissolves. Spoon mixture over hot bread before removing from pan.

Yield: 1 loaf

Popovers with Strawberry Butter

Popovers

1 cup flour

¾ teaspoon salt

1 cup milk

1 tablespoon vegetable oil

3 eggs, room temperature

Strawberry Butter

4 tablespoons butter, softened

1 tablespoon strawberry jam, or fruit jam of choice

Popovers

Sift together flour and salt. Mix milk and oil and add to dry ingredients. Add eggs, one at a time, beating well after each addition. Beat 2 minutes longer. Grease a muffin or popover pan. Place empty greased pan in a 415 degree oven for 1 minute. Remove from oven and fill cups with batter. Bake at 415 degrees for 30 to 40 minutes or until brown. Do not open oven door while baking, as this will cause popovers to fall. After baking, transfer muffin pan to a wire rack. Cut a ½ inch slit in top of each popover to allow steam to escape. Serve immediately with Strawberry Butter.

Strawberry Butter

Mix together butter and jam. Spread over hot popovers.

Yield: 6 popovers

Friendship Cranberry Cake

Cake

1½ sticks butter, softened	1½ teaspoons baking soda
1½ cups sugar	¾ teaspoon salt
3 eggs, room temperature	1½ cups sour cream
1½ teaspoons almond extract	1 (16 ounce) can whole berry cranberry sauce
3 cups all-purpose flour	½ cup chopped walnuts
1½ teaspoons baking powder	

Glaze

¾ cup powdered sugar	½ teaspoon almond extract
1 tablespoon warm water	

Cake

Cream butter and sugar until light. Add eggs, one at a time, beating well after each addition. Add extract. In a separate bowl, sift together flour, baking powder, baking soda and salt. Alternately add dry ingredients and sour cream to creamed mixture. Spoon one third of batter into a greased and floured Bundt pan. Crumble one third of cranberry sauce over batter. Repeat layers twice, ending with sauce. Sprinkle with walnuts. Bake at 350 degrees for 1 hour. Cool in pan 5 minutes. Remove from pan and cover with glaze.

Glaze

Combine sugar, water and almond extract and spread over warm cake.

Yield: 15 servings

Key Notes

Baked French Toast with Maple-Praline Sauce

Unanimously, the cookbook committee's favorite from our weekend retreat.

French Toast

½ (8 ounce) package cream cheese, softened

½ cup sifted powdered sugar

1 (16 ounce) loaf unsliced French bread

8 eggs, lightly beaten

¾ cup half-and-half

1 teaspoon vanilla

¼ teaspoon cinnamon

Maple-Praline Sauce

1 stick butter

½ cup packed light brown sugar

½ cup maple syrup

1 cup chopped pecans

French Toast

Combine cream cheese and powdered sugar in a small bowl; set aside. Cut bread into 1 inch thick slices to yield 20 slices. Spread cream cheese mixture onto top of 10 slices. Top with remaining bread slices to resemble a sandwich. Combine eggs, half-and-half, vanilla and cinnamon in a 9x13 inch baking dish. Add bread sandwiches, turning several times to coat. Cover and refrigerate 8 hours or overnight.

When ready to bake, remove bread sandwiches from dish, discarding any excess liquid. Place bread on a lightly greased baking sheet. Bake at 375 degrees for 20 to 25 minutes or until golden brown. Serve with Maple-Praline Sauce.

Maple-Praline Sauce

Combine butter, brown sugar, syrup and pecans in a small saucepan. Cook over medium-low heat, stirring often, until well blended.

Yield: 10 servings, 1¾ cups sauce

Christmas Morning Coffee Cake

Filling

2 tablespoons butter, melted	1 cup broken pecans
2 tablespoons all-purpose flour	2 to 3 tablespoons strong coffee
1 cup packed light brown sugar	

Batter

2 sticks butter, softened	2 teaspoons vanilla
1 cup sugar	2 cups all-purpose flour
3 eggs	1 teaspoon baking soda
1 cup sour cream	1 teaspoon baking powder

Filling

Combine butter, flour, brown sugar, pecans and coffee; set aside.

Batter

In a mixing bowl, cream butter, sugar, eggs and sour cream. Mix in vanilla. In a separate bowl, sift together flour, baking soda and baking powder. Blend dry ingredients into creamed mixture. Beat 10 minutes.

Pour half of batter into a greased and floured 10 inch tube pan. Top with half of filling. Repeat layers. Bake at 350 degrees for 50 to 60 minutes.

Yield: 15 servings

Cranberry Pecan Cake

3 eggs	2 cups all-purpose flour
2 cups sugar	2½ cups fresh or frozen cranberries
1½ sticks butter, softened	⅔ cup chopped pecans
1 teaspoon almond extract	

Beat eggs and sugar for 5 minutes or until thick and light in color. Add butter and extract and beat 2 minutes longer. Stir in flour just until combined. Fold in cranberries and pecans. Spread batter into a greased 9x13 inch baking pan. Bake at 350 degrees for 45 to 50 minutes or until a toothpick inserted in the center comes out clean.

Yield: 15 to 18 servings

We grew up having Christmas coffee cake and juice while sitting on the floor surrounded by our gifts. We wondered if Santa had enjoyed eating this cake also.

Orange Kiss-Me Cake

Cake

1 orange	1 teaspoon baking soda
1 cup raisins	1 teaspoon salt
⅓ cup walnuts	1 cup milk
2 cups all-purpose flour	1 stick butter, softened
1 cup sugar	2 eggs

Topping

Reserved ⅓ cup orange juice	1 teaspoon cinnamon
⅓ cup sugar	¼ cup finely chopped walnuts

Cake

Squeeze juice from orange, reserving ⅓ cup for topping. Remove seeds from orange and place orange peel and pulp in a food processor with raisins and walnuts. Process and set aside. In a large bowl, combine flour, sugar, baking soda, salt, milk, butter and eggs. Mix with an electric mixer on medium speed for 3 minutes. Stir in orange-nut mixture. Pour batter into a greased and floured 9x13 inch pan. Bake at 350 degrees for 35 to 45 minutes.

Topping

While still warm, drizzle orange juice over baked cake. Combine sugar and cinnamon and mix well. Stir in walnuts. Sprinkle mixture on top of cake.

Yield: 15 to 18 servings

Meringue Torte

Perfect for a ladies' luncheon.

1½ cups egg whites
    (about 9 to 11 eggs)
¼ teaspoon cream of tartar
1½ cups sugar
1 teaspoon vanilla extract
½ teaspoon almond extract

1 cup heavy cream
1 tablespoon sugar
3 (10 ounce) packages frozen
    raspberries
1½ cups sugar
2 tablespoons kirsch

Beat egg whites with an electric mixer on medium speed until frothy. Add cream of tartar and continue beating. Increase mixer to high speed while gradually adding 1½ cups sugar. Beat in extracts. Beat until mixture is very stiff and glossy. Pour mixture into an angel food cake pan that has been greased with butter. Smooth down batter in pan. Place in a 425 degree oven. Allow temperature to reach 425 after closing door, then turn off oven and leave torte in oven overnight without opening door.

When torte is removed from the oven, it will look like a disaster. Push up on the removable bottom and liquid will come out of pan. Using a knife, slice around top to cut away the crust, saving all the crumbs. Slide knife between the bottom of cake and tin. Loosen cake and unmold onto a platter. Whip cream, adding 1 tablespoon sugar while beating. Ice torte with whipped cream. Sprinkle reserved crumbs on top. Mix raspberries with 1½ cups sugar and kirsch. Serve torte with raspberries spooned over each serving or with raspberries on the side.

Yield: 15 servings

Sparkling Fruit Compote

Red ripe strawberries and luscious blueberries sparkle in champagne in this elegant fruit compote.

½ cup sugar

1 cup water

Zest and juice of 1 lemon

4 oranges, peeled and sectioned

2 cups seedless grapes, halved

2 cups fresh pineapple, cubed

1 cup fresh strawberries, sliced

1 cup fresh blueberries

2 kiwi, peeled and sliced

2 cups dry champagne, or sparkling cider, chilled

Combine sugar and water in a saucepan. Bring to a boil, cover and cook 5 minutes. Uncover and cool. Stir in lemon zest and juice. In a large bowl, mix together oranges, grapes and pineapple. Pour sugar mixture over fruit and toss to coat. Cover and chill. Just before serving, add berries and kiwi. Pour champagne on top.

Yield: 8 to 10 servings

Apple Raspberry Compote

A delicious topping for homemade waffles.

4 Granny Smith apples, peeled and
    chopped
½ cup apple cider
3 tablespoons brown sugar
½ teaspoon fresh ginger, grated

Zest and juice of 1 lemon
½ teaspoon ground nutmeg
¼ teaspoon ground allspice
8 ounces frozen raspberries

Combine apples, cider, brown sugar, ginger, lemon zest, lemon juice, nutmeg and allspice in a medium saucepan. Bring to a boil over medium heat. Cook 10 to 12 minutes or until apples are tender. Reduce heat to low and stir in raspberries. Cook and stir 3 to 4 minutes or until heated through. Cool to room temperature. Serve with waffles, French toast or pancakes.

Yield: 4 servings

Scalloped Pineapple

A tried and true recipe from Grandmother's collection.

8 slices white bread
1 (20 ounce) can crushed pineapple

1 stick margarine, melted
1 cup sugar

Remove crusts and cut bread slices into cubes. Mix bread cubes, pineapple, margarine and sugar and place in a baking dish. Bake at 350 degrees for 1 hour. Serve immediately as a side dish.

Yield: 8 servings

Key Notes

Grand Marnier Strawberry Preserves

Wrapped in colored cellophane and ribbon, this is an unforgettable Christmas gift.

3 (10 ounce) packages frozen sliced strawberries, thawed
¼ cup water
1 (1¾ ounce) package powdered pectin

6 cups sugar
⅓ cup Grand Marnier or to taste
3 tablespoons fresh lemon juice
Paraffin wax, melted

Combine strawberries, water and pectin in a stockpot. Bring to a boil, stirring occasionally. Boil 1 minute. Stir in sugar and bring to a full, rolling boil that cannot be stirred down. Boil hard 1 minute. Remove from heat and stir in Grand Marnier and lemon juice. Let stand 5 minutes, stirring occasionally. Skim off foam. Pour preserves into 6 half-pint hot sterilized glass jars. Seal with paraffin wax. Store up to 6 months with seal intact. Preserves will keep up to 1 month in refrigerator after paraffin is removed.

Yield: 6 half-pint jars

Bacon Rounds

1 pound bacon, cooked and
    crumbled
1 bunch green onions, minced
1 cup mayonnaise

Salt and pepper to taste
1 loaf white sandwich bread
1 (1 pint) container cherry
    tomatoes, quartered

Combine bacon, onions, mayonnaise, salt and pepper. Use a 1½ inch biscuit cutter to cut 4 circles out of each slice of bread. This works best if bread is frozen. Spread bacon mixture over bread circles. Top each circle with a tomato quarter.

Yield: 80 rounds

Bread circles can be cut out up to 1 week ahead and frozen until needed. Spread bacon mixture over frozen circles and let stand at room temperature for 2 hours before serving.

Key Notes

Key Notes

N'awlins Bacon

No need to wait for Mardi Gras celebration to enjoy this Bayou favorite. A definite party pleaser.

12 slices thick-sliced bacon   3 tablespoons sugar
1½ teaspoons chili powder   ¼ cup finely chopped pecans

Place bacon on the rack of a broiler pan. Bake at 425 degrees on center rack of oven for 10 minutes or until bacon is golden brown. Combine chili powder and sugar and sprinkle over cooked bacon. Top bacon with pecans and bake 5 minutes longer until bacon is crisp and brown. Drain, sugar-side up, on paper towels and serve.

Yield: 6 servings

The Best Cucumber Sandwiches

1 medium cucumber

½ cup cider vinegar

1 cup water

1 (8 ounce) package cream cheese, softened

¼ cup mayonnaise or mayonnaise-type salad dressing

¼ teaspoon garlic powder

¼ teaspoon onion salt

Dash of Worcestershire sauce

1 loaf sliced firm bread

Thinly sliced pimiento-stuffed olives and paprika for garnish

Score cucumber lengthwise with a fork, then cut crosswise into thin slices. In a medium bowl, combine vinegar and water. Add cucumber slices and let stand at room temperature for at least 30 minutes. Drain well. Meanwhile, combine cream cheese, mayonnaise, garlic powder, onion salt and Worcestershire sauce. Use a 2 inch cutter to cut 2 circles out of each slice of bread. Spread circles lightly with cream cheese mixture. Just before serving, top each circle with a cucumber slice. Garnish with an olive slice or sprinkle with paprika, or both.

Yield: 48 sandwiches

Mexican Mini Muffins

2 cups self-rising cornmeal mix

1 cup self-rising flour

3 tablespoons sugar

3 eggs, beaten

1½ cups milk

1 (8 ounce) container sour cream

1 pound ground beef, browned and drained

1 (17 ounce) can cream style corn

1½ cups sharp Cheddar cheese, shredded

1 large onion, finely chopped

2 jalapeño peppers, seeded and chopped

Combine cornmeal mix, flour, sugar, eggs, milk, sour cream, beef, corn, cheese, onions and jalapeño pepper. Spoon into greased mini muffin cups. Bake at 400 degrees until brown.

Yield: 36 to 40 mini muffins

Delta Breakfast Rolls

1 pound hot or mild sausage

1 (8 ounce) package cream cheese

1 (4 ounce) can chopped green
    chiles, drained

1 (6 ounce) jar sliced mushrooms,
    drained

2 puff pastry sheets

1 egg white

2 tablespoons poppy seeds

Brown sausage in a skillet and drain. Mix cream cheese, chiles and mushrooms into hot sausage and cool. Refrigerate up to 1 day ahead. Roll out a pastry sheet into a rectangle. Place half of sausage mixture lengthwise down the center of rectangle. Roll pastry, starting with long side, to form a log. Repeat with remaining pastry and sausage mixture. Place logs about 3 inches apart on an ungreased baking sheet. Brush lightly with egg white and sprinkle with poppy seeds. Bake at 325 degrees for 45 minutes or until golden brown. Slice and serve.

Yield: 10 to 15 servings

Breakfast Frittata

1 small onion, chopped

1 medium potato, peeled and thinly
    sliced

1 pound sausage, cooked and
    crumbled

3 ounces fresh mushrooms, sliced

1 small zucchini, chopped

1 small red bell pepper, chopped

12 eggs, beaten

⅓ cup freshly grated Parmesan
    cheese

In a greased 12 inch ovenproof skillet or casserole, layer onions, potatoes, sausage, mushrooms, zucchini and bell peppers. Pour eggs over top and sprinkle with cheese. Bake at 350 degrees for 40 to 45 minutes or until set. Transfer to broiler and cook until top is lightly browned.

Yield: 8 to 10 servings

Company Crêpes

1 pound mild sausage

1 onion, minced

1 (8 ounce) package cream cheese

1 (7 ounce) can mushroom stems and pieces, drained

1 (8 ounce) can chopped water chestnuts, drained

¼ teaspoon dried thyme

¼ teaspoon garlic salt

12 store-bought crêpes

½ cup sour cream

1 stick butter, softened

½ cup Cheddar cheese, shredded

Brown sausage and onions in a skillet; drain well. Add cream cheese, mushrooms, water chestnuts, thyme and garlic salt to skillet and mix. Fill each crêpe with 2 tablespoons sausage filling. Roll gently and place crêpes, seam-side down, in a large glass baking dish. Blend sour cream and butter and pour over crêpes. Garnish with Cheddar cheese. Heat in a microwave or oven until warm.

Yield: 4 to 6 servings

We have enjoyed these crêpes each year when fishing on the White River in the Ozarks.

Quiche with Mushroom Crust

8 ounces mushrooms, chopped

3 tablespoons butter

½ cup saltine crackers, finely crushed

2 tablespoons butter

½ cup green onions, chopped

2 cups Monterey Jack cheese, shredded

1 cup cottage cheese

3 eggs

¼ teaspoon cayenne pepper

¼ teaspoon paprika

Sauté mushrooms in 3 tablespoons butter in a skillet over medium heat. Remove from heat and stir in cracker crumbs. Press mixture into the bottom and up the sides of a greased 10 inch pie pan. Grease fingers to prevent crust from sticking as you press.

Melt 2 tablespoons butter in a skillet. Add onions and sauté until limp. Spread onions over crust. Sprinkle Monterey Jack cheese on top. Blend cottage cheese, eggs and cayenne in a food processor until smooth. Pour mixture into crust. Sprinkle with paprika. At this point, quiche can be refrigerated until ready to bake. Bake at 350 degrees for 20 minutes. Increase oven to 400 degrees and bake 10 minutes longer or until top is brown. Remove from oven and let stand 10 minutes before cutting.

Yield: 6 to 8 servings

Quiche can be baked ahead. To reheat, bake at 300 degrees for 20 minutes.

Savory Mushroom Roll Ups

Batter

½ cup plain yogurt

½ cup milk

¼ cup quick-cooking grits

⅔ cup Cheddar cheese, shredded

4 egg yolks

Salt and pepper to taste

6 egg whites

Filling

2 cups fresh mushrooms, sliced

4 tablespoons butter

½ cup cooked ham, chopped

½ cup all-purpose flour

4 tablespoons butter, melted

2 cups milk

2 (6 ounce) cans chopped green chiles, drained

Dash of cayenne pepper

1 cup Cheddar cheese, shredded

Batter

Bring yogurt and milk to a boil in a saucepan. Add grits and cook according to package directions. Remove from heat and stir in cheese. Mix in yolks one at a time. Season with salt and pepper. Beat egg whites until stiff and gradually fold into grits. Spread batter into a greased 10x15 inch jelly-roll pan lined with greased wax paper. Bake at 350 degrees for 20 to 25 minutes. Do not overcook. Remove from oven and turn pan upside-down onto wax paper. Remove baked grits from pan and strip off paper.

Filling

Sauté mushrooms in 4 tablespoons butter in a skillet until tender. Stir in ham. Combine flour and 4 tablespoons melted butter in a saucepan. Blend in milk and bring to a boil. Cook and stir until thickened. Add mushroom mixture, chiles and cayenne. Spread filling over baked grits. Sprinkle with cheese and roll up jelly-roll style. Let stand 5 minutes before slicing.

Yield: 8 to 10 servings

Punched Up Java

5 tablespoons instant coffee

2 cups hot water

1 cup sugar

½ teaspoon salt

6 cups cold water

½ teaspoon almond extract

½ gallon vanilla ice cream

½ gallon chocolate ice cream

1 pint half-and-half

Dissolve coffee in hot water. Add sugar and salt and stir until dissolved. Add cold water and almond extract. Chill. When ready to serve, place vanilla and chocolate ice cream in a punch bowl. Add half-and-half to coffee mixture. Pour mixture over ice cream.

Yield: 40 to 50 servings

Hot Buttered Rum

4 sticks butter, softened

1 (16 ounce) package light brown sugar

1 (16 ounce) package powdered sugar

2 teaspoons ground nutmeg

2 teaspoons cinnamon

1 quart vanilla ice cream, softened

Light rum

Boiling water

Whipped cream and cinnamon for garnish

Cream butter, sugars, nutmeg and cinnamon until smooth. Add ice cream and mix well. Spoon mixture into a 2 quart container and freeze.

For each serving, place 3 tablespoons of frozen mixture and a jigger of rum in a mug. Fill with boiling water and stir. Top with whipped cream and sprinkle with cinnamon.

Yield: 16 to 20 servings

Brunch Punch

1 (64 ounce) can pineapple juice, chilled

1 (2 liter) bottle ginger ale, chilled

1 (0.34 ounce) package artificially sweetened strawberry kiwi powdered drink mix

1 quart water

Combine pineapple juice, ginger ale, drink mix and water in a punch bowl. Double recipe if using a large bowl.

Yield: 24 to 30 servings

Easy punch for a large gathering. Plan on two four-ounce servings of punch per person.

Holiday Eggnog

Young children, pregnant women, the elderly and anyone with immune disorders should avoid eating raw egg.

8 eggs, separated

2 cups sugar

1 quart milk

½ pint bourbon

1 pint heavy cream

Nutmeg

Beat egg yolks. Blend in sugar. Stir in milk, then bourbon. Refrigerate until ready to serve. When ready to serve, whip cream until stiff. In a separate bowl, beat egg whites. Fold egg whites into whipped cream. Pour eggnog into a punch bowl or into individual glasses. Top with whipped cream mixture. Sprinkle with nutmeg.

Yield: 24 servings

Wassail

3½ quarts water

2 cups sugar

2 cinnamon sticks

1 teaspoon whole cloves

1 (48 ounce) can pineapple juice

1 (6 ounce) can frozen orange juice concentrate

1 (6 ounce) can frozen limeade concentrate

Combine water, sugar, cinnamon and cloves in a stockpot. Bring to a boil. Boil 10 minutes. Remove cinnamon and cloves. Add pineapple juice and concentrates. Heat and serve.

Yield: 36 servings

Meats

*Beef Tournedos with
Gorgonzola and Cranberry-Port Sauce*

1996

*O*ne mother of two "miracle" children has seen first-hand what Le Bonheur can do. When her son was just 2½ years old, he was diagnosed with a rare form of hemophilia. Not long after, his sister began a long, hard battle against a list of illnesses. Eventually, she was diagnosed with osteomyelitis, a bone marrow disease, complicated by an immune deficiency.

Her daughter's experience - 18 surgeries, extended hospital stays, close calls with death - has given this mother a personal knowledge of the miracles Le Bonheur can achieve. "All I can say to someone who isn't familiar with Le Bonheur is, 'just walk through the halls,'" says the mother. "You will see what it means to a child and the parents."

Recently the daughter was the youngest rider to be inducted into the United States Equestrian Team at the age of twelve. This is a tremendous accomplishment. Both children are stronger today, but they will always need the ongoing care of Le Bonheur.

Beef Tournedos with Gorgonzola and Cranberry-Port Sauce

Cranberry-Port Sauce

3 tablespoons butter

3 large cloves garlic, sliced

1 large shallot, sliced

1 cup canned beef broth

1 cup ruby port

¼ cup dried cranberries

Beef

3 tablespoons butter

4 (5 to 6 ounce, 1 inch thick) beef
    tenderloin steaks

Salt and pepper to taste

½ teaspoon fresh rosemary, minced

¼ cup canned beef broth

½ cup Gorgonzola cheese, crumbled

Fresh rosemary sprigs for garnish

Cranberry-Port Sauce

Melt butter in a saucepan over medium-high heat. Add garlic, shallot, broth, port and cranberries. Boil 8 minutes or until reduced to ½ cup. Set aside.

Beef

Melt butter in a large skillet over medium-high heat. Season beef with salt and pepper. Cook beef in butter to preferred degree of doneness, about 5 minutes per side for medium-rare. Remove beef from skillet and cover loosely with foil. Add sauce, rosemary and broth to skillet. Boil 1 minute, scraping up any brown bits. Spoon sauce over beef. Sprinkle with cheese and garnish with rosemary sprigs.

Yield: 4 servings

Port is a sweet, fortified red wine made from red and white wine grapes. True port is produced in Portugal and appears in three types. The finest is vintage port made from a single grape harvest, bottled after two years of aging and left on its side to bottle age for 10-20 years. You would not cook with it. For the average consumer, tawny port is a blended wine and aged until the color matures from purple to ruby to golden to tawny. Ruby port is the younger sibling of tawny and is aged for only three years.

"A little consideration
for others makes all
the difference"

Do calligraphy or hand
made artwork on place
cards for guests.

Honor someone's
birthday with his or her
special menu request.

Set your table early.

Place a container of
soapy water under
cabinet. Drop silverware
in between courses and
enjoy your dessert!

Pick ivy, greenery
and flowers from your
yard to work into an
arrangement.

Elegant Beef

You don't need to have a black tie dinner to serve this dish.

4 (6 ounce) beef tenderloin steaks
2 teaspoons fresh thyme, finely
    chopped
¼ teaspoon salt
¼ teaspoon black pepper
1 tablespoon butter
1 tablespoon olive oil

2 cups dry white wine
1 cup beef consommé
1 cup half-and-half
8 small asparagus spears, trimmed
    and steamed to crisp-tender
2 ounces bleu cheese, crumbled

Rub steaks with thyme, salt and pepper. Melt butter in a large skillet over medium heat. Add oil. Cook steaks in skillet to desired degree of doneness. Remove steaks and keep warm, reserving drippings in skillet. Stir wine and consommé into skillet. Increase heat to high and cook until reduced to about ½ cup. Keep sauce warm. To serve, top each steak with 2 asparagus spears and sprinkle with cheese. Broil 6 inches from heat source until cheese melts. Serve steaks immediately with sauce.

Yield: 4 servings

Marinated Beef Tenderloin

6 tablespoons olive oil
3 tablespoons soy sauce
2 teaspoons seasoned salt
¼ teaspoon black pepper

⅛ teaspoon garlic powder
⅛ teaspoon dried thyme
1 (4 pound) beef tenderloin

Combine olive oil, soy sauce, seasoned salt, pepper, garlic powder and thyme to make a marinade. Pour marinade over beef and refrigerate at least 8 hours, turning occasionally. Drain beef, discarding marinade. Bake at 425 degrees for 30 to 40 minutes or grill 10 to 15 minutes on each side.

Yield: 6 to 8 servings

Roasted Tenderloin

Clarified Butter

4 sticks salted or unsalted butter

Tenderloin

1 (4 to 5 pound) beef tenderloin, room temperature

⅔ cup clarified butter, warmed

Equal amounts of salt, pepper and granulated garlic

Clarified Butter

Cut butter into pieces and place in a deep saucepan. Bring to a hard boil. Allow to cool and skim off any foam. Pour off the clear, yellow liquid and discard milk solids at bottom of pan. Store clarified butter indefinitely in an airtight container in the refrigerator.

Tenderloin

Drench beef with butter. Rub seasoning mixture over meat and place on a rack on a baking pan. Bake at 425 degrees for 45 to 60 minutes or until internal temperature reaches 140 to 150 degrees for medium rare.

Yield: 8 to 10 servings

Marinated Grilled Rib-Eye Steak

½ cup olive oil

½ cup soy sauce

½ cup dry sherry wine

2 to 3 teaspoons fresh ginger, grated

2 to 3 teaspoons fresh orange zest

1½ teaspoons cracked black pepper

1½ teaspoons fresh garlic, minced

1½ teaspoons fresh thyme, minced

¼ cup packed brown sugar

4 (14 ounce) beef rib-eye steaks

Combine olive oil, soy sauce, sherry, ginger, orange zest, pepper, garlic, thyme and brown sugar to make a marinade. Pour marinade over beef and refrigerate 24 hours. When ready to cook, grill to desired degree of doneness.

Yield: 4 servings

Marinated Flank Steak Béarnaise

Easy and impressive dinner.

Marinade

1 onion, chopped

1 clove garlic, chopped

½ cup soy sauce

⅔ cup water

1 tablespoon ground ginger

3 tablespoons sugar

Steak

1 to 1½ pounds beef flank steak

1 (8 ounce) package cream cheese, cubed

¼ cup milk

1 tablespoon green onions, sliced

½ teaspoon dried tarragon, crushed

2 egg yolks, beaten

2 tablespoons dry white wine

1 tablespoon lemon juice

Marinade

Mix together onions, garlic, soy sauce, water, ginger and sugar. Use as a marinade for beef, pork, chicken or venison. This recipe will marinate 2 to 3 pounds of meat.

Steak

Pour marinade over steak and refrigerate 8 hours or overnight.

Combine cream cheese, milk, onions and tarragon in a saucepan. Stir over low heat until cheese melts. Stir a small amount of hot cheese mixture into egg yolks, then stir back into cheese mixture. Mix in wine and lemon juice. Continue to cook and stir over low heat for 1 minute or until sauce is thickened.

Drain steak and score on both sides. Place steak on a broiler pan rack. Broil on each side for 5 minutes or to desired degree of doneness. Cut steak across the grain into thin slices. Serve with cheese sauce.

Yield: 6 servings

Grilled Sirloin with Roasted Red Pepper Relish

This flavorful relish complements any grilled meat.

2 tablespoons olive oil

1 large yellow bell pepper, finely chopped

1 medium shallot, minced

1 large clove garlic, minced

Salt and pepper to taste

1 (7 ounce) jar roasted sweet red peppers, drained and chopped to equal ½ cup

1 jalapeño pepper, seeded and minced

1 tablespoon sherry vinegar

½ teaspoon oregano

2 pounds boneless sirloin, 1½ to 2 inches thick

1 tablespoon olive oil

3 tablespoons sliced almonds, toasted

Heat 2 tablespoons oil in a large skillet. Add bell peppers, shallots, garlic, salt and pepper. Cook over low heat for 7 minutes. Add roasted peppers, jalapeño peppers and vinegar. Cover and cook 10 minutes or until vegetables are tender. Stir in oregano and set aside. Rub steaks with 1 tablespoons oil. Season with salt and pepper. Grill over high heat to desired degree of doneness; 7 to 8 minutes per side for medium-rare. Steak is medium rare when the juices begin to collect on the surface of the steak. Remove from grill and allow to rest 5 minutes. Slice steak into ¼ inch slices. Fan about 5 slices on each plate. Spoon red pepper relish on top and sprinkle with almonds.

Yield: 6 to 8 servings

Beef and Scallop Stir-Fry

¼ cup chicken broth

3 tablespoons soy sauce

2 tablespoons rice vinegar

2 teaspoons cornstarch

1 teaspoon sugar

½ teaspoon dried red pepper flakes

2 tablespoons vegetable oil

2 cloves garlic, minced

10 ounces beef tenderloin, ¾ inch diced

10 ounces sea scallops, patted dry

2 tablespoons vegetable oil

2 cloves garlic, minced

1 large red bell pepper, ½ inch diced

1 cup white corn kernels

6 green onions, cut into 1 inch lengths

¼ cup fresh basil, chopped

2 cups cooked rice

In a small bowl, combine broth, soy sauce, vinegar, cornstarch, sugar and pepper flakes; set aside. Heat 2 tablespoons oil in a wok. Add 2 cloves garlic and sauté 30 seconds. Add beef and scallops and cook 3 minutes or until meat is no longer pink. Transfer to a plate. Add remaining 2 tablespoons oil and 2 cloves garlic to wok and cook 30 seconds. Add bell peppers, corn and onions and stir fry 2 to 3 minutes. Stir the soy sauce mixture and add to wok. Cook about 2 minutes or until sauce thickens. Return beef and scallops to wok and stir to coat. Mix in basil. Serve over rice.

Yield: 4 servings

Windy City Meatloaf

My friend says, "This is meatloaf like we make in Chicago. You will love it."

2 pounds ground beef sirloin or round

2 pounds ground lean turkey

1 cup low fat cottage cheese

1 cup bread crumbs

1 large yellow onion, finely chopped

1 green bell pepper, finely chopped

3 eggs, beaten

1 (12 ounce) bottle chili sauce

1 tablespoon salt

1 teaspoon dried thyme

Black pepper to taste

½ cup dry red wine

½ cup tomato sauce

Combine beef and turkey. Mix in cottage cheese, bread crumbs, onions, bell peppers, eggs and about half (¾ cup) the bottle of chili sauce. Season with salt, thyme and pepper. Form mixture into two or three loaves and place in 9x5 inch loaf pans or freeze. Pour red wine over loaves. Combine remaining chili sauce and tomato sauce and spoon over loaves. Adjust wine and sauce amounts accordingly if one or more loaves are being frozen for future use.

Bake at 400 degrees for 30 minutes. Reduce heat to 350 degrees and bake 60 minutes longer. Remove from oven and let stand a few minutes before slicing.

Yield: 12 to 15 servings

Rosemary and oregano can also be used to season meatloaf.

Provençal Beef Burgundy

2 pounds boneless beef sirloin

¼ cup all-purpose flour

6 tablespoons margarine

1 onion, sliced

3 stalks celery, diced

3 carrots, chopped

1 (10½ ounce) can beef consommé

1 cup red wine

1 (7 ounce) can mushrooms, drained

Salt and pepper to taste

Garlic powder to taste

Dredge beef in flour. Melt margarine in a skillet. Add beef to skillet and brown. Transfer beef to a 3 quart saucepan, reserving drippings in skillet. Add onions to skillet and sauté. Add skillet contents to beef. Mix celery, carrots, consommé, wine and mushrooms into saucepan. Season with salt, pepper and garlic powder. Simmer at least 2 hours. Serve over noodles or mashed potatoes.

Yield: 6 servings

Stuffed Leg of Lamb

1 (6 pound) boned leg of lamb

Salt and pepper to taste

1½ cups bread crumbs

½ cup extra virgin olive oil

½ cup garlic, minced

1 cup Parmesan-Romano cheese,
    freshly grated

3 tablespoons fresh parsley leaves,
    chopped

Pat dry lamb and season thoroughly with salt and pepper. In a skillet over medium heat, cook bread crumbs in oil until golden brown. Transfer to a bowl and add garlic, cheese and parsley. Season with salt and pepper. Spread the bread crumb mixture on the cut side of the lamb. Roll lamb to enclose bread stuffing and tie with string. Save any remaining stuffing. Arrange lamb on a rack in a roasting pan. Add about 1 inch of water to the pan. Bake at 375 degrees for 1 hour to 1 hour, 30 minutes or until meat is medium-rare. Remove from oven and let stand 10 minutes before carving. Heat extra stuffing to serve on the side.

Yield: 10 to 12 servings

Tangy Rack of Lamb

Glaze

3 tablespoons olive oil

½ red onion, finely chopped

2 cloves garlic, minced

⅓ cup blackberry jam

¼ cup packed dark brown sugar

2 tablespoons red wine vinegar

2 teaspoons kosher salt

2 teaspoons freshly ground black pepper

Lamb

2 racks of lamb, chine bone removed

Salt and pepper to taste

3 tablespoons olive oil

1 cup pecans, toasted and finely chopped

Glaze

Heat olive oil over low heat. Add onions and garlic and sauté 3 minutes or until softened. Stir in jam, sugar, vinegar, salt and pepper. Bring to a boil. Reduce heat to a simmer and cook 3 minutes or until glaze thickens.

Lamb

Season lamb with salt and pepper. Heat olive oil in a pan for 3 minutes or until it just starts to smoke. Sear lamb in oil for about 2 minutes per side. Place lamb, fat-side up, on a rack in a roasting pan with the bones crossing. Brush lamb thoroughly with glaze. Coat with pecans. Bake at 425 degrees for 20 to 25 minutes or until lamb is cooked to 130 degrees for medium-rare. Remove from oven and let stand 5 minutes before carving.

Yield: 4 servings

To prevent drippings from burning, add a little wine or juice to the bottom of the pan before roasting. After roasting, deglaze pan with a bit more wine or juice and spoon over the slices of lamb.

1. When buying a rack of lamb, ask the butcher to trim the fat and French the bones or remove the fat and meat from the tips of the bones. This will allow you to cross the bones while roasting and will make for a more dramatic and stunning presentation.

2. Using a brown sugar glaze on meat or poultry during roasting will help create a crispy, sweet crust. As the sugar bakes, it becomes hardened and adds great flavor to the meat.

Grilled Lamb Chops

1 medium clove garlic	1 teaspoon mint jelly
1 medium shallot, quartered	¼ cup olive oil
1 tablespoon fresh mint, finely chopped	8 thick lamb chops
¼ cup red wine	

Chop garlic and shallot in a food processor. Add mint, red wine, jelly and oil and process. Adjust seasonings to taste. Place lamb chops in a single layer in a glass dish. Cover both sides of chops with wine mixture. Marinate in refrigerator for 4 hours. When ready to cook, drain chops. Grill over medium-high heat to desired degree of doneness.

Yield: 4 servings

If desired, season chops with minced fresh rosemary just prior to grilling.

Veal Scaloppine in Lemon Sauce

1¾ pounds veal cutlets	½ cup dry white wine
⅓ cup all-purpose flour	Juice of 1 large lemon
½ teaspoon salt	2 tablespoons fresh parsley, chopped
¼ teaspoon freshly ground black pepper	1 large clove garlic, pressed
2 tablespoons margarine	2 tablespoons capers
1 tablespoon olive oil	Fresh parsley sprigs and lemon slices for garnish
1 tablespoon margarine	

Use a meat mallet or rolling pin to flatten veal cutlets between 2 pieces of heavy duty plastic wrap to ¼ inch thickness. Combine flour, salt and pepper. Dredge veal in flour mixture. Heat 2 tablespoons margarine and oil in a large skillet over medium heat. Add veal in batches and cook 1 minute on each side or until golden. Remove from skillet and keep warm. Add 1 tablespoon margarine, wine and lemon juice to skillet. Stir to loosen brown bits. Cook until thoroughly heated. Stir in parsley, garlic and capers. Spoon over veal. Garnish as desired with parsley sprigs and lemon slices.

Yield: 4 servings

Pork Tenderloin with Cream Sauce

2 tablespoons vegetable oil

1¼ pounds pork tenderloin

2 tablespoons butter

¼ cup shallots, chopped

½ cup dry white wine

1 (10½ ounce) can chicken broth

½ cup beef broth

1 cup half-and-half

2 tablespoons fresh lime juice

Salt and pepper to taste

Heat oil in an ovenproof skillet or Dutch oven over high heat. Add pork and brown on all sides, turning frequently. Bake pork in skillet at 400 degrees for 20 minutes or until cooked through. In a separate skillet, melt butter over medium heat. Add shallots and sauté 3 minutes. Add wine and bring to a boil. Cook and stir 5 minutes or until reduced by half. Add broths and bring to a boil. Cook and stir 13 minutes or until reduced to 6 tablespoons. Stir in half-and-half and boil 7 minutes or until sauce is reduced to 1 cup. Mix in lime juice and season with salt and pepper. Cut pork into ¼ inch slices. Spoon sauce over pork.

Yield: 4 servings

Pineapple Salsa

½ fresh medium pineapple, peeled and coarsely chopped

1 red bell pepper, chopped

1 jalapeño pepper, seeded and chopped

4 green onions, thinly sliced

¼ cup red onion, finely chopped

2 tablespoons fresh cilantro, chopped

2 tablespoons fresh lime juice

Combine pineapple, peppers, onions, cilantro and lime juice. Cover and chill. Great served with grilled pork tenderloin.

Yield: 4½ cups

Ancho Chiles

Dried poblanos are known as ancho chiles and are toasted to bring out their flavor, then reconstituted in warm water. The chiles are then pureed and strained before using.

Tailgate Tenderloins with Ancho Honey Mustard

Tenderloins

½ cup sherry

½ cup packed brown sugar

1 cup soy sauce

1 teaspoon salt

¼ teaspoon black pepper

1 onion, diced

2 (1 pound) boneless pork tenderloins

Ancho Honey Mustard

2 dried ancho peppers, stemmed and seeded

¼ cup honey, or to taste

¼ cup mustard, or to taste

Tenderloins

Stir together sherry, sugar, soy sauce, salt and pepper until dissolved. Add onions. Place tenderloins in a roasting pan lined with foil. Pour marinade mixture over pork and cover. Refrigerate 2 hours. Bake at 400 degrees for 10 minutes, turning once. Reduce heat to 325 degrees and bake 1 hour, 30 minutes to 1 hour, 45 minutes or until done. Remove from oven and chill thoroughly before cutting into thin slices. Serve at room temperature with Ancho Honey Mustard.

Ancho Honey Mustard

Place peppers in a glass bowl. Cover with boiling water to reconstitute. Drain peppers and place in a blender or small food processor. Add honey and mustard and blend thoroughly. Adjust honey and mustard to taste.

Yield: 10 servings

Crusted Pork Loin with Pepper Jelly Glaze

1 clove garlic, minced

½ teaspoon fresh rosemary, finely chopped

¼ teaspoon salt

¼ teaspoon black pepper

1 to 1½ pounds boneless pork loin roast

1 tablespoon olive oil

2 tablespoons Dijon mustard

¼ cup bread crumbs

1 cup jalapeño pepper jelly

1 cup apple cider or juice

1 cup cider vinegar

Combine garlic, rosemary, salt and pepper. Rub seasoning mixture into pork. Stir together oil and mustard and spread over pork. Roll pork in bread crumbs, coating evenly. Bake at 350 degrees for 1 hour, 15 minutes or until just done; do not overbake. Heat jelly, apple cider and vinegar together and pour over pork during last 30 minutes, basting every 10 minutes.

Yield: 4 to 6 servings

Pork Chops with Apple Glaze

4 (1 inch thick) boneless pork chops

Salt and pepper to taste

¼ to ½ teaspoon dried thyme

1 to 2 tablespoon olive oil

1 cup apple juice

2 tablespoons packed brown sugar

2 tablespoons cider vinegar

½ teaspoon mustard seeds

½ teaspoon cornstarch

1 tablespoon water

Thinly sliced apples for garnish

Season pork with salt, pepper and thyme. In a skillet, brown chops in oil over medium-high heat for 5 minutes on each side. Stir apple juice and brown sugar together and add to skillet. Simmer 3 minutes, turning pork once. Remove chops. Add vinegar and mustard seeds to skillet. Bring to a boil and cook 5 minutes or until reduced to ⅓ cup. Return chops to skillet. Stir in cornstarch dissolved in water and cook 2 minutes. Serve sauce over chops. Garnish with apple slices.

Yield: 4 servings

Convection Ovens

How to convert conventional oven recipes for a convection oven. Heat the convection oven to 25 degrees (or per manufacturers instruction) lower than the recipe calls for. Also, expect food to be done in 25% less time than it would be in a conventional oven. Start checking for doneness about 10 minutes before the food is scheduled to be done. Check sooner for foods that cook for extended periods, such as roasts.

Ginger Mustard Pork Chops

4 (4 ounce, ½ inch thick) boneless,
    pork loin chops

2 tablespoons flour

1 tablespoon butter

1½ cups chicken broth

4 teaspoons fresh ginger, minced

4 teaspoons Dijon mustard

4 teaspoons grainy mustard

4 green onions, minced

Salt and freshly ground pepper to
    taste

Dust chops lightly with flour. Melt butter in a large skillet. Add chops and sauté over medium-high heat for 2 to 3 minutes per side or until done. Remove chops from skillet and keep warm. Add broth to skillet. Increase heat and bring to a boil, scraping up brown bits from bottom of pan. Add ginger and cook, stirring frequently, for 2 minutes. Stir in mustards and onions. Season with salt and pepper. Spoon sauce onto individual serving plates and top with chops.

Yield: 4 servings

Cranberry Chutney

1 (12 ounce) bag fresh cranberries

2 Granny Smith apples, peeled and
    chopped

1 onion, chopped

1 cup orange marmalade

½ cup dried currants

⅓ cup packed brown sugar

¼ cup cider vinegar

¼ teaspoon nutmeg

¼ teaspoon allspice

½ teaspoon dried red pepper flakes

Combine cranberries, apples, onions, marmalade, currants, brown sugar, vinegar, nutmeg, allspice and pepper flakes in a large pot. Cover and cook over medium heat for 30 minutes, stirring occasionally, or until mixture thickens. Cool. Cover and refrigerate. Serve warm over pork tenderloin or pork chops.

Yield: 3 to 4 cups

Pork Fricassee

3½ pounds boneless pork loin, cut into 2 inch pieces

1 large onion, chopped

2 stalks celery, chopped

1 bay leaf

4 cups chicken broth

4 cups water

8 large carrots, cut diagonally into 1 inch pieces

1 pound mushrooms, sliced

4 tablespoons butter

¼ cup flour

1 cup heavy cream

1 tablespoon lemon juice

Salt and pepper to taste

2 cups dry rice, cooked

½ cup fresh parsley, minced

Brown pork in batches in a large Dutch oven. Transfer pork to a large bowl. Pour off fat from pot and return pork to pot. Add onion, celery, bay leaf, broth and water. Simmer 1 hour, 30 minutes or until pork is tender. Add carrots and simmer 15 minutes. Remove pork and carrots from pot with tongs. Strain liquid from pot and return strained liquid to pot. Bring to a boil and cook until reduced to about 3 cups. In a large skillet, sauté mushrooms in butter. Cook over medium heat until most of the liquid evaporates. Sprinkle mushrooms with flour and sauté about 3 minutes, scraping up brown bits. Stir in cream until combined. Add mushroom mixture to liquid in pot. Simmer and stir until thickened. Stir lemon juice, pork and carrots into pot. Season with salt and pepper. Serve over rice with parsley sprinkled on top.

Yield: 8 to 12 servings

This is our traditional Christmas Eve meal. I make it ahead and warm it in the oven while we are attending church.

Grilled Tarragon Ham Steak with Sautéed Apples

Appealing Apples

How to preserve apples: peel, core and cut the apples into wedges. Toss in lemon juice, and then sugar. Spread on a baking sheet and freeze until firm. Transfer to a zipper-lock freezer bag and freeze for up to six months.

Ham Steak

4 tablespoons butter, melted

1 tablespoon dried tarragon

Black pepper to taste

2 (¾ to 1 pound, ½ inch thick) fresh ham steaks

Sautéed Apples

2 tablespoons butter

2 crisp apples, peeled and thinly sliced

¼ cup heavy cream

Salt and white pepper to taste

2 tablespoons fresh chives, chopped

Ham Steak

Combine melted butter, tarragon and pepper. Brush mixture on steaks. Grill steaks, uncovered, for 1 minute on each side. Cover and grill 4 minutes longer on each side. Baste with butter sauce while cooking. Serve with Sautéed Apples on top.

Sautéed Apples

Melt butter in a skillet over medium heat. Add apples and sauté, tossing carefully, for 3 minutes or until just wilted. Add cream and cook another 1 to 2 minutes or until most of cream is cooked off but apples are still intact. Season with salt and pepper and sprinkle with chives.

Yield: 4 servings

Bourbon Glazed Ham

1 (8 to 10 pound) bone-in cooked ham
Whole cloves
1 (16 ounce) package dark brown
    sugar

1 cup spicy brown mustard
1 cup apple cider
½ cup bourbon
1 cup brewed coffee

Trim excess fat from ham. Score ¼ inch thick into a diamond pattern and stud with cloves. Place ham in a shallow roasting pan. Combine sugar, mustard, cider and bourbon. Spread mixture evenly over ham. Bake at 350 degrees, basting frequently, for 1 hour, 30 minutes to 2 hours or until thoroughly heated. Transfer ham to a warm serving platter. Add coffee to pan drippings. Bring mixture to a boil and simmer 5 minutes. Using a gravy separator, pour sauce into a bowl or sauceboat.

Yield: 12 to 15 servings

Quick Brunch Method: Prepare ham a day ahead. Slice ham into serving sizes. Brush slices with sauce and place in sliced dinner rolls. Stack on an ovenproof platter and cover platter with foil. Bake at 350 degrees for 15 to 20 minutes or until hot. Serve with remaining sauce, honey mustard or other condiments.

Key Notes

Seafood

Pan Seared Sea Bass with Chipolte Aïoli and Squash Salsa

2000

*N*obody loves kids like Le Bonheur! I am fortunate enough to know that statement to be true because my son recites the hospital's motto, "Believe in Miracles," from his heart since he experienced it firsthand.

I took my four-year-old son to our pediatrician with some odd symptoms. The doctor quickly determined that something was going on with his liver. The initial blood work indicated that it was some form of hepatitis and it would run its course. After three days, the doctor called to say it was not Hepatitis A or C. At that moment I had a sinking feeling that something was wrong with my son.

We were sent to Le Bonheur Children's Medical Center for IV fluids and were greeted by friendly nurses and calm, reassuring doctors. My son started feeling better, and I was thinking maybe the test results were falsely negative, meaning he really did have Hepatitis A. After getting him through four hours of constant nausea that night, I called the emergency room and our doctor quickly came to the phone. He simply and firmly said, "Bring him back right now and I'll be waiting for you." The same nurse made sure she was assigned to us again. It was such a relief to have the same doctor and nurse who knew our situation and obviously cared about my son. Le Bonheur has a policy to provide consistent care to its patients by assigning the same doctors and nurses to patients who are admitted repeatedly. Over the next few months, that came to mean the world to us.

In the ICU, we learned my son's liver was failing, and he needed an almost immediate transplant. Our son would become Memphis' first pediatric living donor liver recipient. We did not fathom that my son's donor would not be Mom or Dad, but his uncle, my sister's husband. His uncle is now and forever our hero. We pray our son will grow up to emulate his uncle's selflessness and to recognize the amazing leap of faith he took for us.

The incredible transplant team saved our child's life. We encountered many kind gestures everyday, and the superior medical care assured my son's miraculous recovery. Le Bonheur Children's Medical Center is an outstanding facility, and its existence played the most vital role in our family's miracle.

Pan Seared Sea Bass with Chipotle Aïoli and Squash Salsa

Chipotle Aïoli

2 egg yolks

⅓ cup olive oil

¾ cup chipotle salsa

2 teaspoons garlic, minced

2 tablespoons fresh cilantro, chopped

Juice of 1 lime

Juice of 1 lemon

Juice of 1 orange

Salt and pepper to taste

Squash Salsa

1 yellow squash, diced

1 zucchini, diced

½ red onion, diced

2 tomatoes, diced

1 tablespoon lime juice

¼ cup fresh cilantro, chopped

2 tablespoons garlic, minced

Salt and pepper to taste

Sea Bass

1 tablespoon olive oil

6 (8 ounce) sea bass fillets

Chipotle Aïoli

Whisk together egg yolks and oil. Add salsa, garlic, cilantro, citrus juices, salt and pepper. Blend until well mixed.

Squash Salsa

Combine squash, zucchini, onions, tomatoes, lime juice, cilantro, garlic, salt and pepper in a bowl.

Sea Bass

Heat oil in a large skillet. Add fillets and cook about 1 minute on each side. Place fish in a baking dish and spread aïoli evenly over each fillet. Broil at 425 degrees for 10 to 12 minutes. Serve immediately with Squash Salsa.

Yield: 6 servings

Sea Bass with Soy Beurre Blanc

Savory and sophisticated!

Rice

3 cups chicken broth

½ teaspoon chicken base

1 cup dry Black Thai rice, red rice or wild rice

Soy Beurre Blanc

6 tablespoons dry white wine

2 tablespoons white wine vinegar

3 tablespoons minced shallots

Salt and white pepper to taste

1 tablespoon heavy cream

1 stick unsalted butter, cold and cubed into 16 pieces

1½ tablespoons soy sauce, or to taste

Sea Bass

1 cup all-purpose flour

½ teaspoon salt

½ teaspoon white pepper

3 tablespoons unsalted butter

2 (7 ounce) sea bass fillets

Rice

Bring broth and chicken base to a boil in a medium saucepan. Add rice, reduce heat to a simmer and cover. Cook 25 to 30 minutes. Drain excess liquid and set aside.

Soy Beurre Blanc

Combine wine, vinegar, shallots, salt and pepper in a small skillet. Simmer over medium heat until reduced by three-fourths. Stir in cream. Remove from heat and whisk in butter, one piece at a time. Whisk constantly until sauce is creamy and whitened. Whisk in soy sauce.

Sea Bass

Combine flour, salt and pepper in a shallow dish. Melt butter in an ovenproof skillet over medium-high heat. Dredge sea bass in flour mixture. When butter is sizzling, add fillets to skillet and cook for 1 minute on each side or until browned. Broil at 425 degrees for 10 to 12 minutes.

To serve, spoon rice into the center of 2 serving plates. Spoon Soy Beurre Blanc around the outside of the rice. Place a fillet over rice and serve immediately.

Yield: 2 servings

Halibut Topped with Caramelized Onions

Don't overlook this simple, yet scrumptious, white fish.

1½ tablespoons olive oil

2 cups onions, thinly sliced

1 tablespoon dried dill

4 halibut steaks

Combine oil, onions and dill in a 9 inch square baking dish. Bake at 400 degrees for 15 minutes or until onions are lightly browned. Remove onion mixture from dish and place halibut in dish. Top steaks with onions. Bake 15 to 20 minutes or until fish flakes.

Yield: 4 servings

Halibut Provençal

1 cup dry white wine

6 (6 ounce) halibut steaks

6 cups tomatoes, diced

2 cups onions, finely chopped

¼ cup fresh basil, chopped, or
    4 teaspoons dried

¼ cup fresh parsley, chopped, or
    4 teaspoons dried

2 tablespoons kalamata olives, minced

1 tablespoon olive oil

½ teaspoon salt

½ teaspoon anchovy paste

⅛ teaspoon black pepper

2 cloves garlic, minced

¼ cup bread crumbs

1 tablespoon Parmesan cheese, grated

1 teaspoon olive oil

Pour wine into a greased 9x13 inch baking dish. Arrange steaks in dish. In a bowl, combine tomatoes, onions, basil, parsley, olives, 1 tablespoon olive oil, salt, anchovy paste, pepper and garlic. Stir well and spoon mixture over steaks. Bake at 350 degrees for 35 minutes or until fish flakes easily with a fork. Combine bread crumbs, cheese and 1 teaspoon olive oil in a bowl and stir well. Sprinkle bread crumb mixture over fish. Broil until crumbs are golden. Serve immediately.

Yield: 6 servings

Grilled Yellowfin Tuna with Tomato Pineapple Sauce

1 (14½ ounce) can Roma tomatoes, juice reserved

1 fresh pineapple, diced, or 1 (20 ounce) can pineapple tidbits, drained

1 tablespoon garlic, minced

3 tablespoons fresh cilantro, minced

1 tablespoon shallots, minced

1 tablespoon fresh ginger, grated

3 tablespoons olive oil

1 cup fish fumet or stock

1½ cups heavy cream

Salt and pepper to taste

6 (8 ounce) yellowfin tuna fillets

Puree tomatoes; set aside. Sauté pineapple, garlic, cilantro, shallots and ginger in olive oil. Add pureed tomatoes and bring to a simmer. Add reserved tomato juice and fish fumet and simmer. Stir in cream and simmer until sauce is reduced. Season with salt and pepper. Grill tuna to desired degree of doneness. Serve tuna with sauce.

Yield: 6 servings

Parmesan Crusted Fish

¾ cup Parmesan cheese, shredded

1 stick butter, softened

3 tablespoons green onions, chopped

3 tablespoons mayonnaise

2 teaspoons chives, chopped

4 (6 ounce) fish fillets, such as scrod, orange roughy or grouper

3 tablespoons lemon juice

¼ teaspoon black pepper

Mix together cheese, butter, onions, mayonnaise and chives; set aside. Arrange fish in a single layer in a lightly greased 9x13 inch baking dish. Pour lemon juice over fish and sprinkle with pepper. Broil fish 6 to 10 minutes or until fish flakes easily with a fork. Remove from oven and spread cheese mixture over fish. Broil 2 to 3 minutes longer or until cheese is lightly browned and bubbly.

Yield: 4 servings

Grilled Tuna with Sun-Dried Tomatoes

1 large lemon, thinly sliced

4 (6 to 8 ounce) tuna steaks

2 tablespoons olive oil

2 tablespoons oil from oil-packed tomatoes

2 teaspoons fresh rosemary, chopped

Salt and pepper to taste

3 tablespoons sun-dried tomatoes packed in oil

1 tablespoon oil from oil-packed tomatoes

1 clove garlic

Lay lemon slices in the bottom of a baking dish. Arrange tuna on top. Combine olive oil and 2 tablespoons tomato oil and pour over tuna. Sprinkle with rosemary and season with salt and pepper. Let stand at room temperature for 1 hour. Combine sun-dried tomatoes, 1 tablespoon tomato oil and garlic in a food processor. Process until smooth; set aside. When ready to cook, remove steaks from baking dish. Grill tuna, rosemary-side up, for 4 minutes. Turn steaks and top with tomato mixture. Cook 3 to 4 minutes longer.

Yield: 4 servings

Fish For Two

Little preparation for a satisfying weeknight meal.

2 (8 ounce) orange roughy fillets

2 tablespoons butter or margarine, melted

2 tablespoons lemon juice

⅛ teaspoon lemon pepper

¼ teaspoon garlic salt

Paprika

1 green onion, sliced

1 tablespoon fresh parsley, chopped

Lemon wedges for garnish

Place fillets in a lightly greased baking dish. Pour butter and lemon juice over fillets. Sprinkle lemon pepper, garlic salt, paprika, onions and parsley evenly on top. Bake at 350 degrees for 20 to 25 minutes. Broil 3 to 5 minutes or until lightly browned. Garnish with lemon wedges.

Yield: 2 servings

Herbed Tilapia

Excellent with roasted potatoes and sautéed green beans or sugar snap peas.

2 tilapia fillets

4 tablespoons butter, melted

¼ cup olive oil

½ tablespoon rice vinegar or white wine vinegar

¼ teaspoon lemon juice

¼ teaspoon dried basil

¼ teaspoon dried tarragon

⅛ teaspoon black pepper

1 clove garlic, crushed

Lemon pepper

Freshly grated Parmesan cheese (optional)

Place fillets in a baking dish. Combine butter, olive oil, vinegar, lemon juice, basil, tarragon, pepper and garlic and pour over fish. Sprinkle with lemon pepper and cheese. Broil 5 to 8 minutes.

Yield: 2 servings

This recipe can easily be doubled or tripled.

Grilled Salmon Steaks

2 bunches watercress, tough stems removed, minced

1 stick unsalted butter, softened

2 tablespoons minced shallots

2 tablespoons Dijon mustard

¼ teaspoon salt

¼ teaspoon freshly ground black pepper

6 (8 ounce, 1 inch thick) salmon steaks

¼ teaspoon salt

Watercress sprigs for garnish

Combine watercress, butter, shallots, mustard, ¼ teaspoon salt and pepper in a bowl. Refrigerate mixture at least 1 hour. When ready to cook, season salmon with ¼ teaspoon salt. Dot one side of salmon with half the butter mixture. Arrange salmon, butter-side up, on a grill. Cook 4 minutes. Turn salmon and dot with remaining butter mixture. Cook 3 minutes longer. Garnish with sprigs of watercress and serve immediately.

Yield: 6 servings

Trout with Lemon Cream Sauce

4 slices bacon
½ cup all-purpose flour
1 teaspoon salt
½ teaspoon black pepper
4 (4 ounce) trout fillets

¾ cup heavy cream
2 tablespoons fresh lemon juice
2 tablespoons fresh chives or green onions, chopped

Cook bacon in a skillet until crisp. Drain bacon on paper towels, reserving drippings in skillet. Crumble bacon and set aside. Combine flour, salt and pepper in a shallow dish. Dredge trout in flour mixture, shaking off excess. Cook trout in bacon drippings in skillet over medium heat for 6 to 8 minutes or until golden on both sides. Remove trout and keep warm. Add cream to skillet. Simmer, stirring constantly, for 2 to 3 minutes or until thickened. Stir in lemon juice. Pour sauce over fish. Sprinkle bacon and chives on top.

Yield: 4 servings

The first time my five-year old went fishing, she loved it until the caught fish flopped onto the ground. After that, the fish went back into the river and the local fish market provided our dinner.

Salmon Florentine

1 pound salmon fillet
1½ cups white vermouth cooking wine

1 (10 ounce) package frozen creamed spinach, thawed
Pine nuts to taste
Garlic powder to taste

Place salmon in a glass baking dish. Pour in wine. Spread creamed spinach over salmon and sprinkle pine nuts and garlic powder on top. Cover with foil. Bake at 425 degrees for 20 to 30 minutes. Uncover and bake 5 minutes longer.

Yield: 4 servings

Papaya

Papaya is a medium sized, smooth skinned, well-colored fruit. It should be ripened in a perforated bag at room temperature until yellow all over. Refrigerated, ripened papayas will keep for a week.

Tropical Salmon

Salsa

1 large ripe papaya, peeled, seeded and diced

1 tablespoon lime juice

1 tablespoon fresh cilantro, chopped

Salmon

1 tablespoon olive oil

1 teaspoon ground ginger

¾ teaspoon ground cumin

¾ teaspoon ground coriander

¼ teaspoon cayenne pepper

Dash of black pepper

2 (6 ounce) salmon fillets

Salsa

Combine papaya, lime juice and cilantro.

Salmon

Mix together oil, ginger, cumin, coriander, cayenne and black pepper. Spoon mixture over salmon in a shallow dish and marinate in refrigerator for no longer than 30 minutes. Drain salmon and place on a broiler pan, skin-side down. Broil for about 12 minutes. Serve with salsa.

Yield: 2 servings

Sante Fe Salmon

6 salmon fillets

¼ cup bottled teriyaki sauce

1 tablespoon olive oil

1 red bell pepper, chopped

4 green onions, sliced

1 (16 ounce) can black beans, rinsed and drained

3 tablespoons seasoned rice wine vinegar

3 tablespoons fresh cilantro, chopped

Brush fillets with half of teriyaki sauce. Broil 5 to 8 minutes on one side. Turn and brush with remaining teriyaki sauce. Broil 5 to 8 minutes longer or until done. Heat oil in a skillet. Add bell peppers and green onions and sauté 4 minutes or until softened. Add beans, vinegar and cilantro. Cook until heated through. Spoon mixture onto a serving platter. Top with salmon.

Yield: 6 servings

Broiled Salmon with Ginger Glaze

3 tablespoons fresh ginger, minced
3 tablespoons honey
¼ cup hoisin sauce
2 tablespoons Dijon mustard

2 tablespoons fresh lemon juice
½ teaspoon salt
1 (2 pound) salmon fillet

Combine ginger, honey, hoisin sauce, mustard, lemon juice and salt. Pat salmon dry with paper towels and place on a lightly greased broiler rack. Spoon ginger mixture over salmon. Bake at 450 degrees for 8 minutes. Broil 5 inches from a heat source for 1 minute or until glaze starts to brown.

Yield: 6 servings

Lagniappe Salmon

Lagniappe means "something extra." When you open the parchment, you are greeted with an array of vegetables.

6 salmon fillets
4 tablespoons butter, softened
2 tablespoons prepared mustard
½ teaspoon garlic, minced
1 cup carrots, julienned

1 cup green onions, julienned
1 cup zucchini, julienned
¼ cup fresh herbs, such as dill, thyme or parsley, chopped

Place each fillet on a separate sheet of parchment paper. Combine butter, mustard and garlic and place 1 tablespoon of mixture on each fillet. Mix together carrots, onions, zucchini and herbs. Spoon vegetable mixture over fillets. Fold long sides of parchment paper over fish and roll outer edges to seal. Place salmon on a baking sheet. Bake at 375 degrees for 10 to 15 minutes, depending on thickness of fillets.

Yield: 6 servings

Tropical Salsa

1 (10 ounce) can peaches in juice, drained and chopped
4 fresh plum tomatoes, chopped
4 green onions, chopped
2 tablespoons pickled jalapeño peppers, chopped
1 tablespoon fresh cilantro, finely chopped
1 tablespoon olive oil
1 tablespoon lime juice
1 teaspoon honey
¼ teaspoon salt
¼ teaspoon black pepper

Combine peaches, tomatoes, onions, jalapeño peppers, cilantro, olive oil, lime juice, honey, salt and pepper and stir gently to mix. Refrigerate up to 3 days. Serve with Broiled Salmon with Ginger Glaze.

Flipping Grilled Fillets

Place a large strip of heavy-duty foil on the grill to use as a sling. Carefully slide the fillet onto the foil. Grab the ends of the foil and gently flip. Avoid spatulas, which tend to tear the fish.

Firecracker Grilled Salmon

This hot and spicy salmon is a heart-healthy addition to your July 4th cookout.

4 (6 ounce) salmon fillets
¼ cup olive or vegetable oil
2 tablespoons soy sauce
2 tablespoons balsamic vinegar
2 tablespoons green onions, chopped
1½ teaspoons packed brown sugar

1 teaspoon garlic, minced
¾ teaspoon fresh ginger, grated
1 to 2 teaspoons crushed red pepper flakes
½ teaspoon sesame oil
⅛ teaspoon salt

Place fillets in a glass dish. Whisk together olive oil, soy sauce, vinegar, green onions, brown sugar, garlic, ginger, pepper flakes, sesame oil and salt and pour over fillets. Cover and refrigerate 4 to 6 hours. When ready to cook, drain salmon. Grill over medium heat for 10 minutes per inch thickness, turning halfway through cooking time.

Yield: 4 servings

Light Lemon Catfish

4 (5 ounce) catfish fillets
⅓ cup lemon juice
2 tablespoons reduced-calorie margarine, melted

¼ teaspoon garlic powder
¼ teaspoon dried tarragon
¼ teaspoon dried marjoram
1 tablespoon fresh parsley, minced

Place fillets in a greased 11x7 inch glass baking dish. Combine lemon juice, margarine, garlic powder, tarragon and marjoram and pour over fillets. Bake at 350 degrees for 15 to 17 minutes or until fish flakes easily with a fork. Sprinkle with parsley.

Yield: 4 servings

To cook in microwave, prepare as directed. Cover dish with wax paper. Microwave on high for 5 to 6 minutes or until fish flakes easily with a fork. Let stand 3 minutes. Sprinkle with parsley and serve.

Salmon Burgers with Basil Aïoli

Surprise your family with this fresh seafood alternative to the boring burger.

Salmon Burgers

2 pounds fresh salmon fillets, finely chopped

½ cup red bell pepper, finely chopped

½ cup green bell pepper, finely chopped

¼ cup green onions, finely chopped

2 tablespoons heavy cream

2 teaspoons Tabasco sauce

½ teaspoon salt

½ teaspoon freshly ground black pepper

1 egg white, beaten stiff

1 tablespoon vegetable oil

1 tablespoon butter

Basil Aïoli

3 tablespoons mayonnaise

1 teaspoon lemon juice

1 teaspoon white wine vinegar

Dash of garlic powder

3 tablespoons prepared basil pesto

Salmon Burgers

Combine salmon, bell peppers, onions, cream, Tabasco, salt and pepper. Fold in egg white. Form mixture into 6 patties. Heat oil and butter in a large skillet. Add patties to skillet and cook until done. Serve on buns with Basil Aïoli.

Basil Aïoli

Combine mayonnaise, lemon juice, vinegar, garlic powder and pesto.

Yield: 6 servings

Catfish Creole

Creole Sauce

1 cup onions, chopped	4 bay leaves
1 cup green onions, chopped	½ teaspoon dried thyme
1 cup green bell pepper, chopped	½ teaspoon dried oregano
¼ cup celery, chopped	1 teaspoon paprika
2 teaspoons garlic, pureed	1 teaspoon hot pepper sauce
1 stick butter	1 teaspoon Creole seasoning
2 cups chicken broth	1 tablespoon cornstarch
2 cups tomatoes, peeled and diced	

Catfish

2 eggs, beaten	¼ cup chopped pecans (optional)
2 tablespoons white wine	1½ tablespoons Greek seasoning
¾ cup butter-type crackers, crushed	1 tablespoon fresh parsley, minced
6 tablespoons Parmesan cheese, grated	6 large catfish fillets
	3 tablespoons unsalted butter, melted

Creole Sauce

Sauté onions, bell peppers, celery and garlic in butter in a saucepan for 5 minutes or until translucent. Reserve 1 tablespoon chicken broth and set aside. Add remaining broth, tomatoes, bay leaves, thyme, oregano, paprika, hot sauce and Creole seasoning to saucepan. Simmer 15 minutes. Combine reserved tablespoon of broth with cornstarch and stir into sauce.

Catfish

Beat together eggs and wine in a shallow dish. In a separate dish, combine cracker crumbs, cheese, pecans, Greek seasoning and parsley. Dip fillets in egg mixture, then dredge in cracker mixture. Place in a greased 9x13 inch baking dish and drizzle with butter. Bake at 350 degrees for 30 minutes. Serve with Creole Sauce.

Yield: 6 servings

Creole Sauce can be prepared a day in advance or frozen.

Baked Catfish in Citrus Sauce

Tangy citrus sauce proves there is more than one way "to cook a catfish."

1 (6 ounce) can frozen orange juice
    concentrate, thawed

Juice of 1 lemon

Juice of 1 lime

Juice of 1 orange

2 tablespoons orange zest

1½ teaspoons nutmeg, freshly grated

Salt and pepper to taste

Cayenne pepper to taste

4 (4 ounce) catfish fillets

Fresh parsley sprigs for garnish

Combine orange juice concentrate, citrus juices, zest, nutmeg, salt, pepper and cayenne; set aside. Season fillets with salt and pepper. Arrange fillets in a greased baking dish. Spoon juice mixture evenly over fillets and cover dish with foil. Bake at 450 degrees for 15 minutes. Uncover and bake 5 minutes longer. Garnish with parsley.

Yield: 4 servings

Seafood Ragoût

2 tablespoons olive oil

1 onion, chopped

3 cloves garlic, chopped

1 red bell pepper, chopped

1 carrot, sliced

4 tomatoes, peeled, seeded and
    chopped, or 1 (35 ounce) can

1½ cups chicken broth

1 cup white wine

1 jalapeño pepper, chopped, or dash
    of cayenne pepper

Salt and pepper to taste

1 pound (21/25 count) shrimp

2 pounds firm fish, such as sea bass,
    redfish or haddock, cubed

Chopped parsley for garnish

Heat oil in a large skillet. Add onions and garlic and sauté. Stir in bell peppers, carrots, tomatoes, broth, wine, jalapeño pepper, salt and pepper. Bring to a boil. Reduce heat to low, cover and simmer 15 minutes. Just before serving, uncover and add shrimp. Cook 4 minutes. Stir in fish and cook 4 minutes longer. Serve immediately in bowls by itself or over rice. Garnish with parsley.

Yield: 4 servings

Jockey Club Crab Cakes

Crab Cakes

¾ cup heavy cream

½ cup red bell pepper, diced

½ cup yellow bell pepper, diced

1 tablespoon butter

1 pound lump crabmeat, picked through

2 tablespoons fresh chives, finely chopped

Salt and pepper to taste

1 tablespoon Dijon mustard

½ teaspoon Worcestershire sauce

2 dashes of Tabasco sauce

2 eggs, slightly beaten

3 cups panko bread crumbs or as needed

Vegetable or canola oil for sautéing

Rémoulade Sauce

1 cup light mayonnaise

1 teaspoon dry mustard

1 teaspoon lemon juice

1 teaspoon garlic, minced

1 tablespoon capers, minced

2 teaspoon dried tarragon

1 tablespoon fresh parsley, minced

2 hard-boiled eggs, finely chopped

Crab Cakes

In a heavy saucepan, reduce cream by half over medium heat. Chill well. Sauté bell peppers in butter until tender but not browned. Cool 5 minutes. Gently combine chilled cream, bell peppers, crabmeat, chives, salt, pepper, mustard, Worcestershire sauce, Tabasco, eggs and about 1 cup of bread crumbs. Form mixture into desired size crab cake patties. Place the remaining bread crumbs on a large plate. Coat the crab cakes with crumbs, pressing crumbs in lightly to stick. At this point, cakes can be covered and refrigerated until ready to use.

To cook, add oil to a skillet to ¼ inch deep. Heat over medium-high until oil is hot but not smoking. Add crab cakes and cook until first side is nicely browned. Turn over and cook until done. Serve hot with Rémoulade Sauce.

Rémoulade Sauce

Blend mayonnaise, mustard, lemon juice, garlic, capers, tarragon, parsley and eggs together well. Refrigerate until ready to use. This sauce is best if made in advance to allow flavors to combine.

Yield: 12 to 15 servings

Panko are Japanese bread crumbs. If not available, substitute fresh coarse white bread crumbs that have been dried in a low oven. Do not allow to burn.

Seafood Casserole

1 teaspoon olive oil	*2 teaspoons lemon juice*
½ cup celery, diced	*¼ cup pimiento, chopped*
¼ cup green bell pepper, chopped	*½ cup milk*
¼ cup green onions, chopped	*¼ cup mayonnaise*
1 clove garlic, minced	*¼ cup egg substitute*
2 cups fresh mushrooms, sliced	*2 tablespoons dry milk powder*
8 ounces shrimp, peeled and deveined	*2 teaspoons Worcestershire sauce*
4 ounces bay scallops	*½ teaspoon cayenne pepper*
4 ounces crab	*1½ to 2 cups cooked rice*
2 tablespoons sherry	*¼ cup bread crumbs*

Heat oil in a skillet. Add celery, bell peppers, onions and garlic and sauté. Stir in mushrooms, shrimp and scallops. Remove from heat. Gently stir in crab, sherry, lemon juice and pimiento. In a large bowl, combine milk, mayonnaise, egg substitute, milk powder and Worcestershire sauce. Add seafood mixture, cayenne and cooked rice to bowl. Mix until blended. Transfer to a 9x9 inch baking dish. Sprinkle with bread crumbs. Bake at 350 degrees for 20 minutes.

Yield: 4 servings

Crabmeat and Shrimp Stuffed Flounder

Stuffing

4 tablespoons butter

1 small onion, chopped

8 ounces medium shrimp, cooked
    and chopped

8 ounces crabmeat

1 tablespoon fresh parsley, chopped

Salt and pepper to taste

½ cup dry white wine

1¼ cups bread crumbs

Flounder

6 flounder fillets

3 tablespoons lemon juice

Salt and pepper to taste

1 cup fresh bread crumbs

1 stick butter, melted

Stuffing

Melt butter in a large saucepan over medium-high heat. Add onions and sauté 3 to 4 minutes. Stir in shrimp, crabmeat and parsley. Season with salt and pepper. Add wine and reduce heat to medium. Cook, stirring often, for 5 minutes or until heated throughout. Remove from heat and stir in bread crumbs.

Flounder

Spread each fillet with 3 tablespoons of stuffing. Roll fillets and secure with toothpicks. Place rolls in a greased 2-quart baking dish and season with lemon juice, salt and pepper. Sprinkle bread crumbs on top and drizzle with melted butter. Bake at 375 degrees for 20 minutes or until fish flakes easily with a fork.

Yield: 6 servings

Caribbean Crab Cakes

Spice and citrus flavors explode in this island version of an American favorite.

8 ounces lump crabmeat

¼ cup green onions, minced

¼ cup red bell pepper, minced

2 tablespoons jerk seasoning

2 teaspoons honey

1 egg

¼ cup mayonnaise

1½ cups bread crumbs

3 tablespoons butter

Juice of 1 lime

2 tablespoons peach or apricot jam

Lime wedges for garnish

Combine crabmeat, onions, bell peppers, jerk seasoning, honey, egg, mayonnaise and bread crumbs in a bowl. Gently mix and form into 16 patties. Sauté patties in butter over medium heat for 4 to 5 minutes on each side. Mix together lime juice and jam. Garnish crab cakes with lime wedges and serve with lime sauce on the side.

Yield: 16 crab cakes

Fired-Up Shrimp

Ice down your summertime beverages to accompany this "dressed up" shrimp.

1 pound Gulf shrimp

3 tablespoons extra virgin olive oil

2 tablespoons lemon zest

¼ teaspoon cayenne pepper, or to taste

2 teaspoons fresh thyme, minced

2 tablespoons fresh parsley, minced

5 ounces pancetta, thinly sliced

Juice of 1 lemon

Peel and devein shrimp, leaving tails intact. In a medium bowl, combine olive oil, lemon zest, cayenne, thyme and all but 2 teaspoons parsley. Add shrimp and stir to coat. Marinate for 2 hours. Wrap each shrimp in a slice of pancetta, overlapping pancetta slightly with each turn to completely cover the shrimp. Thread shrimp onto skewers. Grill shrimp over high heat for 2 minutes on each side or until the pancetta begins to color and the shrimp are pink and opaque throughout. Remove shrimp from skewers and toss with lemon juice and reserved parsley. Serve immediately.

Yield: 6 servings

Key Notes

Shrimp in Red Thai Curry Sauce

1 tablespoon butter

1 bunch green onions with tops, chopped

1 cup fresh mushrooms, sliced

1 teaspoon red curry paste, or more to taste

1 (14 ounce) can lite coconut milk

1 pound medium to large peeled shrimp

1 (12 ounce) bag rice noodles or angel hair pasta, cooked al dente

Melt butter in a large saucepan. Add onions and mushrooms and sauté until tender. Add curry paste and cook and stir for about 2 minutes. Add coconut milk and stir well over medium heat for 2 minutes or until well mixed. Add shrimp and cook until shrimp are cooked through. Adjust seasoning as needed, adding more paste for a spicier flavor. Serve warm over cooked noodles.

Yield: 4 servings

Look for red curry paste in the ethnic section of the grocery store.

Spicy Shrimp Stir-Fry

⅓ cup honey

¼ cup soy sauce

1 tablespoon rice wine vinegar

2 teaspoons cornstarch

2 teaspoons orange zest

¼ teaspoon dried red pepper flakes

1 tablespoon vegetable oil

4 cloves garlic, minced

2 teaspoons fresh ginger, grated

1 red bell pepper, chopped

1 cup snow peas, cut into 1 inch pieces

1½ pounds shrimp, peeled and deveined

3 green onions, cut into 1 inch pieces

Cooked white rice (optional)

Whisk together honey, soy sauce, vinegar, cornstarch, orange zest and pepper flakes until thoroughly mixed; set aside. Heat oil in a wok. Add garlic and ginger and stir-fry 1 minute. Add bell peppers and peas and stir-fry 1 minute. Add shrimp and onions and stir-fry until shrimp turn pink. Stir in reserved soy sauce mixture. Cook and stir until sauce boils and thickens. Serve over rice.

Yield: 4 servings

Dixie Shrimp and Grits

A contrast in textures adored by Southerners.

Grits

Quick grits

2 cups milk

2 cups chicken broth

1 cup fresh Parmesan cheese, shredded

1 cup white Cheddar cheese, shredded

1 egg, beaten

2 tablespoons minced garlic

Salt and pepper to taste

Shrimp

1 pound bacon

½ cup slivered almonds

2 teaspoons hot pepper sauce

¾ cup green bell pepper, chopped

¾ cup red bell pepper, chopped

¾ cup yellow bell pepper, chopped

2 tablespoons garlic, minced

2 pounds medium shrimp, peeled and deveined

1 cup yellow Cheddar cheese, shredded

1 cup green onions, finely chopped

Grits

Use amount of grits indicated on package for a 4 cup serving. Bring milk and broth to a boil in a saucepan. Stir in grits and remove from heat. Mix in cheeses, egg and garlic. Season with salt and pepper. Spread grits in the bottom of a greased 9x13 inch glass baking dish. Set aside.

Shrimp

Cook bacon in a skillet, drain and crumble. Reserve 2 tablespoons bacon grease in the skillet. Add almonds, hot sauce, bell peppers and garlic to skillet and sauté. Add shrimp and cook until pink but still tender. Spread shrimp mixture over grits. Sprinkle with cheese, onions and crumbled bacon. Bake at 350 degrees until cheese melts and shrimp and grits are heated through.

Yield: 10 servings

Steamed Mussels with Cilantro Cream Sauce

Cilantro Cream Sauce

½ bunch fresh cilantro

½ cup chicken broth

2 teaspoons garlic, minced

1⅓ to 1½ cups heavy cream

Kosher salt and pepper to taste

Mussels

40 mussels

2 teaspoons olive oil

2 teaspoons garlic, minced

½ cup chicken broth or fish stock

½ cup white wine

Cilantro Cream Sauce

Puree cilantro in a food processor. Combine cilantro, broth and garlic in a saucepan. Reduce liquid by half. Add cream and simmer until thickened. Season with salt and pepper.

Mussels

Sauté mussels in a skillet in olive oil and garlic for 1 minute. Add broth and wine. Steam mussels 3 to 5 minutes or until they open. Transfer mussels into individual serving bowls. Reduce broth in skillet by half. Add cream sauce and cook 2 minutes to thicken. Pour sauce over mussels.

Yield: 10 to 12 servings

Mussels

When buying live mussels, tap the shells. They should snap shut, indicating that the mussel is alive. Avoid mussels with broken shells. Smaller mussels are usually more tender than larger ones.

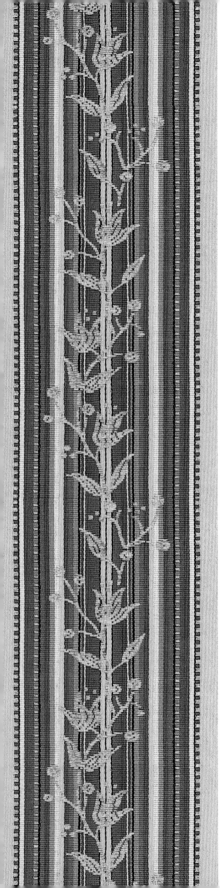

Poultry & Game

Grilled Orange Sesame Chicken

1994

*M*any different illnesses are diagnosed and treated at
Le Bonheur each day. Though many children enter
Le Bonheur's door, each child and family is treated with special care
and attention.

We would like to share our story of our oldest son, who has
hydrocephalus (water pressure on the brain). He has a VP shunt that
was inserted when he was 4 months old. Without the Le Bonheur
doctors, nurses and equipment, my son would not be alive today. We
thank God everyday for the life that He has given us at the hands of the
caring Le Bonheur staff. I must admit that it was a very trying time for us
and our families, and Le Bonheur gave us much support even after we
brought our son home. Our son is now seven years old and is living a
healthy, normal and happy life. We would like to show our gratitude
and offer support to our hospital. Le Bonheur truly is a blessing to our
lives, and we want to say, "Thank you so much for all you do and keep
on caring for our children."

Grilled Orange Sesame Chicken

3 oranges

Juice of 1 lemon

1 tablespoon white wine vinegar

¼ teaspoon freshly ground black pepper

2 teaspoons Dijon mustard

2 tablespoons toasted sesame oil

6 boneless, skinless chicken breast halves

2 bunches asparagus

6 small zucchini, sliced on diagonal ¼ inch thick

1 teaspoon extra virgin olive oil

½ teaspoon salt

2 teaspoons toasted sesame seeds

Cut 1 orange, unpeeled, into wedges; set aside. Remove zest of 1 orange and juice of 2 oranges. Place zest and juice in a glass bowl. Add lemon juice, vinegar, pepper and mustard. Whisk to mix. Slowly whisk in sesame oil. Place chicken in a separate glass bowl. Pour half of vinaigrette mixture over chicken, reserving half of marinade for later. Coat thoroughly, cover with plastic and refrigerate 2 to 3 hours.

When ready to cook, coat asparagus and zucchini with olive oil and sprinkle with salt. Grill vegetables and reserved orange wedges until tender. Drain chicken, discarding marinade. Grill chicken until browned and cooked through. Arrange chicken and vegetables on a serving platter. Sprinkle with sesame seeds and garnish with grilled orange wedges. Serve with reserved vinaigrette.

Yield: 6 servings

Freddie's Flavoring Mix

10 tablespoons chili powder

10 tablespoons Creole seasoning

10 tablespoons seasoned salt

1 tablespoon monosodium glutamate flavor enhancer

1 tablespoon cayenne pepper

1 tablespoon black pepper

1 tablespoon ground cumin

Combine chili powder, Creole seasoning, seasoned salt, monosodium glutamate, cayenne pepper, black pepper and cumin in a small bowl. Sprinkle on chicken prior to grilling for a delicious taste. Store dry mix in an airtight container in refrigerator for up to 2 months. Always ready to use!

Key Notes

Pecan Chicken with Caribbean Salsa

Island flavored salsa and pecan crusting create chicken with a reggae beat!

Chicken

½ cup milk

1 egg

1½ cups bread crumbs

1½ cups pecans, chopped and toasted

6 boneless, skinless chicken breast halves

Salt and pepper to taste

3 tablespoons Dijon mustard

½ cup all-purpose flour

3 tablespoons vegetable oil

Caribbean Salsa

⅓ cup red bell pepper, chopped

⅓ cup yellow bell pepper, chopped

1½ jalapeño peppers, seeded and chopped

3 tablespoons cilantro, chopped

3 cups bananas, thinly sliced

Juice of 1½ limes

1½ tablespoons brown sugar

Salt and pepper to taste

Chicken

Beat milk and egg together in a bowl. Combine bread crumbs and pecans in a shallow dish. Season chicken with salt and pepper. Spread mustard over chicken and coat each breast lightly with flour. Dip breasts in egg mixture, then dredge in crumb mixture, pressing mixture onto chicken gently to coat thoroughly.

Heat oil in a nonstick skillet. Add chicken and sauté, turning once, until golden brown on both sides. Transfer chicken to a baking dish. Bake at 350 degrees for 15 to 20 minutes or until cooked through. Serve with Caribbean Salsa.

Caribbean Salsa

Combine all peppers, cilantro, bananas, lime juice, brown sugar, salt and pepper. Let mixture stand at room temperature for at least 1 hour to allow flavors to blend.

Yield: 6 servings

Mediterranean Chicken

6 boneless, skinless chicken breast
    halves
1 cup sun-dried tomatoes, chopped
½ cup red wine
8 ounces feta cheese
¼ cup pine nuts, toasted

1 cup kalamata olives, pitted and
    chopped
1 teaspoon dried marjoram
1 egg, beaten
Bread crumbs
Olive oil
½ cup red wine

Slice a pocket into the side of each chicken breast. Reconstitute tomatoes in ½ cup wine; do not drain. Combine cheese, pine nuts, olives, marjoram and tomatoes with liquid. Stuff mixture into breasts. Dip breasts in egg, then dredge in bread crumbs. Brown breasts on both sides in olive oil. Transfer chicken to a 9x13 inch baking dish. Add ½ cup wine and cover with foil. Bake at 350 degrees for 30 minutes. Uncover and bake 10 minutes longer.

Yield: 6 servings

Pesto Pepper Chicken Rolls

6 boneless, skinless chicken breast
    halves
1 (15 ounce) jar mild pesto sauce
2 cups Monterey Jack cheese, shredded

1 (16 ounce) jar roasted red
    peppers, drained
2 tablespoons peppercorns, crushed

Pound each chicken breast to about one-fourth inch thickness between 2 sheets of plastic wrap. Generously spread breasts with pesto and sprinkle with cheese. Top with large pieces of peppers and sprinkle with peppercorns. Roll each breast jelly-roll style and secure with toothpicks. Place in a shallow baking pan. Bake at 350 degrees for 45 minutes.

Yield: 6 servings

Helpful Hints

Freeze chicken
stock in ice cube trays.
Pop out and store in
plastic bags to season
soups or sauces.

Grate cheese in
food processor and
store in plastic bags
to have ready for
toppings.

Marinated Grilled Chicken

For full flavor, marinate the chicken for 48 hours.

1 cup soy sauce

1¾ cups pineapple juice

½ cup sugar

1¼ cups cooking sherry

½ cup wine vinegar

1½ teaspoon garlic powder

10 to 12 chicken breast halves

Combine soy sauce, pineapple juice, sugar, sherry, vinegar and garlic powder in a dish or zip-top plastic bag. Add chicken and marinate in refrigerator for 1 to 2 days. When ready to cook, drain chicken, reserving marinade. Bake at 400 degrees for 45 minutes, basting every 10 minutes with marinade, or cook on a grill.

Yield: 10 to 12 servings

Citrus Chicken

4 large chicken breast halves

Salt

All-purpose flour

¼ cup peanut oil (do not substitute)

3 tablespoons unsalted butter

6 tablespoons brown sugar

2 large oranges, peeled and sectioned

4 large peaches, peeled and sliced, or 8 ounces frozen peaches, thawed

½ cup Grand Marnier

½ cup almonds, toasted

Lightly season chicken with salt and coat with flour. Fry chicken in oil over medium heat until brown and almost cooked. Remove chicken from skillet and set aside. Drain oil from skillet. Add butter and brown sugar to skillet and simmer and stir until smooth. Add chicken and orange sections. Place peaches on top and pour Grand Marnier over all. Simmer, basting with pan liquid, for 5 minutes. Arrange chicken and fruit on a platter. Sprinkle with almonds.

Yield: 4 servings

Herb Chicken with Roasted Tomato Sauce

Chicken

4 bone-in, skinless chicken breast
    halves
¼ cup vegetable oil

1 small onion, diced
1½ teaspoons dried rosemary
1½ teaspoons dried thyme

Roasted Tomato Sauce

10 Roma tomatoes
½ cup olive oil
4 cloves garlic

1½ tablespoons dried basil
Salt and pepper to taste

Chicken

Brown chicken in oil with onions. Transfer chicken and onions to a baking dish. Sprinkle with rosemary and thyme. Bake at 350 degrees for 30 minutes or until done. Spoon Roasted Tomato Sauce over each chicken breast on individual serving plates.

Roasted Tomato Sauce

Cut stem end from tomatoes and remove seeds. Place tomatoes in a roasting pan and drizzle with oil. Bake at 450 degrees for 15 minutes or until done. Remove tomatoes from pan and reserve oil. Puree tomatoes in a food processor. Add garlic and basil to tomatoes and puree until smooth. Add reserved oil to puree as needed to reach desired consistency. Season with salt and pepper.

Yield: 4 servings

Cornish Hens with Cranberry-Orange Sauce

Cornish Hens

4 (1 pound, 6 ounce) Cornish game
    hens

¼ cup frozen orange juice
    concentrate, thawed

¼ cup water

Cranberry-Orange Sauce

1½ cups fresh or frozen cranberries,
    coarsely chopped

1 teaspoon orange zest

¾ cup unsweetened orange juice

2 tablespoons packed light brown
    sugar

2 teaspoons cornstarch

Cornish Hens

Remove giblets from hens. Rinse hens with cold water and pat dry. Split each hen in half lengthwise using an electric knife. Place hens, cut-side down, on a rack in a shallow roasting pan. Combine orange juice concentrate and water in a small bowl. Bake hens at 350 degrees for 1 hour or until done, basting occasionally with orange juice mixture. Transfer hens to a serving platter. To serve, spoon about 2½ tablespoons of sauce over each hen half.

Cranberry-Orange Sauce

Combine cranberries, orange zest and juice, brown sugar and cornstarch in a small saucepan. Stir well and bring to a boil. Reduce heat to medium and cook, stirring constantly, for 1 minute or until thickened. Serve warm.

Yield: 8 servings, 1⅓ cups sauce

Southern Chicken and Dumplings

Make this on Sunday afternoons in honor of your grandmother.

Chicken

1 (3 to 4 pound) whole chicken	4 cups water
1 yellow onion, quartered	1 bay leaf
2 slices lemon	⅛ teaspoon ground sage
Salt and white pepper to taste	½ teaspoon dried thyme

Dumplings

¼ cup shortening	⅛ teaspoon dried thyme
2 cups all-purpose flour	⅓ to 1 cup water
1 teaspoon salt	

Chicken

Place chicken in a heavy pot with a lid. Add onions, lemons, salt, pepper, water, bay leaf, sage and thyme. Cover and boil for 20 minutes. Reduce heat and simmer 40 minutes or until chicken is cooked through.

Dumplings

Make dumplings while chicken cooks. In a medium mixing bowl, cut shortening into flour, salt and thyme. Stir in water, starting with ⅓ cup and adding more as needed until a soft dough forms. Pinch off dough into 1 inch pieces. Let dough rest and dry out on counter as chicken cooks.

Let chicken cool slightly in the pot. Remove chicken from pot. Discard skin and remove meat from bones. Cube meat. Discard onions, lemons and bay leaf. Pour broth into a large bowl. Cool broth and skim off fat. Return skimmed broth to pot along with cubed chicken. Simmer over low heat for 10 minutes. Drop dumpling pieces into pot. Simmer, uncovered, for 20 minutes. Cover and simmer 10 minutes longer. Season with salt and pepper. Serve immediately.

Yield: 4 servings

Never Fail Roast Turkey

1 small turkey (up to 14 pounds)
2 cups kosher salt or 1 cup table salt
4 medium onions, coarsely chopped
2 medium carrots, coarsely chopped

2 stalks celery, coarsely chopped
5 sprigs thyme
5 tablespoons unsalted butter, melted
Salt and pepper to taste

Well, it did fail once, because my oven broke halfway through cooking it. It happened the first Thanksgiving I cooked as a new wife, in my new home, for my family. Thank goodness we had an already cooked ham!

Rinse turkey thoroughly. Remove giblets, neck and tailpiece and reserve to make gravy. Dissolve salt in 2 gallons of very cold water in a large stockpot or a clean cooler. Add turkey and refrigerate 12 hours or overnight.

Remove turkey from brine water and rinse cavity and skin under cool running water for several minutes until all traces of salt are gone. Pat turkey dry inside and out with a lint-free towel. Mix one third each of onions, carrots, celery and thyme with 2 tablespoons of melted butter. Place mixture in turkey's body cavity and truss the legs. Place remaining onions, carrots, celery and thyme in a roasting pan. Add 1½ cups water. Place a V-rack in pan. Brush entire breast-side of turkey with about half of the remaining butter. Season with salt and pepper. Place turkey, breast-side down, on rack. Brush entire backside of turkey with remaining butter and season with salt and pepper.

Place oven rack in the lowest position. Roast turkey at 400 degrees for 45 minutes without opening the door while baking. Remove pan from oven and baste with pan juices. Add water to pan as needed while cooking. Turn turkey a quarter turn, leg/thigh-side up, and return to oven. Roast 15 minutes. Remove from oven, baste and turn turkey so that other leg/thigh-side is up. Roast 15 minutes longer. Remove from oven and baste. Turn turkey so breast-side is up. Roast 30 minutes or until a thermometer registers 165 degrees when inserted into the breast and 170 to 175 degrees when inserted into the thigh. Remove turkey from pan, cover loosely with foil and let rest at least 20 minutes or until ready to carve.

Yield: 10 to 12 servings

For a larger bird (18 to 20 pounds), follow recipe, roasting breast-side down at 250 degrees for 3 hours, basting every hour. Then turn breast-side up and roast another hour, basting once or twice. Increase oven to 400 degrees and roast about 1 hour longer or until done. Serves 18 to 20.

The secret to this recipe is the brine. It makes the meat stay very moist throughout. Although it requires a bit of work, it never fails! It is perfect for Thanksgiving dinner.

Chicken Couscous

1¼ cups water

2 teaspoons butter or olive oil

1 (10 ounce) package frozen chopped spinach, thawed and drained

1 (10 ounce) can tomatoes with diced green chiles, undrained

1 (5.9 ounce) package Parmesan-flavored couscous

1½ cups cooked chicken breast halves, chopped

Grated Parmesan cheese

Combine water, butter, spinach, tomatoes and flavor packet from couscous package in a medium saucepan. Bring to a slow boil, then remove from heat. Stir in couscous and chicken. Cover and let stand 5 minutes or until liquid is absorbed. Serve with Parmesan cheese.

Yield: 4 servings

Turkey with Artichokes

4 cups cooked turkey or chicken,
  chopped
2 (15½ ounce) cans artichoke
  hearts, drained
¼ cup all-purpose flour

4 tablespoons butter, melted
¼ teaspoon garlic salt or powder
2 cups chicken broth
6 ounces Cheddar cheese, shredded
1 (8 ounce) can mushrooms, drained

Topping

2 tablespoons butter
¼ teaspoon savory

¼ teaspoon dried thyme
½ cup bread crumbs

Combine turkey and artichokes in a large casserole dish. Blend flour, melted butter and garlic in a medium saucepan. Add broth and cook and stir until thickened. Blend in cheese and mushrooms and pour over turkey and artichokes.

Topping

Melt butter with savory and thyme in a small saucepan. Mix in bread crumbs. Sprinkle over top of casserole. Bake at 350 degrees for 20 minutes or until bubbly. Serve over rice or noodles.

Yield: 8 servings

Feast on Pheasant

This is a wonderful dish to accompany your traditional Thanksgiving dinner.

1 (6 ounce) package wild rice
12 ounces mild sausage
1 large onion, chopped
½ pound mushrooms, chopped
1 (8 ounce) can sliced water chestnuts
2 cups cooked pheasant, chopped
½ lemon

4 tablespoons butter
¼ cup all-purpose flour
¼ cup milk
1¾ cups chicken broth
1 teaspoon salt
⅛ teaspoon black pepper
½ cup slivered almonds, toasted

Cook rice according to package directions; set aside. Brown sausage in a skillet. Remove sausage and set aside, reserving fat in skillet. Add onions and mushrooms to skillet and sauté. Add water chestnuts and sausage to skillet. Add pheasant and lightly toss mixture. Squeeze lemon half over mixture. Stir cooked rice into mixture.

To make a white sauce in a medium saucepan, melt butter. Blend in flour and milk. Add broth, salt and pepper. Cook and stir until thickened. Combine sauce with pheasant. Pour mixture into a casserole dish. Bake at 350 degrees for 1 hour. Remove from oven and sprinkle with almonds before serving.

Yield: 8 to 10 servings

Fool Proof Pheasant

2 pheasants
Olive oil
Salt and pepper
to taste
2 cinnamon sticks
2 (14 ounce) cans
chicken broth
½ cup
cooking sherry
1 stick butter

Clean and wash pheasant, pat dry. Grease with olive oil and rub in salt and pepper. Place cinnamon stick in each cavity. Place in a Dutch oven and cover with chicken broth and sherry. Add butter. Cover and cook at 325 degrees for 1½ to 2 hours or until tender. Baste with stock every 10 minutes during last 30 minutes of cooking. Cool and pull meat off bone for casserole.

Quail

There are several varieties of quail, the best known in America being the bobwhite. Its name is derived from its clear, piercing call which sounds like a young girl calling to Bob White with the last name a rising, shrill note.

Braised Quail with Cider Sauce

Quail

2 teaspoons shallots, chopped

3 tablespoons butter

8 mushrooms, finely chopped

1 cup bread crumbs

Dash of nutmeg

1 teaspoon dried tarragon

Salt and pepper to taste

¼ cup sliced blanched almonds

⅓ cup dry white wine

6 quail

1 stick butter

1 cup dry white wine

Cider Sauce

1 teaspoon garlic, minced

2 shallots, roasted

1 tablespoon olive oil

1 orange, halved

1 cup boiled apple cider

¼ cup whole grain mustard

2 tablespoons molasses

1 (7 ounce) bottle duck sauce or similar glaze

Salt and pepper to taste

Quail

Sauté shallots in 3 tablespoons butter. Mix sautéed shallots with mushrooms and bread crumbs. Season mixture with nutmeg, tarragon, salt and pepper. Add almonds and ⅓ cup wine. Mix well. Stuff mixture into quail.

Melt stick of butter in a heavy skillet. Brown quail on all sides in butter. Transfer quail, breast-side down, to a 9x13 inch casserole dish. Add 1 cup wine to dish. Bake at 350 degrees for 20 minutes. Serve with cider sauce.

Cider Sauce

Sauté garlic and shallots in oil in a skillet. Squeeze juice from orange halves into skillet, then add halves to skillet. Stir in cider, mustard and molasses. Bring mixture to a simmer. Add duck sauce and return to a simmer. Season with salt and pepper and continue to simmer sauce until ready to serve. Strain sauce through a mesh strainer. Serve warm over quail.

Yield: 6 servings

Greenbriar Duck Kabobs

1 cup canola oil

1 white onion, coarsely chopped

⅔ cup sugar

⅓ cup tamari soy sauce

1 tablespoon all-purpose flour

2 cloves garlic

2 tablespoons sesame seeds, toasted

10 duck breasts, cut into 1 inch cubes

1 (8 ounce) can pineapple chunks, drained

Combine oil, onions, sugar, soy sauce, flour and garlic in a food processor. Blend until smooth. Pour mixture into a glass dish or large plastic zip-top bag. Stir in sesame seeds. Reserve ½ cup of marinade mixture, cover and chill. Add duck to remaining marinade and stir to coat. Cover and refrigerate for 6 hours or overnight.

When ready to cook, soak 12 wooden skewers for 30 minutes; drain. On each skewer, alternate several duck pieces with 1 or 2 pineapple chunks. Grill kabobs for 15 to 20 minutes or until medium-rare, turning kabobs constantly and basting several times with reserved marinade. Do not overcook and be careful of flare-ups, although some charring is acceptable. Remove meat and pineapple from skewers and serve on a lettuce-lined platter with toothpicks.

Yield: 6 to 8 servings

Key Notes

A bowl of this gumbo stirs memories of the mornings in the duck blind for my husband and sons. One favorite memory is of our youngest son's first duck hunting trip. He came home so excited to tell me how Dad shot a duck called "Suzie" and even the duck cleaner knew her name. Imagine that!

Duck Gumbo

2 to 3 ducks

2 (10½ ounce) cans consommé

2 consommé cans water

¾ cup vegetable oil

⅔ cup all-purpose flour

2 onions, chopped

2 cups celery, chopped

2 cups okra, sliced

3 cloves garlic, minced

1 (16 ounce) can tomatoes, chopped

1 (10¾ ounce) can condensed
   tomato soup

½ teaspoon black pepper

½ teaspoon Tabasco sauce

½ teaspoon cayenne pepper

1 teaspoon dried thyme

1 teaspoon poultry seasoning

1 teaspoon cumin

3 (14 ounce) cans chicken broth

2½ cups water

1 pound sausage, cooked

Pinch of filé powder

Cooked rice

Simmer ducks in consommé and 2 cans of water for 3 hours; cool. Remove meat from bones and cut into bite-size pieces, discard cooking liquid. In a stockpot, make a roux by blending oil and flour. Cook and stir until brown. Add onions, celery, okra, garlic, tomatoes, soup, black pepper, Tabasco, cayenne, thyme, poultry seasoning, cumin, broth, 2½ cups water and duck meat. Simmer 3 hours. Add sausage and filé powder and simmer 30 minutes longer. Serve over rice.

Yield: 12 to 15 servings

Venison Tenderloin with Tarragon

This is fabulous and we think it is better than beef tenderloin with béarnaise sauce. Hunters die over it!

½ cup dry red wine

2 tablespoons soy sauce

2 tablespoons Worcestershire sauce

2 cloves garlic, minced

1 medium onion, sliced

½ teaspoon ground thyme

2 (1 pound) venison tenderloins, trimmed

1½ cups bread crumbs

1 tablespoon fresh tarragon, chopped

½ teaspoon salt

1 teaspoon black pepper

1 tablespoon butter

1 tablespoon vegetable oil

3 tablespoons sour cream

Chopped parsley for garnish

Combine wine, soy sauce, Worcestershire sauce, garlic, onion and thyme in a glass dish or zip-top bag. Add tenderloins and marinate in refrigerator for at least 6 hours or overnight, turning occasionally. Drain venison, reserving marinade. Slice venison into 1 inch thick medallions and set aside.

Mix together bread crumbs, tarragon, salt and pepper. Place mixture on a sheet of wax paper near stovetop. Heat butter and oil until foamy in a large nonstick skillet over medium-high heat. Dredge venison medallions in bread crumb mixture and place close together in skillet. Cook 3½ minutes on each side or until medium-rare. Remove meat from skillet and keep warm.

Pour ½ cup of reserved marinade into hot skillet and stir to deglaze. Boil marinade for 5 minutes or until reduced by half. Remove skillet from heat and whisk in sour cream. To serve, place 3 to 4 medallions on each individual serving plate. Top venison with sauce and sprinkle with parsley.

Yield: 6 servings

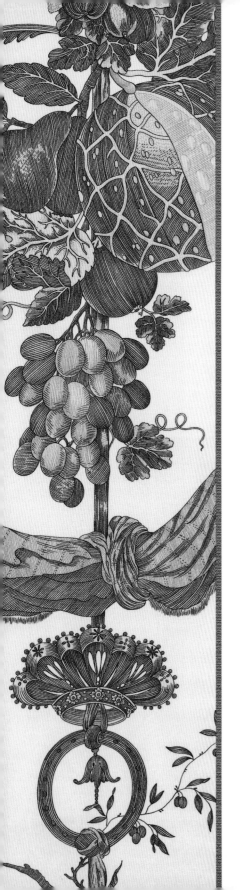

Pasta

Creamy Fettuccine with Prosciutto,
Asparagus, Mushrooms and Peas

1998

I never dreamed I would need the services of Le Bonheur Children's Medical Center. However, after my son's accidental hunting gunshot wound to the pelvis, we found ourselves a long way from home, surrounded by total strangers whom we had to rely on to care for him. For two weeks, my son had round-the-clock care in the Trauma Unit in another hospital. The doctors agreed the best place for my son was Le Bonheur. He was taken out of the unit and security of the staff I had come to know and trust. I was scared, unsure and alone.

A wonderful nurse calmed my fears and assured me that he would be well cared for. My son made a real connection with this special nurse and their friendship continues even today. Our new pediatrician worked diligently to control the pain in my son's feet and legs, guiding us through the coming weeks, preparing us for eventual discharge and rehabilitation. He continued his long distance care on several occasions. Above all, he never doubted my son would walk, even though we had been told the probability was low.

A dear staff member spent time teaching my son the art of fly tying, a craft he continues today. A Le Bonheur Club volunteer sat with me and talked about shopping and events outside the hospital. Even the cooks became involved! My son had blue Jell-O on his food tray everyday. An X-ray technician gave him his Pooh tie saying it looked better on my son anyway. I'll never forget the staff associate who would whisper something to my son every morning. Later, I found out she was telling him not to ever give up hope, because someday he would walk again.

On a stormy afternoon, a funnel cloud had been spotted just a couple of blocks from the hospital. Our special nurse friend, who was off shift, called to tell me to move away from the windows and cover with blankets and pillows. Thankfully, another nurse was already there, calming me because she found out I was terrified of storms. When my son wished for Sara Lee Cherry Cheesecake, this incredibly special nurse spent the day looking for the cheesecake to bring to him. On our discharge day, she was concerned that my son would have to ride home in an ambulance alone or with someone who was unaccustomed to his care. Amazingly, she took the day off and rode to Alabama with him in the ambulance.

In the weeks I spent at my son's side, I learned a lot by watching the people of Le Bonheur. The staff doesn't go there just to work. There is a dedication involved that seems to be powered by the heart. There was a great celebration when my son was able to get into a wheelchair after 41 days in bed. He was surprised with a birthday party complete with gifts and cake. It is these heartfelt gestures that we will never forget. The doctors, nurses and ancillary staff cared for us in many ways. They laughed with me. They cried with me. And when the weight of the world was too heavy, they carried me.

In the midst of all our blessings, Le Bonheur Children's Medical Center is truly our greatest gift. They gave me back my child that should not have survived.

Creamy Fettuccine with Prosciutto, Asparagus, Mushrooms and Peas

8 ounces thin asparagus, trimmed and cut into ½ inch lengths

4 tablespoons unsalted butter

4 ounces thinly sliced prosciutto, cut into ¼ inch strips

1 cup fresh mushrooms, sliced

1 cup frozen petite peas, thawed

1 cup heavy cream

16 cherry tomatoes, halved

1 pound fettuccine

Salt and pepper to taste

¾ cup Parmesan cheese, grated

¼ cup fresh chives, chopped

Cook asparagus in a large pot of boiling salted water for 3 minutes or until crisp-tender. Using a slotted spoon, transfer to a bowl, reserving cooking water in pot. Melt butter in a large skillet over medium-low heat. Add prosciutto and stir 1 minute. Add mushrooms and sauté about 3 minutes. Add asparagus, peas and cream and simmer 2 minutes or until cream is reduced by one third. Remove from heat and stir in tomatoes. Bring reserved cooking water to a boil. Add fettuccine and cook until tender; drain. Add fettuccine to cream sauce and toss over low heat until coated. Season with salt and pepper. Remove from heat and stir in cheese. Transfer to a large bowl and sprinkle with chives.

Yield: 4 servings

Four Star Manicotti

Prepare this marvelous Manicotti the day ahead so you can enjoy a glass of your favorite Italian red wine with your guests.

Tomato Sauce

1 cup onions, chopped

¼ cup olive oil

3 (14 ounce) cans diced plum
    tomatoes, undrained

1 (6 ounce) can tomato paste

2 teaspoons dried basil

2 teaspoons sugar

Salt and pepper to taste

Filling

¼ cup onions, chopped

1 teaspoon garlic, chopped

2 tablespoons olive oil

1 (10 ounce) package frozen spinach,
    thawed and squeezed dry

8 ounces sausage

8 ounces ground beef chuck

2 tablespoons heavy cream

½ cup Parmesan cheese, grated

2 eggs, slightly beaten

1 teaspoon dried oregano

Salt and pepper to taste

Béchamel Sauce

1 stick butter

½ cup all-purpose flour

1 cup half-and-half

1 cup heavy cream

1 teaspoon salt

1 (10 ounce) container Alfredo sauce

1 (16 ounce) package manicotti shells

Tomato Sauce

Sauté onions in olive oil. Add tomatoes, tomato paste, basil and sugar. Season with salt and pepper. Simmer, uncovered, for 45 minutes.

Filling

Sauté onions and garlic in olive oil until softened. Add spinach and cook 5 minutes. Brown sausage and beef, drain and add to spinach mixture. Stir in cream, cheese, eggs and oregano. Season with salt and pepper.

Béchamel Sauce

Melt butter in a saucepan. Blend in flour and cook and stir until bubbly and well combined. Pour in half-and-half and cream. Season with salt. Cook over low heat, whisking constantly, until sauce is thick and smooth. Stir in Alfredo sauce.

To assemble, cook manicotti shells and drain. Fill each shell with filling. Pour a thin layer of tomato sauce over the bottom of a 9x13 inch baking dish. Lay stuffed manicotti side by side on top of sauce. Pour Béchamel sauce over shells and spoon remaining tomato sauce on top. Bake at 350 degrees for 20 to 30 minutes.

Yield: 6 to 8 servings

Fancy Farfalle

1½ pounds medium shallots, peeled and halved lengthwise

2 tablespoons olive oil

Salt and pepper to taste

1 cup fresh bread crumbs made from French bread

2 tablespoons olive oil

1½ pounds farfalle (bow tie) pasta

1 (14 ounce) can artichoke hearts, quartered

2 pounds bleu cheese, crumbled

Toss shallots with 2 tablespoons olive oil on a baking sheet. Spread into a single layer and season with salt and pepper. Bake at 375 degrees, stirring occasionally, for 35 minutes or until tender and golden brown. Combine bread crumbs and 2 tablespoons olive oil in a skillet. Cook and stir over medium heat for 4 minutes or until browned. Cook pasta in a large pot of boiling salted water until tender. Add artichokes to boiling water near end of cooking time and cook until tender-crisp. Drain and transfer pasta and artichokes to a large bowl. Immediately add cheese and shallots and toss until cheese melts and pasta is well coated. Season with salt and pepper. Transfer to bowls and sprinkle with bread crumbs.

Yield: 4 servings

Shallots and bread crumbs can be prepared 8 hours in advance, covered separately and kept at room temperature.

Cavatini

Another great make ahead tasty dish. This makes a large amount to feed a crowd or divide and share with family and friends.

1 pound ground beef

1 pound ground mild turkey or pork sausage

1 medium onion, chopped

1 green bell pepper, chopped

1 (3½ ounce) package sliced pepperoni, chopped

1 (28 ounce) can spaghetti sauce

1 (16 ounce) jar mild salsa

1 (4 ounce) can sliced mushrooms, drained

1 (10 ounce) jar pepperoncini salad peppers, drained and sliced

1 (16 ounce) package shell macaroni, cooked and drained

1 cup Parmesan cheese, grated

4 cups mozzarella cheese, shredded

Brown beef and sausage with onions and bell peppers. Drain and set aside. Combine pepperoni, spaghetti sauce, salsa, mushrooms and pepperoncini in a large bowl. Stir in meat mixture and cooked macaroni. Divide half of the macaroni mixture among 3 greased 8x8 inch baking pans. Combine Parmesan and mozzarella cheeses. Sprinkle half of cheese mixture over macaroni. Top with remaining macaroni mixture. Cover with foil. At this point, dish may be frozen and thawed prior to baking. Bake at 350 degrees for 30 minutes. Uncover and sprinkle remaining cheese mixture on top. Bake 5 minutes longer.

Yield: 10 to 12 servings

Spaghettini à la Puttanesca

Saying the name of this dish will impress your guests but not as much as the taste!

Marinara

1 clove garlic, halved

¼ cup olive oil

1 (28 ounce) can Italian tomatoes
    with basil, coarsely chopped

2 tablespoons fresh basil, chopped

1 tablespoon dried oregano

1 bay leaf

½ teaspoon salt

¼ teaspoon black pepper

2 tablespoons fresh parsley, chopped

¾ cup white wine

Olive Mixture

2 cloves garlic, minced

1 to 3 dried red peppers, seeded

3 tablespoons olive oil

6 large green olives, chopped

6 large black olives, chopped

2 tablespoons capers

½ cup white wine

1 pound linguine

Marinara

Brown garlic halves in olive oil in a medium skillet. Remove skillet from heat and add tomatoes. Return to medium heat and stir in basil, oregano, bay leaf, salt and pepper. Simmer 15 to 20 minutes. Add parsley and wine and simmer 10 minutes longer. Discard garlic and bay leaf.

Olive Mixture

Slowly brown garlic and red peppers in olive oil in a small skillet. Add olives and capers and sauté 10 minutes. Add wine and simmer 10 minutes. Remove red peppers.

Cook linguine in boiling water until tender; drain. Combine marinara and olive mixture. Toss with hot linguine.

Yield: 4 to 6 servings

Gnocchi

Italian for "dumplings," gnocchi (NYOH-kee) can be made from dough of potatoes and flour with or without eggs. Cheese and finely chopped spinach are popular additions to the dough. Gnocchi are shaped into small oval balls and cooked in boiling water. The dough can be chilled, sliced and baked. Gnocchi makes an excellent accompaniment for meat or poultry.

Gnocchi with Chicken

1 pound dry gnocchi pasta

½ cup oil packed sun-dried tomatoes, drained and chopped, 2 tablespoons oil reserved

4 boneless, skinless chicken breast halves

4 cloves garlic, minced

½ cup chicken broth

¾ cup Gorgonzola cheese, crumbled

Salt and pepper to taste

¼ cup pine nuts, toasted

¼ cup Gorgonzola cheese, crumbled

Cook pasta in a large pot of boiling salted water until tender; drain and keep warm. Meanwhile, heat 1 tablespoon reserved tomato oil in a large heavy skillet over medium-high heat. Add chicken and sauté 4 to 5 minutes on each side or until cooked through. Transfer chicken to a plate and cool. Cut chicken into bite-size pieces. Heat remaining tablespoon tomato oil in same skillet over medium-high heat. Add garlic and sauté 1 minute or until tender. Add tomatoes, chicken broth and ¾ cup cheese. Bring to a boil. Add chicken pieces and simmer 2 minutes or until heated through. Transfer pasta to a large bowl. Add cheese sauce and toss. Season with salt and pepper. Sprinkle pine nuts and ¼ cup cheese on top.

Yield: 4 to 6 servings

Tuxedo Chicken

2 cups bow tie pasta

4 boneless, skinless chicken breast
    halves

Salt and pepper to taste

¼ cup oil from oil-packed sun-dried
    tomatoes

6 cloves garlic, thinly sliced

2 cups dry white wine

1½ cups heavy cream

¾ cup sun-dried tomatoes, drained
    and thinly sliced

3 tablespoons dried basil

Cook pasta as directed on package. Season chicken with salt and
pepper. Heat tomato oil in a heavy medium skillet over medium-high
heat. Add chicken and sauté 5 minutes on each side or until golden. Add
garlic and sauté 1 minute longer. Add wine, cream, tomatoes and basil
and bring to a boil. Reduce heat and simmer 4 minutes or until chicken in
cooked. Transfer chicken to a plate and keep warm. Increase heat and boil
sauce until thickened. Season with salt and pepper. Serve chicken over
pasta with sauce spooned over the top. Serve immediately.

Yield: 4 servings

Chicken Caesar Pasta

2 boneless, skinless chicken breast
    halves, thinly sliced

1 (8 ounce) bottle Caesar salad
    dressing

2 green onions, thinly sliced

1 (10 ounce) package frozen sugar
    snap peas

1 carrot, thinly sliced

1 cup fresh spinach, torn

8 ounces bow tie pasta, cooked al dente

Sauté chicken in 3 tablespoons Caesar dressing until almost done. Add
onions, peas and carrots and stir-fry until vegetables are crisp-tender. Add
spinach and cook 1 to 2 minutes or until wilted. Toss with remaining
Caesar dressing and pasta.

Yield: 2 to 4 servings

Key Notes

The small amount of Tequila cooks away giving a south of the border flavor. What becomes of the leftover Tequila is up to you and your guests.

Tortellini with Drunken Chicken

2 (9 ounce) packages refrigerated spinach-cheese tortellini

1¼ pounds boneless, skinless chicken breast, diced into ¾ inch pieces

3 tablespoons soy sauce

½ cup fresh cilantro, chopped

2 tablespoons fresh garlic, minced

3 tablespoons jalapeño pepper, minced

2 tablespoons unsalted butter

½ cup chicken broth

2 tablespoons gold tequila

2 tablespoons freshly squeezed lime juice

¼ medium onion, diced

½ green bell pepper, diced

½ yellow bell pepper, diced

½ red bell pepper, diced

2 tablespoons unsalted butter

2 tablespoons chopped fresh cilantro for garnish

Cook tortellini in a large pot of boiling water for 6 to 8 minutes or until tender. Drain, rinse and set aside. Meanwhile, combine chicken and soy sauce in a small bowl and marinate 5 minutes.

Sauté cilantro, garlic and jalapeño in 2 tablespoons butter over medium heat for 4 to 5 minutes. Add broth, tequila and lime juice. Bring to a boil. Reduce heat and simmer until reduced to a paste-like consistency. Set aside.

In a large skillet, sauté onions and bell peppers in 2 tablespoons butter until tender. Add chicken and soy sauce. Stir in tequila mixture and bring to a boil. Boil gently for 3 to 5 minutes or until chicken is cooked through. Add tortellini and toss to mix. Heat until heated through. Garnish with cilantro.

Yield: 4 to 6 servings

Chicken Penne Pesto

Pesto

25 fresh basil leaves

15 fresh parsley leaves

3 tablespoons pine nuts

½ cup mayonnaise

¼ cup olive oil

2 cloves garlic, peeled

¼ cup Parmesan cheese, grated

Salt and pepper to taste

Chicken Penne

1 pound green beans, trimmed

8 ounces penne pasta, cooked al dente

3 cups cooked chicken, diced

2 tablespoons pine nuts, toasted for garnish

Freshly grated Parmesan cheese for garnish

Pesto

Place basil, parsley, pine nuts and mayonnaise in a food processor. Process until creamy. With motor running, slowly add oil. Add garlic and process, then cheese. Season with salt and pepper.

Chicken Penne

Cook green beans until crisp-tender. Combine beans, pasta and chicken in a bowl. Add pesto and toss. Top with pine nuts and cheese.

Yield: 4 to 6 servings

Key Notes

Lasagna Florentine

1 pound mushrooms, sliced

2 cloves garlic, minced

½ cup onion, chopped

3 tablespoons olive oil

3 cups chicken breast halves, cooked and cubed

2 (10 ounce) packages frozen chopped spinach, thawed and drained

1 cup mozzarella cheese, shredded

1 cup Parmesan cheese, grated

Béchamel sauce

9 lasagna noodles, cooked al dente

¼ cup bread crumbs

¼ cup grated Parmesan cheese

Béchamel Sauce

3½ cups milk

½ cup onion, chopped

2 bay leaves

¼ teaspoon ground thyme

½ teaspoon nutmeg

3 tablespoons butter

⅓ cup all-purpose flour

½ teaspoon salt

¼ teaspoon black pepper

Sauté mushrooms, garlic and onions in olive oil. Add chicken, spinach, mozzarella cheese, 1 cup Parmesan cheese and half the béchamel sauce. Spread one fourth cup of remaining béchamel sauce in the bottom of a greased 9x13 inch baking dish. Place 3 noodles over sauce. Top with one third of chicken mixture. Repeat noodle and chicken layers 2 more times. Spread remaining béchamel sauce on top. Sprinkle with bread crumbs. Bake, covered, at 350 degrees for 45 minutes. Uncover and sprinkle with ¼ cup Parmesan cheese. Bake, uncovered, for 10 to 15 minutes longer.

Béchamel Sauce

Combine milk, onion, bay leaves, thyme and nutmeg in a saucepan. Bring to a boil over medium heat. Remove from heat and cool. Melt butter in a heavy saucepan over low heat. Slowly blend in flour until smooth and cook 1 minute. Gradually add milk mixture while stirring constantly. Cook over medium heat until thick and bubbly. Add salt and pepper. Remove bay leaves. Cool slightly.

Yield: 6 to 8 servings

Potpourri Penne

½ cup boiling water

¼ cup sun-dried tomatoes

4 boneless chicken breast halves

¼ cup dry white wine

1 tablespoon Italian seasoning

3 tablespoons onion, chopped

1¼ cups portobella mushrooms, chopped

½ cup fresh or frozen green peas

5 cloves garlic, minced

1 tablespoon all-purpose flour

1 (12 ounce) can evaporated skim milk

⅛ teaspoon nutmeg

⅛ teaspoon dried red pepper flakes

½ cup fresh basil, chopped

8 ounces penne paste, cooked al dente

5 medium-size black olives, sliced

Pour boiling water over tomatoes and set aside to soften. Combine chicken, wine and Italian seasoning in a shallow 8x10 inch baking dish. Bake at 350 degrees for 15 to 20 minutes or until done but still juicy. Remove chicken, reserving cooking juices. Cut chicken into thin slices. Drain tomatoes and thinly slice. Sauté onions, mushrooms, peas and sliced tomatoes in reserved cooking juices until liquid is absorbed and vegetables are wilted. Remove from heat and keep warm.

Sauté garlic and flour in a saucepan sprayed with cooking spray. Whisk in milk until smooth. Add nutmeg and pepper flakes. Cook and stir until thickened. Reduce heat and add basil. Toss together drained pasta, sliced chicken, sautéed vegetables and white sauce. Garnish with olives.

Yield: 4 servings

Family Night Barbecue Chicken Pasta

A quick and easy family meal sure to please all ages.

½ cup onion, chopped

1 cup tomato juice

2 tablespoons packed brown sugar

1 teaspoon paprika

½ teaspoon salt

1 teaspoon dry mustard

Dash of cayenne pepper

3 tablespoons Worcestershire sauce

½ cup ketchup

¼ cup vinegar

6 boneless, skinless chicken breast halves

2 (8 ounce) cans sliced mushrooms, drained

1 (14 ounce) can artichoke hearts, drained and sliced

1 (15 ounce) package spaghetti or egg noodles, cooked al dente

In a saucepan, sauté onions in tomato juice until softened. Add sugar, paprika, salt, mustard, pepper, Worcestershire sauce, ketchup and vinegar. Add chicken and cook over low heat for about 30 minutes. Stir in mushrooms and artichokes and simmer 10 to 15 minutes. Place pasta on individual serving plates. Spoon chicken and sauce over pasta.

Yield: 6 servings

Turkey Pasta Bake

4 tablespoons butter

2 medium-size green bell peppers, diced

6 tablespoons all-purpose flour

3 cups hot chicken broth

4 ounces baked ham, julienned

1 pound cooked turkey, julienned

1 tablespoon fresh parsley, chopped

2 teaspoons Worcestershire sauce

½ teaspoon salt

¼ teaspoon white pepper

1 cup milk

10 ounces thin noodles

¼ cup dry bread crumbs

2 tablespoons grated Parmesan cheese

Melt butter in a 3 quart saucepan. Add bell peppers and sauté 5 minutes. Blend in flour. Stir in broth and bring to a boil. Cook and stir 5 minutes or until smooth. Add ham, turkey, parsley, Worcestershire sauce, salt and pepper. Bring to a boil. Gradually add milk, stirring gently. Simmer 5 minutes. Meanwhile, cook noodles in 2 quarts of boiling salted water for 7 minutes; drain well. Spread noodles in a greased shallow casserole dish. Spread turkey mixture evenly over noodles. Sprinkle with bread crumbs and cheese. Bake at 375 degrees on the center rack of oven for 20 minutes or until heated through and lightly browned on top. Serve warm with a green salad or tomatoes and vinaigrette.

Yield: 6 to 8 servings

Pesto Prosciutto Fettuccine

Fettuccine

8 ounces dry fettuccine, cooked al dente

Fresh Pesto

⅓ cup slivered prosciutto

¼ cup sliced sun-dried tomatoes packed in oil

Freshly grated Parmesan cheese

Fresh Pesto

1 clove garlic

1 cup lightly packed fresh basil

¼ cup pine nuts or pecans

¼ cup olive oil

⅓ cup freshly grated Parmesan cheese

1 teaspoon lemon juice

½ teaspoon salt

Fettuccine

Combine pasta, pesto, prosciutto and tomatoes and toss to coat. Sprinkle with cheese.

Fresh Pesto

Combine garlic, basil and nuts in a food processor. Pulse several times until coarsely chopped. Add oil, cheese, lemon juice and salt and pulse until finely ground.

Yield: 4 servings, ¾ cup pesto

Substitute orzo for fettuccine and serve cold as a salad.

Pasta Gamberetti

This shrimp and pasta ensemble evokes memories of warm summer nights vacationing on the Gulf.

Juice of 1 lemon

1 teaspoon lemon zest

4 tablespoons butter, softened

2 sticks butter

8 ounces mushrooms, sliced

4 teaspoons garlic, chopped

1 pound shrimp, peeled and deveined

2 cups fresh spinach, torn into large pieces

3 tablespoons pine nuts

2 teaspoons salt

2 teaspoon black pepper

1 pound dry vermicelli, cooked al dente

Whip lemon juice, zest and 4 tablespoons butter together to make a lemon butter.

Melt 2 sticks butter in a large skillet over medium heat. Add mushrooms and sauté briefly. Add garlic and shrimp and cook just until shrimp begin to color. Stir in spinach and pine nuts. Add lemon butter, salt and pepper. Bring to a simmer. Cook 2 minutes or just until shrimp are done. Serve immediately over cooked vermicelli.

Yield: 6 servings

Pasta with Shrimp and Goat Cheese

1 medium onion, diced

2 tablespoons olive oil

1 pound large shrimp, peeled and deveined

1 clove garlic, minced

1 teaspoon dried basil

½ cup milk

4 ounces goat cheese

8 ounces dry rotini, cooked al dente

1 tablespoon chopped fresh parsley

½ teaspoon salt

¼ teaspoon black pepper

Sauté onions in olive oil until tender in a large skillet over medium heat. Stir in shrimp, garlic and basil and sauté 4 minutes or until shrimp are pink. Remove from heat. In a small saucepan, cook milk and goat cheese over low heat for 5 to 7 minutes or until cheese melts. Stir cheese mixture into skillet with shrimp. Toss shrimp mixture with rotini. Sprinkle with parsley, salt and pepper and serve immediately.

Yield: 3 to 4 servings

Shrimp in Pesto

Shrimp and Pasta

6 tablespoons olive oil

6 tablespoons butter

1 pound raw shrimp, peeled and deveined

Juice of 1 lemon

Salt and pepper to taste

¼ cup or more Pesto Sauce

8 ounces dry rotini noodles, cooked al dente

Pesto Sauce

2 cups firmly packed fresh basil leaves

⅓ cup pine nuts

3 medium cloves garlic

½ cup freshly grated Parmesan cheese

½ cup olive oil

Salt and pepper to taste

Shrimp and Pasta

Heat oil and butter in a skillet. When hot, add shrimp. Sauté 1 minute or until shrimp turn pink. Season with lemon juice, salt and pepper. Continue to sauté about 5 minutes. Add pesto and toss and cook 2 to 3 minutes. Serve immediately over rotini.

Pesto Sauce

Blend basil, nuts, garlic and cheese in a food processor until pureed. With motor running, slowly add oil. If sauce seems dry, add more oil. Season with salt and pepper. Use immediately or refrigerate in a glass jar for up to 1 week.

Yield: 3 to 4 servings

Pesto can be frozen in ice cube trays for later use. If freezing, add nuts and cheese after thawing.

Key Notes

Key Notes

Coastal Shrimp Fettuccine

Garlic Butter

1½ sticks unsalted butter, softened

2 teaspoons garlic, minced

3 tablespoons shallots, minced

½ cup fresh parsley, chopped

⅛ teaspoon salt

Freshly ground black pepper to taste

Fettuccine

4 tablespoons unsalted butter

2 tablespoons olive oil

1 pound large raw shrimp, peeled and deveined

½ cup dry white wine

1 pound fettuccine, cooked al dente
Garlic Butter

¼ cup heavy cream

⅔ cup Parmesan cheese, freshly grated

⅓ cup fresh parsley, chopped

Salt and pepper to taste

⅓ cup fresh parsley, chopped for garnish

Garlic Butter

Combine butter, garlic, shallots, parsley, salt and pepper. If not using right away, cover and refrigerate. When ready to use, bring garlic butter to room temperature.

Fettuccini

Heat butter and oil in a skillet over medium heat. Add shrimp and sauté 2 to 3 minutes or until shrimp are pink. Add wine and cook 2 minutes. Remove from heat and toss with pasta in a bowl. Stir in garlic butter until melted. Stir in cream, cheese and ⅓ cup parsley. Toss well. Season with salt and pepper. Top with ⅓ cup parsley.

Yield: 4 servings

Spicy Linguine with Halibut and Tomato

1 pound white fish fillets, such as halibut or cod, cut into ¼ inch strips

2 tablespoons olive oil

¼ cup fresh basil, finely chopped

1 clove garlic, crushed

1 small dried red chile, seeded, or more, if desired

2 tablespoons olive oil

1 small onion, finely chopped

4 cloves garlic, minced

1 pound plum tomatoes, peeled, seeded and chopped, or 1 (14½ ounce) can diced, drained

1 cup dry white wine

12 ounces dry linguine

Salt and pepper to taste

Toss fish with 2 tablespoons olive oil and basil; set aside. In a large skillet, combine crushed garlic, red chile and 2 tablespoons olive oil. Cook over medium heat until garlic turns golden brown. Discard garlic and chile. Add onions and minced garlic to skillet. Cook 4 minutes or until softened. Stir in tomatoes and wine. Reduce heat and simmer 15 minutes. Meanwhile, cook linguine in a large pot of boiling water until al dente; drain. Increase heat of skillet with vegetable mixture to medium-high. Add fish and cook and stir for 5 minutes or until fish is opaque. Season with salt and pepper. Add pasta to fish sauce and toss well.

Yield: 4 servings

Key Notes

Crabmeat Cannelloni

3 tablespoons butter
½ cup onion, finely chopped
½ cup celéry, finely chopped
3 cloves garlic, minced
1 pound fresh lump crabmeat
1 tablespoon Dijon mustard
1 (12 ounce) can evaporated skim milk
2 eggs, slightly beaten
Juice of 1 lemon

2 tablespoons fresh parsley, minced
½ cup bread crumbs
Dash of dried red pepper flakes
Salt and pepper to taste
12 cannelloni shells, cooked al dente
1 stick butter
Juice and zest of 1 lemon
Pinch of salt
Grated Parmesan cheese

Melt 3 tablespoons butter in a saucepan. Add onions, celery and garlic and sauté over low heat. Set aside. In a medium bowl, combine crab, mustard, ¼ cup of milk, eggs, juice of 1 lemon, parsley, bread crumbs, pepper flakes, salt and pepper. Add sautéed vegetables and mix well. Fill cannelloni shells with crab mixture. Place shells in a single layer in a greased 9x13 inch baking dish. Melt 1 stick butter and combine with remainder of evaporated milk, juice and zest of 1 lemon and salt. Mix well and pour over pasta shells. Bake at 350 degrees for 45 minutes. Sprinkle with Parmesan cheese before serving.

Yield: 6 to 8 servings

Szechwan Noodle Toss

1 (12 ounce) package thin spaghetti

2 tablespoons sesame oil

1 large red bell pepper, julienned

4 green onions, cut into 1 inch pieces

1 clove garlic, crushed

1 (10 ounce) package fresh spinach, torn into pieces

2 cups cooked chicken breast halves, cubed

1 (8 ounce) can sliced water chestnuts, drained

2 tablespoons sesame oil

¼ cup soy sauce

2 tablespoons rice vinegar

¼ teaspoon dried red pepper flakes

1 teaspoon fresh ginger, minced

Salt and pepper to taste

Cook spaghetti according to package directions. Drain, rinse with cold water and drain again. Place spaghetti in a large bowl and set aside. Heat 2 tablespoons sesame oil in a large skillet. Add bell peppers, onions and garlic. Sauté 2 minutes. Stir in spinach, cover and cook over medium heat for 3 minutes or until spinach wilts. Remove from heat and cool. Spoon mixture over spaghetti. Add chicken and water chestnuts. Combine 2 tablespoons sesame oil, soy sauce, vinegar, pepper flakes, ginger, salt and pepper. Pour over pasta mixture and toss gently to coat.

Yield: 4 to 6 servings

Little ones may not like this too spicy, but Asian food lovers can turn up the heat by adding more red pepper flakes.

Vegetables
& Side Dishes

Snow Peas with Red Peppers

Stuffed Squash Boats

1979

*W*hen my daughter was 15 days old, she was admitted to Le Bonheur and diagnosed with whooping cough. She was the youngest patient ever to be diagnosed with this and was in the special care unit for 15 days. We received numerous letters from the doctors after her dismissal telling us that they were using her case to teach doctors and students at Le Bonheur.

We know that without the Le Bonheur doctors' and nurses' care, we would have lost our daughter. She is now 21 and has a son, 14 months old, who also has been in Le Bonheur four times since birth. Thank you for your help when we needed it the most.

1999

*M*yotubular myopathy, a form of muscular dystrophy, is an inherited muscle disorder with no known cause. Before the baby is born, the child's muscle cells cease to develop fully. The most severe form of this disease affects baby boys. In the past, most boys with this condition died shortly after birth or before their first birthday. Now, with early diagnosis and state-of-the-art treatment found at Le Bonheur Children's Medical Center, these little boys are living longer, better lives.

I would like to say that Le Bonheur is the best children's hospital. My son comes to Le Bonheur at least three times a month. He has myotubular myopathy. The trip takes us at least three hours one way. I would not have it any other way except for my son to receive his care at Le Bonheur. My local doctors told me that he would not live and they gave up on him. The doctors at Le Bonheur told me that it was all up to my son. Now, he is a happy little boy, and I want to thank each and everyone at Le Bonheur for giving me hope and for believing in him.

Stuffed Squash Boats

8 to 10 medium yellow squash
¼ cup green bell pepper, chopped
¼ cup red bell pepper, chopped
1 medium tomato, chopped
½ cup onion, chopped
4 slices bacon, cooked and crumbled

½ cup sharp Cheddar cheese,
    shredded
½ teaspoon salt
¼ teaspoon white pepper
2 tablespoons butter, melted

Cook whole squash in boiling salted water for 10 minutes or until tender. Drain and cool. Cut squash in half lengthwise and remove and discard seeds. In a bowl, combine bell peppers, tomatoes, onions, crumbled bacon, cheese, salt and pepper. Mix well. Spoon filling into squash shells. Drizzle with butter. Bake at 400 degrees, uncovered, for 20 minutes.

Yield: 8 to 16 servings

Snow Peas with Red Peppers

This colorful side dish makes any meal picture perfect.

14 ounces snow peas, ends and
    strings removed

Zest of 1 orange

Juice of 2 oranges

6 tablespoons butter

1 red bell pepper, thinly sliced and
    cut into 1 inch pieces

Salt and pepper to taste

Cook peas in boiling salted water for 3 to 4 minutes. Drain and set aside. Combine orange zest and juice in a saucepan. Bring to a boil and cook until reduced to 2 tablespoons. Strain juice and return to saucepan, discarding zest. Add butter to juice and whisk until creamy. Add bell peppers and peas and cook until heated through. Season with salt and pepper.

Yield: 4 servings

Grilled Asparagus with Saffron Aïoli

Saffron Aïoli

2 tablespoons red wine vinegar

1½ teaspoons honey

Pinch of saffron

½ cup mayonnaise

1 clove garlic, minced

Salt and pepper to taste

Asparagus

2 pounds asparagus, ends trimmed

3 tablespoons olive oil

Salt and pepper to taste

1 small red bell pepper, finely chopped

Saffron Aïoli

Whisk vinegar, honey and saffron in a heavy saucepan over medium-high heat. Bring to a boil. Remove from heat and cool completely. Mix mayonnaise and garlic together in a medium bowl. Stir in cooled vinegar mixture. Season to taste with salt and pepper. **Aïoli** can be prepared up to 1 day ahead and stored in the refrigerator.

Asparagus

Toss asparagus with olive oil. Sprinkle with salt and pepper. Grill asparagus over medium-high heat, turning occasionally, for 5 minutes or until crisp-tender. Transfer to a serving platter. Drizzle **aïoli** over asparagus. Sprinkle with bell peppers.

Yield: 6 servings

Roasted Asparagus with Thyme

2 pounds asparagus, thin stalks, ends trimmed

2 tablespoons olive oil

½ teaspoon dried thyme, or 1 teaspoon fresh, chopped

Salt and pepper to taste

Drizzle asparagus with oil and toss lightly to coat. Place in a single layer in a shallow baking pan. Sprinkle with thyme, salt and pepper. Bake at 425 degrees for 15 minutes or until tender.

Yield: 4 servings

Grill Seasoning for Vegetables

3 tablespoons salt

3 tablespoons packed light brown sugar

2 tablespoons paprika

1 tablespoon black pepper

2 tablespoons chili powder

2½ teaspoons garlic powder

1½ teaspoons cayenne pepper

1½ teaspoons dried basil

Combine salt, brown sugar, paprika, black pepper, chili powder, garlic powder, cayenne and basil and mix well. Store in an airtight container in refrigerator. Use on any vegetable you grill. Coat vegetables with oil before sprinkling with seasoning mix.

Grilled Asparagus

½ cup Italian dressing   ½ cup olive oil
½ cup balsamic vinegar   1 pound asparagus, ends trimmed

Combine dressing, vinegar and oil and pour over asparagus. Marinate at least 2 hours. Drain asparagus and grill on a rack for about 7 minutes, turning frequently.

Yield: 3 servings

The marinade could be used for other vegetables suitable for grilling, such as large mushrooms, onions, etc.

Eggplant Creole

1 onion, chopped   ¼ teaspoon dried oregano
1 green bell pepper, chopped   1 cup beef broth
1 stick butter   ½ teaspoon salt
½ cup dry rice   ½ teaspoon black pepper
1 large eggplant, peeled and chopped   2 dashes of hot pepper sauce
1 (14 ounce) can tomatoes, chopped   1 cup sharp Cheddar cheese, shredded
¼ teaspoon dried basil

Sauté onions and bell peppers in butter. Add rice and sauté until rice is golden. Add eggplant, tomatoes, basil, oregano, broth, salt, pepper and hot sauce. Bake at 350 degrees in a greased 2 quart casserole dish for 30 minutes. Sprinkle with cheese and bake 30 minutes longer. Serve hot.

Yield: 6 to 8 servings

Almond Fruit Couscous

These tiny pearls of semolina dough are a staple of the North African diet.

1 (14½ ounce) can chicken broth

3 tablespoons butter

1½ cups couscous

½ cup dried craisins

¼ cup currants or golden raisins

½ cup sliced almonds, toasted

6 green onions, thinly sliced

4 ounces plain yogurt

1 tablespoon lemon juice

Salt and pepper to taste

Bring broth and butter to a boil in a medium saucepan. Remove from heat and stir in couscous. Cover and let stand 5 minutes. Fluff couscous with a fork. Transfer to a bowl and stir in craisins, currants, almonds, onions, yogurt and lemon juice. Season with salt and pepper.

Yield: 8 servings

Grilled Green Beans with Gorgonzola Vinaigrette

1 pound fresh green beans

½ tablespoon olive oil

¼ cup balsamic vinegar

¼ cup Gorgonzola cheese, crumbled

1 tablespoon firmly packed light brown sugar

1 teaspoon garlic, chopped

¾ teaspoon shallots, chopped

¼ teaspoon dried thyme

¼ teaspoon dried basil

½ tablespoon olive oil

Salt and pepper to taste

Blanch beans in lightly salted boiling water for 4 minutes. Drain and immediately immerse in ice water to stop cooking; drain. In a small saucepan, combine ½ tablespoon olive oil, vinegar, cheese, sugar, garlic, shallots, thyme and basil. Cook over medium heat for 5 minutes or until ingredients start to combine. Toss beans with ½ tablespoon olive oil and season with salt and pepper. Quickly grill over high heat for about 30 seconds on each side. Toss beans in warm vinaigrette and serve immediately.

Yield: 6 servings

Honey-Glazed Baby Carrots

1 pound baby carrots

3 tablespoons unsalted butter

3 tablespoons honey

Salt and pepper to taste

In a steamer set over boiling water, steam carrots, covered, for 4 to 8 minutes or until fork-tender. In a small skillet, melt butter with honey over medium-low heat. Add carrots, salt and pepper. Cook, tossing to coat carrots, for 1 minute or until carrots are well glazed. Serve immediately.

Yield: 4 servings

Hazelnut Green Beans

1 pound fresh whole green beans

1 tablespoon olive oil

¼ teaspoon salt

1 red bell pepper, julienned

1 tablespoon hazelnuts, toasted and
    chopped

Cook green beans until crisp-tender; drain. While still warm, combine beans with oil, salt and bell peppers and toss. Sprinkle with hazelnuts.

Yield: 4 to 6 servings

To toast hazelnuts, bake at 275 degrees for 25 to 30 minutes or until skins crack. Remove skins by rubbing warm nuts in a paper towel.

Mushroom Burgers

¼ cup white wine vinegar

2 tablespoons olive oil

1 clove garlic, minced

¼ cup fresh basil, chopped

¼ teaspoon salt

¼ teaspoon freshly ground black
    pepper

1 red bell pepper, cut into 8 strips

1 yellow bell pepper, cut into 8 strips

1 sweet onion, cut into 8 slices

8 portobella mushroom caps

4 slices mozzarella cheese

Combine vinegar, olive oil, garlic, basil, salt and pepper. Pour mixture over bell peppers, onions and mushroom caps. Marinate at least 1 hour, turning occasionally. Drain vegetables. Grill vegetables until partially charred. Place half of the mushroom caps rounded-side down. Top with grilled vegetables and cheese. Place remaining mushroom caps on top, rounded-side up. Grill mushrooms until cheese melts.

Yield: 4 servings

Onion Flowers with Pecans

This is our family's favorite substitute for a baked potato to complement our grilled steak.

6 large sweet onions

6 to 8 tablespoons butter, melted

3 to 4 tablespoons chopped pecans

Peel onions, leaving root end intact. With root end down, cut into onion in parallel slices, ¼ inch apart, cutting from top to the root end without cutting through. Rotate and slice at right angles to the first cut, making a chrysanthemum design. Place onions, root ends down, in a lightly greased baking dish. Drizzle butter on top and season with salt and pepper. Bake at 300 degrees for 1 hour to 1 hour, 30 minutes, basting often. Add pecans in center of each onion and bake 25 to 30 minutes longer.

Yield: 4 to 6 servings

Chantilly Potatoes with a Gruyère Crust

2 pounds Yukon Gold potatoes, peeled and cut into 2 inch pieces

½ cup cold milk

6 tablespoons unsalted butter, softened

¾ cup onions, chopped

2 tablespoons dried parsley

Salt and pepper to taste

1 cup heavy cream

1 tablespoon butter

¾ cup Gruyère cheese, shredded

Cook potatoes in boiling salted water for 12 minutes or until tender. Drain potatoes and place in a large bowl. Mash potatoes. Beat in milk, 6 tablespoons butter, onions and parsley. Season with salt and pepper. In a separate bowl, whip cream until soft peaks form. Beat one-third of cream into potatoes. Fold in remainder of cream. Transfer potatoes into a greased 9x13 inch baking dish. Dot with 1 tablespoon butter and sprinkle with cheese. Bake at 400 degrees for 35 minutes. Broil 2 minutes or until top is browned. Remove from heat and let stand for 10 minutes before serving.

Yield: 6 servings

Stir-Fry Sauce

2½ cups chicken broth

½ cup cornstarch

½ cup light corn syrup

½ cup soy sauce

½ cup dry sherry

¼ cup cider vinegar

¼ teaspoon
ground ginger

2 cloves garlic, minced

¼ teaspoon
cayenne pepper

Combine broth,
cornstarch, corn syrup,
soy sauce, sherry,
vinegar, ginger, garlic
and cayenne in a
1½ quart jar with a
tight-fitting lid. Shake
well. Store in
refrigerator
for up to 3 weeks.
Use with any stir-fry
recipe or vegetable
combinations.

Yield: 4 cups

Fresh Green Peas with Pine Nuts

½ cup chicken broth

3 green onions, thinly sliced

2 pounds fresh green peas, shelled,
 or 2 (10 ounce) packages frozen

3 tablespoons butter

½ cup pine nuts

1 tablespoon dried rosemary

Dash of salt

Dash of black pepper

Combine broth and onions in a medium skillet. Bring to a boil. Add peas, reduce heat and simmer 2 minutes. Drain peas and place in a different container; set aside. In same skillet, melt butter over medium heat. Add pine nuts and rosemary and sauté 2 to 3 minutes or until nuts are lightly browned. Add peas and cook until heated through. Season with salt and pepper and serve immediately.

Yield: 8 servings

Grilled New Potatoes with Italian Parsley

3 pounds small red-skin potatoes

2 tablespoons olive oil

2 tablespoons olive oil

1 cup green onions, thinly sliced

3 tablespoons Italian parsley, chopped

¼ cup Parmesan cheese, grated

4 cloves garlic, finely chopped

½ teaspoon dried oregano

Salt and pepper to taste

Cook potatoes in a large pot of boiling salted water for 15 minutes or until tender. Drain and cool. Cut potatoes in half and place in a large bowl. Add 2 tablespoons oil and toss to coat. Grill potatoes 5 minutes or until golden, turning occasionally. Return to bowl and drizzle with 2 tablespoons olive oil. Add onions, parsley, cheese, garlic and oregano. Toss to coat. Season with salt and pepper and serve warm.

Yield: 8 servings

Plantation Cheese Grits

1 quart milk
1 stick butter
1 cup instant grits
½ teaspoon salt
½ teaspoon white pepper

½ teaspoon garlic, chopped
5 tablespoons butter
4 ounces Gruyère cheese, shredded
½ cup freshly grated Parmesan cheese

Bring milk to a boil in a saucepan. Add 1 stick butter. Stir in grits and cook, stirring constantly, for 5 minutes or until the consistency of cooked oatmeal. Remove from heat and season with salt, pepper and garlic. Beat grits with an electric mixer. Add 5 tablespoons butter. Stir in Gruyère cheese until melted. Pour mixture into a greased 2 quart casserole dish. Sprinkle with Parmesan cheese. Bake at 350 degrees for 1 hour.

Yield: 6 servings

Smashed Potatoes with Roasted Chiles

2 poblano chiles
6 large russet potatoes, peeled and cut into 1 inch cubes
3 cloves garlic, lightly crushed
1 cup half-and-half, warmed

4 tablespoons butter, softened
1 heaping teaspoon horseradish
1 teaspoon salt
1 teaspoon freshly ground black pepper

Broil chiles until blackened on all sides. Immediately place in a bag and let stand for 10 minutes. Peel, seed and coarsely chop chiles. Cook potatoes and garlic in a large pot of boiling water for 15 minutes or until tender; drain. Beat potatoes and garlic with an electric mixer until very smooth. Gradually beat in half-and-half. Add butter and beat until melted. Stir in chiles, horseradish, salt and pepper.

Yield: 4 servings

Old-fashioned stone-ground grits (or hominy grits) are as American as can be.

These will replace the traditional southern cheese grits.

Chiles

There are well over 200 varieties of chiles. These fruits of various members of the Capsicum family are best known for being fiery hot, but many chiles are quite mild and have deep, rich flavors.

Grilled New Potatoes

Throw these potatoes on the grill with your steak or burger.

16 new potatoes

¼ cup olive oil

Salt and freshly ground pepper to taste

⅓ cup extra virgin olive oil

¼ teaspoon mustard seeds

¼ cup fresh parsley, chopped

2 cloves garlic, minced

2 tablespoons freshly squeezed lemon juice

10 dashes Tabasco sauce or to taste

1 tablespoon whole grain Dijon mustard

Cook potatoes in boiling salted water for 15 minutes or until they can be pierced with a fork but are still firm and offer some resistance. Drain and rinse under cold water. Cut potatoes in half and thread onto skewers with cut sides facing the same way. Coat potatoes with ¼ cup olive oil and season with salt and pepper. Grill over medium-high heat for 3 to 5 minutes or until golden brown. Remove potatoes from skewers and place in a medium bowl; set aside.

In a separate bowl, combine ⅓ cup extra virgin olive oil, mustard seeds, parsley, garlic, lemon juice, Tabasco and mustard. Mix well and pour over potatoes. Toss well.

Yield: 4 servings

Braised Spinach

1 cup low-salt chicken broth

1 small onion, chopped

1 cup water

1 (9 ounce) bag fresh spinach

¼ cup apple cider vinegar

Combine broth, onions and water in a large saucepan. Bring to a boil. Add spinach and reduce heat to low. Cover and cook for about 15 minutes. Stir to make sure all spinach is moist. Add vinegar, cover and simmer 5 minutes.

Yield: 4 servings

Sweet Potatoes with Marsala

1 pound sweet potatoes
2 tablespoons packed light brown
    sugar
2 tablespoons buttermilk
2 tablespoons butter or margarine

⅛ teaspoon salt
⅛ teaspoon black pepper
2 tablespoons Marsala wine
Fresh thyme sprigs for garnish
    (optional)

Bake potatoes at 425 degrees for 1 hour, 10 minutes or until tender; cool slightly. Cut each potato in half lengthwise and scoop out pulp; discard skins. Combine potato pulp, sugar, buttermilk, butter, salt, pepper and wine in a small saucepan. Mash to desired consistency. Cook over low heat for 2 minutes or until heated through. Garnish with thyme sprigs.

Yield: 2 servings

Spinach Pecan Bake

1 medium onion, finely chopped
4 tablespoons butter or margarine
3 (10 ounce) packages frozen leaf
    spinach, thawed and drained
½ cup half-and-half
½ cup coarsely chopped pecans

⅓ cup dry bread crumbs
1 teaspoon salt
½ teaspoon ground nutmeg
⅛ teaspoon black pepper
¼ cup dry bread crumbs
2 tablespoons butter or margarine,
    melted

In a skillet, sauté onions in 4 tablespoons butter until tender. In a large bowl, combine sautéed onions, spinach, half-and-half, pecans, ⅓ cup bread crumbs, salt, nutmeg and pepper. Mix well. Transfer mixture to a greased 1½ quart baking dish. Mix together ¼ cup bread crumbs and 2 tablespoons melted butter and sprinkle over spinach mixture. Bake, uncovered, at 350 degrees for 30 minutes or until lightly browned.

Yield: 6 to 8 servings

Sweet Potatoes

There is great confusion about what's a yam and what's a sweet potato. In the early part of the 20th century, a sweet potato with yellow-orange flesh was marketed as a "Louisiana yam" to help it stand out from whiter-fleshed sweet potatoes. True yams are tropical tubers.

Impeccable Rice

One cup of raw rice yields about three cups of cooked rice. Cooked rice freezes well. Cover and reheat in a microwave oven or steam in a covered colander on the stovetop until thoroughly heated.

Rice and Mushrooms

A simple, no-fail rice recipe for any cook.

1 small onion, finely chopped
8 ounces fresh mushrooms, sliced
1 stick butter

1 cup dry white rice
2 (10½ ounce) cans beef consommé

Sauté onion and mushrooms in butter. Add rice and consommé and heat briefly. Pour mixture into a 3 quart casserole dish. Bake at 350 degrees for 1 hour.

Yield: 6 servings

Spinach and Sun-Dried Tomato Risotto

1 tablespoon olive oil
2 cloves garlic, chopped
1 cup dry Arborio rice
2 (16 ounce) cans vegetable or chicken broth
½ (9 ounce) package frozen chopped spinach, thawed

10 sun-dried tomato halves, cut into pieces
½ cup fontina cheese, shredded
¼ cup Parmesan cheese, freshly grated
½ teaspoon freshly ground black pepper

Heat oil in a large saucepan over medium heat. Add garlic and sauté 2 minutes. Add rice and stir until coated. Stir in broth, spinach and tomatoes. Bring to a boil. Reduce to medium heat and simmer, stirring often, for 20 to 25 minutes or until liquid is absorbed and rice is tender. Stir in cheeses and pepper.

Yield: 6 side dish or 4 main dish servings

Irresistible Risotto with Roasted Butternut Squash

1 (2 pound) butternut squash, peeled, seeded and cut into ½ inch cubes

2 tablespoons olive oil

Salt and pepper to taste

6 cups low salt chicken broth

2 tablespoons olive oil

3 large leeks, thinly sliced, white and pale green parts only (about 3 cups)

2 cups dry Arborio or medium grain rice

½ cup dry white wine

½ cup heavy cream

½ cup Parmesan cheese, grated

2 tablespoons fresh sage, chopped

Spread squash cubes on a large, rimmed baking sheet and drizzle with 2 tablespoons olive oil. Sprinkle with salt and pepper and toss to coat. Bake at 400 degrees, stirring occasionally, for 40 minutes or until squash starts to brown. If done in advance, refrigerate until ready to use.

Bring broth to a simmer in a large saucepan. Reduce heat to very low and cover to keep warm. Heat 2 tablespoons olive oil in a separate large saucepan over medium-low heat. Add leeks and sauté 10 minutes or until soft but not brown. Add rice and cook 1 minute. Add wine and simmer, stirring constantly, for 2 minutes or until absorbed. Add one-half cup hot broth and simmer and stir until absorbed. Repeat with remaining broth, adding one-half cup at a time and allowing broth to be absorbed before adding more. Cook and stir 25 minutes or until rice is tender and risotto is creamy. Add squash, cream, cheese and sage. Stir until heated through. Season with salt and pepper. Serve warm.

Yield: 8 servings

Asparagus Risotto

A magnificent, simmering stew of rice, broth, and seasonings, risotto is one of the great dishes of Northern Italy.

1 tablespoon salt

1 pound fresh asparagus, trimmed

1 (32 ounce) can beef broth

1 tablespoon butter

2 tablespoons olive oil

2 tablespoons onion, diced

2 cups dry Italian risotto rice

2 tablespoons butter

½ cup Parmigiano-Reggiano cheese, freshly grated

Salt and pepper to taste

1 tablespoon fresh parsley, minced for garnish

Pour 2 inches of water into a large pot. Add salt and bring to a boil. Add asparagus and cook for 4 to 5 minutes or until asparagus is crisp-tender. Drain and cool asparagus, reserving cooking liquid. Add enough beef broth to cooking liquid to equal 6 cups. Bring to a simmer and keep warm. Cut off about 1½ inches of cooled asparagus tips and set aside. Cut remaining stalks into ½ inch pieces.

Heat 1 tablespoon butter and olive oil in a medium saucepan. Add onions and sauté until transparent. Add asparagus stalks and sauté about 1 minute. Add rice and quickly stir until grains are well coated. Add one half cup of broth mixture and cook, stirring constantly to prevent sticking, until liquid is absorbed. Repeat with remaining broth, adding one half cup at a time and allowing broth to be absorbed before adding more. Cook 20 minutes or until rice is tender but firm and all broth is used. Remove from heat and add reserved asparagus tips, 2 tablespoons butter and cheese. Stir until cheese melts. Season with salt and pepper. Sprinkle parsley on top.

Yield: 4 to 6 servings

Ritzy Spinach and Artichokes

2 (10 ounce) packages frozen
    chopped spinach
1 stick butter, melted
1 (8 ounce) package cream cheese
1 teaspoon lemon juice

1 clove garlic, minced
2 (10 ounce) jars marinated
    artichoke hearts, drained
1 cup butter crackers, crushed
¼ cup Parmesan cheese, grated

Cook spinach and drain. Combine spinach, butter, cream cheese, lemon juice and garlic in a medium bowl. Spread artichoke hearts evenly over the bottom of a greased 8 inch square pan. Pour spinach mixture over artichokes. Mix cracker crumbs with Parmesan cheese and sprinkle over the spinach. Bake at 350 degrees for 20 minutes or until bubbly.

Yield: 6 servings

Spinach Quiche

3 eggs
2 cups half-and-half
¼ cup feta cheese, crumbled
½ cup mozzarella cheese, shredded
¼ cup Swiss cheese, shredded
¼ cup Cheddar cheese, shredded

1 (10 ounce) package frozen
    chopped spinach, thawed and
    well drained
1 (9 inch) deep dish pie crust,
    unbaked
½ teaspoon salt
¼ teaspoon black pepper
Grated Parmesan cheese

Whisk together eggs and half-and-half. Arrange feta, mozzarella, Swiss and Cheddar cheeses and spinach in pie crust. Season with salt and pepper. Pour egg mixture over cheese mixture. Sprinkle with Parmesan cheese. Bake at 350 degrees for 1 hour or until a knife inserted into the center comes out clean.

Yield: 6 servings

Key Notes

Autumn Harvest Squash

1 tablespoon butter

5 slices bacon, chopped

1 cup onions, chopped

1½ pounds butternut squash, peeled, seeded and cut into ⅓ inch cubes

¾ teaspoon dried basil

1 cup packed fresh spinach, chopped

1 (10 ounce) package frozen corn, thawed

Salt and pepper to taste

¼ cup pine nuts, toasted

Melt butter in a large saucepan. Add bacon and sauté over medium heat for 10 minutes. Add onions, squash and basil and sauté 12 minutes or until squash is almost tender. Add spinach and corn. Toss over heat for 5 minutes or until spinach wilts and corn is heated. Season with salt and pepper. Transfer to a serving plate. Sprinkle with pine nuts.

Yield: 6 servings

Zippy Squash Sauté

5 tablespoons butter

1½ pounds zucchini or yellow squash, thinly sliced

1 small red onion, thinly sliced

1 clove garlic, crushed

⅓ cup green onions, chopped

½ teaspoon black pepper

¼ cup spicy vegetable juice

1 teaspoon sugar

2 medium tomatoes, diced

Melt butter in a nonstick skillet over low heat. Add squash, red onions and garlic and sauté 5 minutes. Add green onions, pepper, vegetable juice and sugar. Mix well and cover. Simmer over low heat, stirring occasionally, for 5 minutes or until just tender. Add tomatoes and cook about 2 minutes. Serve immediately.

Yield: 4 to 6 servings

Dilly Squash

6 to 8 squash, yellow or zucchini	1 egg, beaten
1 large onion, chopped	Beau Monde seasoning to taste
½ teaspoon dried dill	Salt and pepper to taste
4 tablespoons butter	Bread crumbs
1 teaspoon sugar	

Cook squash, onions and dill in boiling salted water until tender. Drain well and mash. Add butter, sugar, egg, seasoning, salt and pepper. Pour mixture into a 2-quart casserole dish. Top with bread crumbs. Bake at 300 degrees for 45 minutes or until firm.

Yield: 6 servings

Roasted Vegetables

4 large potatoes, cut into 2 inch chunks, or 8 to 10 small potatoes, halved	1 large red bell pepper, cut into 2 inch chunks
1 medium red onion, cut into 6 to 8 wedges	1 large yellow bell pepper, cut into 2 inch chunks
1 tablespoon vegetable oil	1 large orange bell pepper, cut into 2 inch chunks
½ teaspoon salt	1 tablespoon fresh thyme, minced, or 1 teaspoon dried
2 bunches baby carrots, peeled	½ teaspoon black pepper, coarsely ground
8 ounces baby pattypan squash, or 1 yellow squash, cut into 2 inch chunks	½ large lemon, thinly sliced
8 ounces small green beans, ends trimmed	2 tablespoons vegetable oil

Toss potatoes and onion with 1 tablespoon oil and salt in a large roasting pan. Bake at 425 degrees for 15 minutes. Add carrots, squash, beans, bell peppers, thyme, black pepper and lemon slices. Toss with 2 tablespoons oil until well coated. Bake 45 minutes longer or until vegetables are golden and tender, occasionally turning carefully.

Yield: 6 to 8 servings

Key Notes

Tomatoes Dressed-To-Go

This dish can be served even in winter when tomatoes are out of season.

3 large tomatoes

½ teaspoon salt

¼ teaspoon white pepper

2 cloves garlic, minced

2½ tablespoons green onions, minced

3 tablespoons fresh parsley, minced

Scant ¼ teaspoon dried thyme

⅓ cup extra virgin olive oil

½ cup firmly packed bread crumbs

Cut tomatoes in half crosswise and gently press out juice and seeds. With cut side facing up, sprinkle tomato halves with salt and pepper; set aside. Combine garlic, onions, parsley, thyme, olive oil and bread crumbs. Spread mixture over tomato halves and place on a greased roasting pan. Bake at 400 degrees for 10 to 15 minutes or until tomatoes are barely tender; do not overbake.

Yield: 3 to 4 servings

Broiled Tomatoes with Dill

½ cup sour cream

¼ cup mayonnaise

2 tablespoons onions, chopped

¼ teaspoon dried dill

¼ teaspoon salt

4 large tomatoes, cored

Salt and pepper to taste

¼ cup Parmesan cheese, grated

Melted butter

Combine sour cream, mayonnaise, onions, dill and salt. This sauce may be prepared and refrigerated up to several days in advance. Cut tomatoes in half crosswise and place in a broiler pan, cut-side up. Season tomatoes with salt and pepper. Sprinkle with cheese and drizzle with butter. Broil tomatoes 4 to 5 inches from heat source for 5 minutes. Spoon sauce over broiled tomatoes and serve immediately.

Yield: 3 to 4 servings

Southern Vegetable Pie

Take this to a family reunion and not a crumb will remain!

3 tablespoons extra virgin olive oil

1 large red onion, thinly sliced

3 cloves garlic, minced

3 medium yellow squash, cut into
    ¼ inch slices

3 medium zucchini, cut into
    ¼ inch slices

1 red bell pepper, cut into
    ¼ inch strips

1 yellow bell pepper, cut into
    ¼ inch strips

1 green bell pepper, cut into
    ¼ inch strips

1 cup fresh mushrooms, sliced

6 eggs

¼ cup heavy cream

2 teaspoons salt

2 teaspoons black pepper, freshly
    ground

2 cups stale French bread cubes
    (½ inch)

1 (8 ounce) package cream cheese,
    diced

2 cups Swiss cheese, shredded

Heat oil in a large skillet over medium-high heat. Add onions, garlic, squash, zucchini, bell peppers and mushrooms and sauté 15 to 20 minutes or until crisp-tender. Meanwhile, whisk together eggs, cream, salt and pepper in a large bowl. Stir in bread cubes and cheeses. Add sautéed vegetables and stir until well combined. Pour mixture into a greased 10 inch springform pan, packing mixture tightly. Place pan on a baking sheet. Bake at 350 degrees for 1 hour or until firm to the touch, puffed and golden brown. If top starts to brown too fast, cover with foil. Remove from oven and let stand 10 minutes before removing from pan. Serve hot, cold or at room temperature.

Yield: 8 to 10 servings

Key Notes

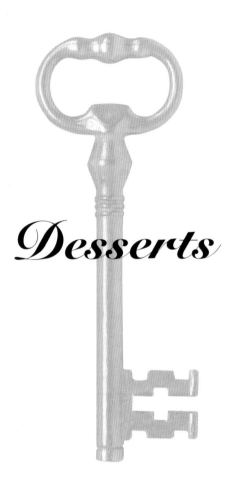

Desserts

Raspberry Swirl Cheesecake
Celebration Stars
Orange Sherbet
Hot Fudge Surprises

1996

The first weeks of my daughter's life progressed quite uneventfully until that day in May when she was admitted to Le Bonheur Children's Medical Center. She was breathing with the assistance of a ventilator and by midnight was given a one percent chance of living through the night. Who would have ever thought that the events that were to unfold would permanently change the lives of a then 19-day-old beautiful baby girl, her family and her surrounding community?

She was diagnosed with Group B Strep meningitis, an often fatal debilitating form of bacterial meningitis. If she could ever be removed from the ventilator, there was doubt she would eat without assistance, talk, walk or have any independence. We were told there was almost no chance that she would survive this horrible disease without being severely disabled. Due to increased brain swelling and the severity of infection in her cerebral spinal fluid, a VP shunt system was placed at the top of her skull. Over the next six months, seven surgeries were performed to add a second VP shunt and eight interconnecting catheters.

At nine months of age, she began an intensive early intervention rehabilitation and therapy program. She was further diagnosed with severe hearing loss, vision impairment, speech and language delay, and fine and gross motor delay. She made progress with the loving guidance and encouragement of the Le Bonheur therapists. At fourteen months of age, she was diagnosed with a bacterial infection in her left leg. The affected major growth plate meant the left leg would be 25% shorter than the right leg.

As parents, we reached a point where we never thought the bad news would end. However, when another door would appear to shut and lock, there was always a key person to unlock it. The day she became ill, miracles began to happen. The keys to my daughter's life proved to be the endless number of loving, dedicated physicians, nurses, therapists and ancillary staff at Le Bonheur Children's Medical Center. She received the gift of life, and we are so incredibly blessed to have such a facility in the Mid-South.

Today, my daughter is a walking, talking, very independent, precious six-year-old girl. She has been left with scars and has multiple learning disabilities, though these seem mild in light of the initial outlook. She has unlocked the doors of possibilities for brain injured children, touched the lives of many people with hope, love and perseverance and unlocked the fear of knowing and loving a physically impaired, developmentally delayed child. We cherish one of the Le Bonheur mottoes: "Believe in Miracles."

White Chocolate Hazelnut Cheesecake

Crust

¾ cup hazelnuts, toasted and chopped

12 whole graham crackers

¼ cup sugar

6 tablespoons butter, melted

Filling

4 (8 ounce) packages cream cheese, softened

1¼ cups sugar

4 eggs

3 ounces imported white chocolate, finely chopped

3 tablespoons Frangelico

Crust

Process hazelnuts, graham crackers and sugar together in a food processor. Add butter and process until crumbs stick together. Wrap foil around the outside of a greased 9 inch springform pan. Press crumb mixture into bottom and 1 inch up sides of pan. Bake at 325 degrees for 10 minutes. Cool on a rack.

Filling

Beat cream cheese until fluffy. Gradually add sugar. Beat in eggs one at a time. Mix in white chocolate and Frangelico. Pour mixture over crust in pan. Bake at 325 degrees for 1 hour, 20 minutes or until edges are set and center moves slightly. Cover and refrigerate at least 8 hours. Run a knife around the sides to loosen. Release sides of pan. Serve with a raspberry sauce. For recipe, see page xxx.

Yield: 10 servings

White Chocolate

French and Swiss white chocolates are high quality chocolate made with cocoa butter. White chocolate is very sweet with a delicate structure, which makes it sensitive to heat and moisture. Use imported white chocolate for this cheesecake to ensure rich flavor.

Raspberry Swirl Cheesecake

Crust

28 vanilla wafers

¼ cup sliced almonds, toasted

3 tablespoons butter, melted

2 tablespoons sugar

Filling

1 (12 ounce) package frozen raspberries, thawed

4 teaspoons cornstarch

1 (12 ounce) package white chocolate chips

4 (8 ounce) packages cream cheese, softened

¾ cup sugar

4 eggs

½ teaspoon almond extract

1 cup sliced almonds, toasted

½ cup heavy cream, whipped (optional)

Whole raspberries or melted chocolate chips for garnish (optional)

Crust

Process wafers and almonds in a food processor until fine crumbs form, yielding about 1½ cups crumbs. Mix crumb mixture with butter and sugar by hand in a 9 inch springform pan. Press mixture into bottom of pan; set aside.

Filling

In a clean blender, process raspberries at high speed. Press raspberry puree through a fine sieve into a 2 quart saucepan to remove seeds. Stir cornstarch into berries. Cook over medium heat, stirring constantly, until mixture comes to a boil. Boil 1 minute or until mixture thickens. Cool.

In a 1 quart saucepan, melt white chocolate over very low heat until smooth. Cool slightly. In a large bowl using a mixer on low speed, beat cream cheese and ¾ cup sugar until smooth. Add melted white chocolate, eggs and almond extract. Beat until smooth. Transfer 1 cup of cream cheese mixture to a small bowl. Reserving 2 tablespoons of berry puree for later, stir remaining berry puree into 1 cup of cream cheese mixture in small bowl.

Pour half of plain cream cheese mixture into springform pan. Drop two-thirds of raspberry-cheese mixture by spoonfuls on top. Use a knife to cut through mix to make a marble effect. Repeat with remaining plain

Raspberry Swirl Cheesecake continued

cheese and raspberry-cheese mixtures. Bake at 300 degrees for 1 hour or until center is just barely firm. Remove cake and cool in pan on a wire rack. Cover and refrigerate at least 4 hours.

To serve, carefully remove cheesecake from pan. Spread reserved 2 tablespoons raspberry puree around side of cake. Press 1 cup almonds onto side. If desired, pipe whipped cream onto top of cheesecake and garnish with whole raspberries or drizzled chocolate.

Yield: 16 servings

Key Notes

Chocolate Chip Cheesecake

1½ cups chocolate wafer sandwich
    cookies, finely crushed
    (about 18 cookies)

4 tablespoons butter, melted

3 (8 ounce) packages cream cheese,
    softened

1 (14 ounce) can sweetened
    condensed milk

3 eggs

2 teaspoons vanilla

1 cup mini chocolate chips

1 teaspoon all-purpose flour

½ cup mini chocolate chips

Chocolate sauce for garnish

Combine cookie crumbs and butter and press firmly into the bottom of a 9 inch springform pan. Beat cream cheese until fluffy. Blend in milk, eggs and vanilla. In a small bowl, toss 1 cup chocolate chips with flour to coat. Add floured chips to cream cheese mixture. Pour batter over crust in pan. Sprinkle ½ cup chocolate chips on top. Bake at 300 degrees for 1 hour. Cool completely before cutting. To garnish, drizzle chocolate sauce on serving plate and place a cheesecake slice on top.

Yield: 8 to 10 servings

Cappuccino Decadence

Even the non-coffee drinker will love this cheesecake.

½ cup chocolate wafers, finely
    crushed

16 ounces semi-sweet chocolate

1 cup heavy cream

1 tablespoon powdered instant coffee

½ teaspoon cinnamon

6 eggs, beaten

¾ cup sugar

⅓ cup all-purpose flour

1 tablespoon orange zest

Coat sides and bottom of a greased 9 inch springform pan with wafer crumbs. Combine chocolate, cream, coffee and cinnamon in a saucepan. Cook and stir over low heat until melted and smooth. In a large bowl, beat together eggs, sugar and flour with an electric mixer on medium speed until thick. Mix in orange zest. Fold a fourth of egg mixture into chocolate mixture. Fold chocolate mixture into remaining egg mixture. Pour batter into springform pan. Bake at 325 degrees for 45 to 50 minutes. Cool in pan to room temperature. Cover and chill completely.

Yield: 10 to 12 servings

Soften one 8 ounce package of cream cheese by microwaving at 30% power for 2 to 2½ minutes. One 3 ounce package of cream cheese will soften in 1½ to 2 minutes.

Chocolate Cheesecake

Crust

1 cup graham cracker crumbs

½ cup finely chopped walnuts

5 tablespoons butter, melted

¼ cup sugar

Filling

5 (8 ounce) packages cream cheese, softened

1¾ cups sugar

3 tablespoons all-purpose flour

5 eggs

2 egg yolks

¼ cup milk

¼ teaspoon salt

1 (8 ounce) package semi-sweet chocolate squares, melted

Crust

Combine cracker crumbs, walnuts, butter and sugar in a medium bowl. Press mixture firmly into the bottom and up the sides to within 1½ inches of the top of a 9 inch springform pan.

Filling

In a large bowl, beat cream cheese with an electric mixer at medium speed until smooth. Reduce speed to low and gradually beat in sugar, flour, eggs, egg yolks, milk, salt and melted chocolate. Beat on high speed for 5 minutes. Pour mixture over crust. Bake at 400 degrees for 12 minutes. Reduce heat to 300 degrees and bake 50 minutes. Turn off oven and leave cheesecake in oven for 30 minutes longer. Cool to room temperature, then cover and refrigerate until chilled. Serve within 1 week.

Yield: 10 to 12 servings

Cooking Cheesecakes

To ensure proper cooking use the right size pan. If the pan is too small, the filling will rise too high and take longer to cook. If the pan is too big, the cake will not rise high enough and may overcook and crack.

Peppermint Cheesecake

Beautiful, festive, NO BAKE dessert.

1 cup chocolate wafers, finely crushed

3 tablespoons margarine, melted

1 (¼ ounce) envelope unflavored gelatin

¼ cup cold water

2 (8 ounce) packages cream cheese, softened

½ cup sugar

¼ cup milk

¼ cup peppermint candy, crushed, plus extra for garnish

1 cup heavy cream, whipped, plus extra for garnish

2 (1.4 ounce) milk chocolate candy bars, finely chopped

Chocolate sauce (optional)

Combine wafer crumbs and margarine and press into the bottom of a 9 inch springform pan. Bake at 350 degrees for 10 minutes; cool. Soften gelatin in cold water in a saucepan. Cook and stir over low heat until dissolved. Using an electric mixer on medium speed, beat cream cheese and sugar together until well blended. Gradually beat in gelatin mixture, milk and crushed candy. Mix until blended. Chill until thickened, but not set. Fold in whipped cream and chocolate. Pour batter over crust in pan. Chill until firm. Remove sides of pan. Garnish with extra whipped cream. Drizzle with chocolate sauce, if desired, and sprinkle extra peppermint candy on top.

Yield: 10 to 12 servings

For Christmas, use green and red peppermints. For Valentine's Day, use red and white peppermints.

Hot Fudge Surprises

Our Four Star Dessert Award.

8 (1 ounce) semi-sweet chocolate
    squares
15 tablespoons butter
4 eggs
4 egg yolks

½ cup sugar
7 tablespoons all-purpose flour
1 cup heavy cream, whipped
2 teaspoons sugar
Fresh strawberries for garnish

Melt chocolate and butter together in the top of a double boiler, stirring occasionally. Cool slightly. In a mixing bowl and using an electric mixer, beat eggs, egg yolks and ½ cup sugar together for 10 minutes or until pale yellow. Reduce mixer speed and gradually add flour. Add chocolate mixture and beat 5 minutes or until glossy. Divide among eight 5 ounce greased ramekins or custard cups. Bake at 325 degrees for 11 to 16 minutes. Center will appear wet. Using a sharp knife, cut around edge of ramekins and invert onto individual serving plates. Whip cream and 2 teaspoons sugar until soft peaks form. Dollop whipped cream on side of serving plates and garnish with fresh strawberries.

Yield: 8 servings

Filled, unbaked ramekins can be refrigerated up to 6 hours. When ready to cook, bake at 325 degrees for 18 to 22 minutes.

Fudge Torte

Torte

12 ounces semi-sweet chocolate	6 egg yolks
5 tablespoons espresso or strong coffee	1 cup all-purpose flour
2 sticks butter, softened	6 egg whites
2 cups sugar	Whipped cream for topping

Glaze (optional)

4 ounces semi-sweet or bittersweet chocolate	2 tablespoons unsalted butter, melted

Torte

Melt chocolate with espresso in the top of a double boiler; cool. In a mixing bowl, cream butter and sugar. Beat in egg yolks, one at a time. Slowly mix in flour. In a separate bowl, beat egg whites until stiff. Fold egg whites into melted chocolate mixture, then fold this mixture into creamed mixture. Pour batter into a greased and floured 9 inch springform pan. Bake at 350 degrees for 60 to 70 minutes or until top is crusty and cracked and center is slightly moist. If desired, top with glaze. Serve with a dollop of whipped cream.

Glaze

Melt chocolate in the top of a double boiler. Add melted butter and whisk until smooth. Pour over torte and spread.

Yield: 8 to 10 servings

White Chocolate and Lime Mousse Cake

Be creative when garnishing this make-ahead, no bake, luscious dessert. Use lime twists, slices or edible flowers.

Crust

2 cups ground gingersnap cookies (about 38 cookies)

2 tablespoons sugar

5 tablespoons unsalted butter, melted

Filling

½ cup Key lime juice

1 (¼ ounce) envelope unflavored gelatin

½ cup heavy cream

9 ounces white chocolate, chopped

1 (8 ounce) package cream cheese, softened

2 (8 ounce) packages reduced fat cream cheese, softened

1 cup sugar

3 tablespoons lime zest

2 cups heavy cream, chilled and whipped

Crust

Combine cookie crumbs and sugar in a food processor. Add butter and pulse processor until moist clumps form. Press mixture into the bottom and 1 inch up the sides of a 10 inch springform pan.

Filling

Place lime juice in a glass bowl. Sprinkle gelatin over top to soften. Bring ½ cup cream to a simmer in a heavy medium saucepan. Remove from heat and add white chocolate. Stir until melted and smooth. Stir in gelatin mixture. Cool slightly. In a large bowl, beat cream cheese, sugar and lime zest with an electric mixer until blended. Slowly beat in white chocolate mixture. Fold in whipped cream. Pour filling over crust in pan. Cover and refrigerate overnight or up to 2 days. Release sides of pan from cake. Transfer to a cake platter and serve.

Yield: 12 to 14 servings

Incredible Eggs

This recipe uses five large eggs, so bring your eggs to room temperature before preparing cake. The eggs will separate more easily and beat to their greatest volume.

Luscious Lemon Cake

Cake

1½ sticks butter, softened

2¼ cups sugar

⅔ cup frozen lemonade concentrate, thawed

2 tablespoons lemon zest

1 teaspoon vanilla

5 eggs

3¾ cups all-purpose flour

1 tablespoon baking powder

Pinch of salt

1½ cups buttermilk

Glaze

1 cup sugar

½ cup fresh lemon juice

Icing

2 (8 ounce) packages cream cheese, softened

1 stick butter, softened

4½ cups powdered sugar

Juice of 2 large lemons

Zest of 2 large lemons

Lemon curls, pansies, blueberries or strawberries for garnish

Cake

Grease three 9 inch round cake pans and line bottoms with wax paper. Grease paper and dust with flour. Cream butter with an electric mixer until fluffy. Gradually beat in sugar. Beat in lemonade, zest and vanilla. Add eggs, one at a time, beating well after each addition. Combine flour, baking powder and salt in a separate bowl. With mixer on low speed, add dry ingredients alternately with buttermilk in 3 batches, starting and ending with dry ingredients. Divide batter among prepared pans. Bake at 350 degrees for 25 minutes. At this point, cake layers can be frozen. Wrap each tightly in plastic wrap and then in foil. Freeze up to 5 days.

Glaze

Combine sugar and lemon juice in a saucepan. Bring to a boil and cook 2 minutes or until dissolved. Remove cakes from oven. With a skewer, poke holes in top of cake. Pour glaze equally over cakes.

Icing

Beat cream cheese and butter with an electric mixer. Add sugar and lemon juice alternately until icing is a spreading consistency. Stir in zest. To assemble, turn one cake onto a cake platter. Peel off wax paper. Spread a layer of icing over cake. Repeat with 2 other layers, stacking on top of each other. Ice top and sides of cake. Garnish with lemon curls, pansies, blueberries or strawberries.

Yield: 8 to 10 servings

Harvest Cake

Cake

1¼ cups vegetable oil	2 teaspoons baking soda
2 cups sugar	¼ teaspoon salt
4 eggs	1 tablespoon cinnamon
2 cups all-purpose flour	1 (16 ounce) can pumpkin

Frosting

2 cups powdered sugar	½ teaspoon vanilla
4 tablespoons butter, softened	1 cup chopped pecans (optional)
1 (8 ounce) package cream cheese, softened	

Cake

Cream oil and sugar. Add eggs, one at a time, beating well after each addition. Sift together flour, baking soda, salt and cinnamon. Add dry ingredients and pumpkin, alternately, to creamed mixture. Pour batter into a greased tube or Bundt pan. Bake at 350 degrees for 1 hour. Cool before frosting.

Frosting

Beat sugar, butter and cream cheese until smooth. Add vanilla and pecans. Frost cake when cooled.

Yield: 16 to 18 servings

Cake can be made in 14 to 16 mini Bundt pans. Bake at 350 degrees for 25 minutes.

Celebrity Carrot Cake

Cake

2 cups all-purpose flour

1½ cups sugar

2 teaspoons baking soda

2 teaspoons cinnamon

½ teaspoon salt

3 eggs

¾ cup vegetable oil

¾ cup buttermilk

2 teaspoons vanilla

1 (8 ounce) can crushed pineapple, drained

2 cups finely chopped carrots

1 cup chopped walnuts or pecans

1 (3½ ounce) can flaked coconut

Glaze

1 cup sugar

½ teaspoon baking soda

½ cup buttermilk

1 stick butter

1 tablespoon corn syrup

1½ teaspoons vanilla

Frosting

1 stick butter, softened

1 (8 ounce) package cream cheese, softened

1 teaspoon vanilla

1 tablespoon orange juice

1½ teaspoons orange zest

1 (16 ounce) package powdered sugar

Cake

Sift together flour, sugar, baking soda, cinnamon and salt in a bowl. In a separate bowl, beat eggs, oil, buttermilk and vanilla. Combine dry ingredients with wet ingredients and mix until smooth. Stir in pineapple, carrots, nuts and coconut. Pour into a greased and floured 9x13 inch baking pan. Bake at 350 degrees for 40 minutes.

Glaze

While cake bakes, prepare glaze. Combine sugar, baking soda, buttermilk, butter and corn syrup in a saucepan. Bring to a boil. Cook and stir 5 minutes. Remove from heat and stir in vanilla. Pour glaze over hot cake as soon as it comes out of oven. Cool completely.

Frosting

Cream butter, cream cheese, vanilla, orange juice and zest. Slowly mix in sugar until smooth. Frost cake in pan or turned out onto a tray when cooled.

Yield: 10 to 12 servings

Summertime Cake

Do you want to impress your tennis or golf team? Surprise them with this refreshing finale to your annual luncheon.

Cake

2 sticks butter, softened	1 teaspoon almond extract
½ cup shortening	1 teaspoon lemon extract
3 cups sugar	3 cups all-purpose flour
5 eggs	½ teaspoon baking powder
1 teaspoon vanilla extract	Pinch of salt
1 teaspoon coconut extract	1 cup evaporated milk

Glaze

1 cup sugar	½ teaspoon coconut extract
½ cup water	½ teaspoon almond extract
½ teaspoon vanilla extract	½ teaspoon lemon extract

Cake

Cream butter, shortening and sugar with an electric mixer at medium speed. Add eggs, one at a time, mixing well after each addition. Mix in extracts. In a separate bowl, combine flour, baking powder and salt. Add dry ingredients and milk, alternately, blending well at low speed. Pour batter into a greased and floured 10 inch tube pan. Bake at 300 degrees for 1 hour, 45 minutes.

Glaze

Combine sugar, water and extracts in a saucepan. Cook over low heat, stirring constantly, until sugar melts. Cool. When done baking, pierce top of cake with a toothpick. Pour glaze over top. Let stand 20 minutes.

Yield: 15 to 20 servings

Apple Brandy Cake

A pretty upside down cake.

Apple Filling

Sugar to coat pan

4 tablespoons butter

¾ cup sugar

⅓ cup water

¾ teaspoon cinnamon

⅛ teaspoon nutmeg

3 to 4 Granny Smith apples, peeled
and thinly sliced

Cake

1 cup all-purpose flour

1 teaspoon baking powder

¼ teaspoon salt

¾ cup sugar

¼ teaspoon ground ginger

3 egg yolks

2 eggs

2 tablespoons brandy

2 teaspoons vanilla

1 stick butter, melted

1 tablespoon brandy

Apple Filling

Sprinkle bottom of a greased 9 inch springform pan with sugar. Place foil around outside of pan to collect any juices that might escape. Melt 4 tablespoons butter in a large skillet over medium heat. Stir in ¾ cup sugar, water, cinnamon and nutmeg. Bring to a slight boil. Add apple slices and cook until tender. Remove apples, leaving liquid in skillet. Arrange apple slices in a decorative pattern in pan. Continue to boil liquid in skillet until thickened. Pour liquid over apples.

Cake

In a bowl, sift together flour, baking powder and salt. In a separate bowl, whisk together ¾ cup sugar, ginger, egg yolks, eggs, 2 tablespoons brandy and vanilla. Slowly mix in dry ingredients. Fold in 1 stick melted butter. Pour batter over apples. Bake at 350 degrees for about 40 minutes. Cool in pan. Brush 1 tablespoon brandy over top of baked cake. Invert onto platter and serve warm.

Yield: 10 to 12 servings

Peaches and Cream Cake

Everybody who has a summertime birthday in my family requests this seasonal cake.

1 (18 ounce) package butter cake mix

½ cup granulated sugar

¼ cup cornstarch

4 cups peeled and sliced fresh peaches

½ cup water

1 cup sour cream

2 cups heavy cream

2 to 3 tablespoons powdered sugar

Fresh peach slices for garnish

Prepare cake mix as directed on package, using two 8 inch cake pans. Cool and split each layer in half horizontally. Combine granulated sugar and cornstarch in a saucepan. Add peaches and water. Cook over medium heat, stirring constantly, until smooth and thickened. Cool completely. Place a cake layer half on a serving plate. Top with a third of peach filling. Spread a third of sour cream over filling. Repeat with remaining cake layers, filling and sour cream, stacking on top of each other and ending with a cake layer. Whip cream with powdered sugar in a medium bowl until stiff peaks form. Frost top and sides of cake with whipped cream. Garnish with fresh peach slices.

Yield: 8 to 10 servings

Brown Sugar Pound Cake

1 (16 ounce) package light brown sugar

1 cup granulated sugar

3 sticks butter, softened

5 eggs

3 cups all-purpose flour

½ teaspoon salt

1 teaspoon baking powder

1 teaspoon vanilla

1 cup milk

Cream sugars and butter. Add eggs, one at a time, beating well after each addition. In a separate bowl, combine flour, salt and baking powder. Combine vanilla and milk in another bowl. Add dry ingredients and milk mixture, alternately, to creamed mixture, beginning and ending with dry ingredients. Beat until just blended. Pour batter into a greased and floured 10 inch tube pan. Bake at 350 degrees for 1 hour to 1 hour, 15 minutes.

Yield: 12 servings

Hold Onto Your Cake!

Place a dab of frosting on the serving platter and place the unfrosted cake on the dab. It will help hold the cake in place while you frost and if you need to transport the cake to a party.

One stick of butter will soften in one minute when microwaved at 20% power.

Fresh Berry Tart

Crust

5 ounces sliced almonds

1 stick butter, softened

2 tablespoons sugar

1¼ cups all-purpose flour

¼ teaspoon salt

1 egg

½ teaspoon almond extract

Filling

8 ounces mascarpone cheese

⅓ cup heavy cream, chilled

1 teaspoon vanilla

¼ cup sugar

1 cup blueberries

1 cup raspberries

1½ to 2 cups strawberries, quartered

2 tablespoons orange marmalade

1½ tablespoons berry liqueur

Crust

Combine almonds, butter, sugar, flour and salt in a food processor. Process until blended. Add egg and almond extract and process until well mixed. Press mixture into the bottom of a greased 11 inch tart pan with a removable bottom. Chill at least 30 minutes. Bake at 350 degrees for 20 to 30 minutes or until browned. Cool.

Filling

Whip cheese, cream, vanilla and sugar in a bowl until stiff peaks form. Spoon over crust. Combine berries in a bowl. In a saucepan, heat marmalade and liqueur to a simmer. Cook until mixture reduces to 3 tablespoons. Pour mixture over berries. Spread berries over filling. Serve at room temperature.

Yield: 8 servings

Island Coconut Lime Pie

Crust

36 vanilla wafers (about 5 ounces)

⅓ cup dry roasted macadamia nuts
(about 2 ounces)

⅓ cup sweetened flaked coconut

4 tablespoons unsalted butter,
melted

Filling

1 (15 ounce) can cream of coconut

⅔ cup vanilla low fat yogurt

½ cup Key lime juice

2 teaspoons lime zest

3 tablespoons cold water

2 teaspoons unflavored gelatin

¾ cup heavy cream, chilled

2 tablespoons powdered sugar

1 lime, thinly sliced into rounds and
powdered sugar for garnish

Crust

Grind wafers and nuts together in a food processor. Pour into a medium bowl and mix in coconut. Add butter and stir until blended. Press mixture into the bottom and up the sides of a 9 inch pie pan. Cover and freeze 30 minutes or up to 1 week. Bake at 350 degrees for 20 minutes or until crust is golden. Cool completely.

Filling

Whisk together cream of coconut, yogurt, lime juice and zest in a large bowl. Pour cold water into a small metal bowl. Sprinkle gelatin over water. Let stand 10 minutes to soften gelatin. Set metal bowl in a small saucepan over barely simmering water. Whisk about 1 minute or until gelatin dissolves. Whisk gelatin into coconut mixture. Pour into crust and chill at least 6 hours or overnight or until set. When ready to serve, whip cream with sugar. Pipe whipped cream onto pie. Garnish with lime slices dipped in powdered sugar.

Yield: 8 to 10 servings

This received rave reviews at the Le Bonheur Club's Sustainer Luncheon and the cooks loved that it could be made a day ahead.

French Apple Tart

Crust

2 egg yolks

2 tablespoons brandy

1¼ cups all-purpose flour

2 tablespoons sugar

¼ teaspoon salt

9 tablespoons unsalted butter, chilled and cut into ½ inch pieces

Filling

1¼ cups blanched slivered almonds

¾ cup sugar

2 eggs

1 tablespoon brandy

1 teaspoon vanilla extract

½ teaspoon almond extract

¼ teaspoon salt

4 tablespoons unsalted butter, softened

3 tart green apples, peeled and sliced ⅛ inch thick

1 tablespoon brandy

1 tablespoon sugar

2 tablespoons butter, melted

1 tablespoon sugar

¼ cup apricot preserves

1 tablespoon brandy

Crust

Stir egg yolks and brandy in a small bowl until blended. Combine flour, sugar and salt in a food processor. Add butter, one piece at a time, and pulse to blend until crumbs are the size of small peas. With machine running, add yolk mixture. Process until mixture forms large, moist clumps. Gather dough into a ball, then flatten into a disk. Wrap in plastic and refrigerate 1 hour or until cold.

Roll out dough on a lightly floured surface into a 14 inch round. Transfer to an 11 inch tart pan with a removable bottom. Fold overhanging dough and press to form double thick sides. Cover and chill while preparing filling.

Filling

Combine almonds, ¾ cup sugar, eggs, 1 tablespoon brandy, extracts and salt in a food processor. Blend until mixture forms a soft paste. Add 4 tablespoons butter and blend 10 seconds. Spread mixture over crust. Chill 45 minutes or until firm.

Meanwhile, mix apple slices, 1 tablespoon brandy and 1 tablespoon sugar in a large bowl. Let stand 30 minutes. Drain apple slices and arrange on top of filling in overlapping concentric circles. Brush 2 tablespoons melted butter over apples and sprinkle with 1 tablespoon sugar.

Bake at 400 degrees for 15 minutes. Reduce temperature to 350 degrees and bake 45 minutes or until apples are tender. Transfer to a wire rack. Melt preserves with 1 tablespoon brandy in a small saucepan over low heat. Strain mixture into a small bowl and brush over tart. Cool. Leave at room temperature and serve within 8 hours.

Yield: 10 to 12 servings

Dough can be prepared up to 1 day ahead, wrapped and refrigerated. Let soften slightly before rolling out.

Nutty Chocolate Chip Pie

1 cup pecans, chopped

1 cup semi-sweet chocolate chips

4 tablespoons margarine or butter, softened

½ cup packed light brown sugar

4 medium eggs

½ cup light corn syrup

1 tablespoon plus 1 teaspoon rum (optional)

½ teaspoon cinnamon

1 teaspoon vanilla

1 (9 inch) frozen deep dish pie crust, baked

Spread pecans on an ungreased baking sheet. Bake at 350 degrees for 4 minutes or until lightly browned, stirring occasionally; set aside. Melt chocolate chips in the top of a double boiler. Cream margarine and sugar with an electric mixer at medium speed for 4 minutes or until light and fluffy. Beat in eggs, one at a time. Add corn syrup, rum, cinnamon, vanilla and melted chocolate. Stir in pecans. Spread mixture in baked crust. Bake at 350 degrees for 45 minutes or until center is set.

Yield: 8 servings

Lemon Tart with Candied Pistachios

Crust

1¼ cups graham cracker crumbs

¼ cup sugar

1 teaspoon cinnamon

4 tablespoons butter, melted

Filling

2 sticks butter

1¼ cups sugar

3 egg yolks

3 eggs

1½ teaspoons vanilla

½ cup lemon juice

1 teaspoon lemon zest

Topping

4 teaspoons water

3 tablespoons sugar

½ cup pistachios, shelled and coarsely chopped

Crust

Mix crumbs, sugar and cinnamon in a bowl. Stir in butter. Press mixture into a tart pan. Bake at 350 degrees for 12 minutes. Cool.

Filling

Melt butter in a saucepan over medium heat. Stir in sugar. Whisk in egg yolks, eggs, vanilla, lemon juice and zest. Whisk 10 minutes or until mixture thickens. Reduce heat to low and cook 2 minutes. Pour hot filling into crust. Refrigerate 2 hours before adding topping.

Topping

Combine water and sugar in a small saucepan. Stir over low heat until sugar dissolves. Increase heat and bring to a boil. Boil, without stirring, until mixture turns amber gold. Remove from heat and stir in pistachios. Toss to coat and pour onto lightly greased wax paper. When cooled, break apart into small pieces. Arrange pistachios in a 1 inch border around outside of tart. Cut tart into wedges and serve.

Yield: 8 to 10 servings

Coconut Cream Pie with Macadamia Crust

The macadamia crust makes this tart an outstanding dessert.

Crust

1 cup all-purpose flour

Pinch of salt

6 tablespoons butter

3 to 5 tablespoons ice water

¾ cup finely chopped macadamia nuts

Filling

1½ cups sugar

2 eggs

½ teaspoon salt

1 stick butter, softened

¼ cup all-purpose flour

½ cup milk

1 cup coconut

½ cup coconut for garnish

Crust

Mix flour and salt in a bowl. Cut in butter until well blended. Gently mix in ice water, adding enough water for dough to form a ball. Transfer dough to a floured surface and knead in macadamia nuts. Roll out dough and transfer to a 9 inch deep dish pie pan. Prick crust and freeze 30 minutes.

Filling

Beat sugar, eggs and salt together. Add butter and flour and mix well. Stir in milk. Fold in 1 cup coconut.

Remove crust from freezer. Bake, unfilled, at 325 degrees for 10 minutes. Remove from oven and add coconut filling. Sprinkle ½ cup coconut on top. Bake 55 to 60 minutes longer or until firm.

Yield: 8 to 10 servings

For Impressive Pastry

For tender, flaky pastry, chill all ingredients before combining and handle sparingly. Roll pastry dough between two pieces of waxed paper lightly dusted with flour or confectioners' sugar. Moisten counter top with water to keep bottom piece of paper from slipping.

Dynasty Pie

Very rich. A small slice will satisfy your sweet craving.

Pie

2 eggs, slightly beaten

¾ cup maple syrup

½ cup granulated sugar

½ cup packed light brown sugar

1 stick butter, melted

1 teaspoon vanilla

1 cup flaked coconut

¾ cup dry rolled oats

½ cup chopped pecans

¾ cup semi-sweet chocolate chips (optional)

1 (9 inch) pie crust, unbaked

Topping

1 cup heavy cream

2 tablespoons powdered sugar

½ teaspoon cinnamon

1 teaspoon vanilla

Pie

Mix together eggs, syrup, sugars, butter and vanilla. Stir in coconut, oats, pecans and chocolate chips. Pour into pie crust. Bake at 375 degrees for 35 to 40 minutes. Cool. Refrigerate pie within 2 hours of baking. Serve with topping or vanilla ice cream.

Topping

Beat cream, sugar, cinnamon and vanilla in a chilled bowl until soft peaks form. Spoon onto pie slices.

Yield: 6 to 8 servings

Old-Fashioned Lemon Chess Pie

3 eggs

6 tablespoons butter, softened

1½ cups sugar

1 tablespoon all-purpose flour

½ teaspoon salt

⅓ cup fresh lemon juice

1 deep dish pie crust, unbaked

Blend eggs, butter, sugar, flour and salt. Mix in lemon juice. Pour mixture into pie crust. Bake at 350 degrees for 50 minutes.

Yield: 8 servings

Chocolate Macadamia Pie

Pie

4 eggs

½ cup packed light brown sugar

¾ cup light corn syrup

4 tablespoons butter, melted

2 tablespoons coffee liqueur

2 teaspoons vanilla

1 (7 ounce) jar macadamia nuts, chopped

1 cup semi-sweet chocolate chips

1 (9 inch) deep dish pie crust, unbaked

Topping

1 cup heavy cream

2 tablespoons powdered sugar

2 tablespoons coffee liqueur

½ cup semi-sweet chocolate chips, melted

Pie

Mix eggs, sugar, syrup, butter, liqueur and vanilla in a bowl. Stir in nuts and chocolate chips. Pour into pie crust. Bake at 425 degrees for 10 minutes. Reduce heat to 350 degrees and bake 45 minutes longer or until set. Cool to room temperature, then refrigerate until chilled.

Topping

Beat cream, sugar and liqueur with an electric mixer on high speed until stiff. Spoon half of cream topping over pie. Drizzle melted chocolate over cream. Serve pie with remaining cream on the side.

Yield: 8 servings

Key Notes

Mouth-Watering Blueberry Pie

1 cup sugar

½ teaspoon cinnamon

5 tablespoons cornstarch

½ teaspoon salt

1 tablespoon fresh lemon juice

4 cups fresh blueberries

Pastry for 9 inch double crust pie

2 tablespoons margarine

1 egg, beaten

1 teaspoon sugar

Combine 1 cup sugar, cinnamon, cornstarch and salt. Mix with lemon juice and blueberries. Spoon mixture into a pastry-lined pie pan. Dot with margarine. Top with remaining pastry crust rolled to ⅛ inch thickness. Cut 2 to 3 gashes in top of crust to allow steam to escape. Brush top of pastry with a small amount of egg. Sprinkle 1 teaspoon sugar on top. Bake at 375 degrees for 40 minutes or until crust is brown.

Yield: 8 servings

For extra decoration, cut top pastry into ½ inch strips and arrange on pie in lattice fashion.

Grandmother's Peach Pie

¾ cup sugar

¾ cup all-purpose flour

4 to 6 ripe peaches, peeled and sliced

1 deep dish pie crust, unbaked

½ cup heavy cream

Mix sugar and flour in a bowl. Add peaches and toss. Spoon mixture into pie crust. Pour cream over peach mixture, lifting peaches to hold cream. Bake at 350 degrees for 40 to 45 minutes or until brown and bubbly. Cool before serving.

Yield: 8 servings

Whenever we have this pie, we always think about our Florida vacations. We would go to a blueberry farm and pick the most delicious, plump blueberries. Remember do not wash fresh blueberries prior to freezing. When you are ready to use them, just remove from freezer bag and gently wash in a colander.

Strawberry Rhubarb Pie

2 cups rhubarb, sliced
   (cut into 1 inch pieces)
1 quart whole strawberries
¼ cup tapioca
1½ cups sugar
¼ teaspoon salt

1 teaspoon nutmeg
1 teaspoon lemon juice
5 drops red food coloring
2 tablespoons butter, melted
1 (9 inch) pie crust, unbaked

Combine rhubarb and strawberries in a bowl. Mix in tapioca, sugar, salt, nutmeg, lemon juice, food coloring and butter. Let mixture stand 5 minutes. Spoon into pie crust. Bake at 375 degrees for 1 hour.

Yield: 6 to 8 servings

When purchasing rhubarb, choose the smallest, thinnest stalks with red color to give a sweeter taste.

Fruit Melange

½ cup sugar
3 tablespoons cornstarch
Pinch of salt
1 egg, beaten
½ teaspoon almond extract
½ cup all-purpose flour
½ cup sugar

½ teaspoon ground ginger
4 tablespoons unsalted butter,
   chilled
2 cups peaches, sliced
2 cups plums, sliced
1½ cups blueberries
½ cup raspberries

Blend ½ cup sugar, cornstarch and salt in a mixing bowl. Add egg and almond extract and mix well. In a separate bowl, combine flour, ½ cup sugar and ginger. Cut in butter with a fork until mixture is finely crumbled. Combine peaches, plums, blueberries and raspberries in a pie plate. Pour egg mixture over fruit. Sprinkle flour mixture on top. Bake at 375 degrees for 45 minutes.

Yield: 8 servings

Your Favorite Fruit Cobbler

2 tablespoons butter

2 cups fruit of choice, such as sliced
    strawberries or peaches,
    blueberries or blackberries

2 tablespoons sugar

1 cup self-rising flour

1 cup milk

1 cup sugar

1 teaspoon cinnamon

4 tablespoons butter

Cinnamon sugar (optional)

My grandfather grew strawberries in South Carolina. During my summer visits, Grandmother would make "my favorite" fruit cobbler especially for me.

Melt 2 tablespoons butter in a saucepan. Add fruit and 2 tablespoons sugar and cook over low heat until fruit is tender. If mixture is too dry, add 1 tablespoon water. In a mixing bowl, combine flour, milk and 1 cup sugar until fairly smooth, but do not overbeat. Stir in cinnamon. Melt 4 tablespoons butter in an 8x11 inch glass baking dish. Pour flour mixture into dish. Spoon fruit mixture on top. Bake at 350 degrees for 30 to 40 minutes or until golden brown. If desired, sprinkle with cinnamon sugar 5 minutes before done baking. Serve warm with vanilla ice cream.

Yield: 6 to 8 servings

Individual Cherry Cobblers

3 (16 ounce) cans pitted Bing
    cherries, drained, juice reserved

2 tablespoons cornstarch

Zest of 1 lemon

¼ cup sugar

¼ teaspoon salt

½ teaspoon almond extract

½ cup all-purpose flour

1 tablespoons sugar

¾ teaspoon baking powder

2 tablespoons butter, softened

1 egg

2 tablespoons milk or buttermilk

Sugar for topping

Combine 1 cup of reserved cherry juice and cornstarch in a 2 quart saucepan. Add lemon zest, ¼ cup sugar and salt. Cook over medium heat for 5 minutes or until mixture thickens. Remove from heat and stir in cherries and almond extract. Divide mixture among eight 12 ounce greased ramekins. In a small bowl or food processor, blend flour, 1 tablespoon sugar, baking powder, butter, egg and milk. Spoon batter over cherries and spread with a knife to cover cherries. Sprinkle with sugar. Bake at 375 degrees for 20 to 25 minutes or until crust is golden brown. Serve with ice cream.

Yield: 8 servings

Fresh pitted cherries can be used; substitute 1 cup water for cherry juice and use about 2 cups fresh cherries instead of canned.

Derby Tarts

Great individual desserts to serve to horse fans at your next Triple Crown Race event.

Pastry for 6 tarts (each pan 4½ inch)
¾ cup semi-sweet chocolate chips
3 eggs, slightly beaten
⅓ cup granulated sugar
3 tablespoons packed light brown sugar

1 tablespoon all-purpose flour
¾ cup light corn syrup
4 tablespoons butter, melted
3 tablespoons bourbon
2 teaspoons vanilla
2 cups pecan halves

Press pastry into 6 tart pans. Divide chocolate chips among pans. Chill 30 minutes. Beat eggs, sugars, flour, corn syrup, butter, bourbon and vanilla with an electric mixer until blended. Pour filling mixture into tart pans, filling each half full. Arrange pecan halves on top. Drizzle tarts with remaining filling. Bake at 350 degrees for 30 to 35 minutes or until set.

Yield: 6 servings

Simple Crème Brûlée

3 cups heavy cream
1½ tablespoons vanilla
9 egg yolks
¾ cup granulated sugar

12 tablespoons packed light brown sugar, divided
Cinnamon (optional)

Combine cream and vanilla in a heavy saucepan. Bring to a rolling simmer over low heat. In a bowl, whisk together egg yolks and granulated sugar. Spoon some of hot cream into yolk mixture. Mix well, then pour back into hot cream. Mix well. Place 1 tablespoon brown sugar in the bottom of 6 ramekins or custard cups. Divide cream mixture among ramekins. Place ramekins in a 9x13 inch baking dish and place in oven. Pour hot water around cups in dish to a depth of 1 inch. Bake at 325 degrees for 30 minutes. Cover ramekins with a sheet of foil, reduce heat to 300 degrees and bake 30 minutes longer or until set. Remove ramekins from oven. Sprinkle 1 tablespoon brown sugar over each ramekin. Broil 3 inches from heat for 20 seconds or until sugar starts to bubble. Sprinkle with cinnamon, if desired. Chill before serving.

Yield: 6 servings

Toffee Bar Cake with Praline Sauce

Cake

2 cups all-purpose flour	1 cup chopped pecans
1 cup packed dark brown sugar	1 teaspoon baking soda
½ cup sugar	1 cup buttermilk
1 stick unsalted butter, softened	1 egg
½ teaspoon salt	1 teaspoon vanilla
4 (1.4 ounce) chocolate covered toffee bars, chopped	

Praline Sauce

1½ cups packed light brown sugar	4 tablespoons butter
⅔ cup light corn syrup	1 (5⅓ ounce) can evaporated milk

Cake

Beat flour, sugars, butter and salt in a large bowl with an electric mixer on low speed until mixture resembles coarse meal. Remove ½ cup of mixture and combine with toffee bars and pecans in a medium bowl; set aside. Stir baking soda into remaining mixture in large bowl. Add buttermilk, egg and vanilla. Beat until just combined. Pour batter into a greased 9x13 inch baking dish. Sprinkle toffee mixture on top. Bake at 350 degrees for 35 minutes or until golden brown on top and a toothpick inserted in the center comes out clean. Cool completely in dish. Cut and serve with Praline Sauce.

Praline Sauce

Combine sugar, corn syrup and butter in a saucepan. Bring to a boil. Remove from heat and cool to lukewarm. Blend in milk. Store in jars in refrigerator until ready to use.

Yield: 10 to 12 servings, 3½ cups sauce

Triple the Praline Sundae Sauce to keep on hand or give as gifts. This sauce is nice to have for last minute company and no time to prepare a fancy dessert.

Chocolate Raspberry Bags

I served this at my son's pre-prom dinner. They all thought I was a great pastry chef!

1 (10 ounce) package frozen raspberries in light syrup, thawed, undrained

1 cup sifted powdered sugar

1 (17 ounce) package frozen puff pastry sheets, thawed

1 cup raspberry-flavored chocolate chips, or semi-sweet chocolate chips

1 cup white chocolate or vanilla chips

1 cup chopped pecans

¼ cup sifted powdered sugar for topping

Combine undrained raspberries and 1 cup sugar in a blender or food processor. Process until smooth. Pour raspberry sauce through a wire mesh strainer and discard seeds. Chill. Roll each pastry sheet into a 12 inch square. Cut each into 4 squares. Combine chocolate chips, white chocolate chips and pecans and divide mixture evenly among the center of pastry squares. Pull up sides of pastry to enclose mixture. Twist ends just above mixture, pinching to seal at "neck" and spreading open top edges of pastry to resemble bags. Place bags on an ungreased baking sheet. Bake at 425 degrees for 20 minutes, covering loosely with foil after 10 minutes to prevent excess browning. Spoon raspberry sauce onto dessert plates. Sprinkle ¼ cup powdered sugar over baked pastry bags. Place a bag in center of sauce on each plate. Serve immediately.

Yield: 8 servings

Not So Tiramisu

A good, low fat alternative to the classic Italian dessert.

1 (8 ounce) package Neufchâtel
    cheese, softened

⅓ cup granulated sugar

5 tablespoons amaretto

½ teaspoon vanilla

1 (8 ounce) container frozen
    whipped topping, thawed

24 ladyfingers

¾ cup strong brewed coffee

¼ cup sifted cocoa

1 tablespoon powdered sugar

2 tablespoons sliced blanched
    almonds

Beat cheese and granulated sugar together until creamy. Add amaretto
and vanilla. Fold in whipped topping. In a 9 inch square dish, layer half
the ladyfingers. Sprinkle with half the coffee. Spread half of cheese
mixture on top. Sprinkle half of sifted cocoa over cheese layer. Repeat
layers. Cover and refrigerate 4 hours or overnight. Sprinkle powdered
sugar and almonds over the top when ready to serve.

Yield: 12 servings

Lemon Trifle

1 (14 ounce) can sweetened
    condensed milk

1 (8 ounce) carton lemon yogurt

⅓ cup lemon juice

2 teaspoons lemon zest

2 cups whipped topping

1 angel food cake, cut into 1 inch
    cubes

2 cups fresh raspberries or
    strawberries

Combine milk, yogurt, lemon juice and zest in a bowl. Fold in
whipped topping. Place half of cake cubes in a trifle bowl or large serving
bowl. Top with half of topping mixture. Repeat layers. Top with berries.

Yield: 8 to 10 servings

**Blanching
Almonds**

To blanch almonds,
plunge the nuts into
boiling water for
1 minute. Drain and
transfer to a clean towel.
Rub the nuts gently to
remove the skin.

Chocolate Mousse in the City

A dear friend served this on a beautiful Royal Crown Derby platter with a crystal bowl filled with whipped cream. It was the most elegant dessert I had ever seen.

8 ounces unsweetened chocolate

8 ounces semi-sweet chocolate

5 egg whites

¾ cup plus 2 tablespoons sugar

1 quart heavy cream, whipped

Whipped cream flavored with amaretto or Grand Marnier

Melt unsweetened and semi-sweet chocolate in the top of a double boiler. Meanwhile, beat egg whites until stiff. Beat in sugar. Pour melted chocolate into a very large bowl. Fold in egg whites. Fold in whipped cream. Pour mixture into a 3 quart mold or into individual ramekins. Refrigerate overnight.

To serve, unmold onto a platter or individual dessert plates. Serve with flavored whipped cream in a bowl on the side or a dollop of cream on individual servings.

Yield: 16 servings

Rum Pots de Crème

8 (1 ounce) squares semi-sweet chocolate

2 cups half-and-half

1 tablespoon sugar

6 egg yolks, slightly beaten

2 tablespoons dark rum

Whipped cream and slivered almonds for garnish

Combine chocolate, half-and-half and sugar in top of double boiler. Bring water to a boil in the bottom of a double boiler. Reduce heat to a simmer. Heat until chocolate melts. Gradually stir a fourth of chocolate mixture into egg yolks in a medium bowl. Pour egg mixture into remaining chocolate mixture. Add rum. Divide mixture among six 4 ounce serving dishes. Chill at least 8 hours. To serve, garnish with whipped cream and almonds.

Yield: 6 servings

Chocolate Fondue

1 (16 ounce) bottle light corn syrup
    (2 cups)

1½ cups heavy cream

3 (12 ounce) packages semi-sweet
    chocolate chips

Dunking Morsels

Angel food or pound cake cubes

Fruits such as apples, pears,
    pineapple, strawberries,
    bananas, cherries or grapes, cut
    into slices or chunks as needed

Marshmallows

Combine corn syrup and cream in a heavy saucepan. Bring to a boil over medium heat, stirring constantly. Remove from heat and add chocolate. Stir with a wire whisk until smooth and glossy. Spoon into a fondue pot or chafing dish and keep warm. Serve with dunking morsels.

Yield: 7 cups

My guests expect this fondue to be on my Christmas buffet at our annual open house. Strawberries are the tastiest dunking morsels.

Frosty Grand Marnier

1 quart vanilla ice cream, softened

24 almond macaroons, crumbled

2 tablespoons Grand Marnier

1 cup heavy cream, whipped

4 teaspoons powdered sugar

¼ cup sliced almonds, toasted

1 quart fresh strawberries

2 tablespoons Grand Marnier

Stir together ice cream and crumbled macaroons. Mix in 2 tablespoons Grand Marnier. Fold in whipped cream. Pour mixture into a 6 cup soufflé mold or serving dish. Cover with plastic wrap and place in freezer. When mixture starts to harden, sprinkle powdered sugar and almonds on top. Return to freezer until hard. Mash strawberries. Blend in 2 tablespoons Grand Marnier. Serve strawberry sauce with frozen dessert.

Yield: 8 to 10 servings

Frozen Macaroon Delight

Macaroons and amaretto - what better way to end a bridge luncheon.

12 coconut macaroons, crushed
1 tablespoon almond extract
1 gallon vanilla ice cream, softened
6 tablespoons amaretto
2 cups heavy cream, whipped

2 (12 ounce) packages frozen
    raspberries, thawed
½ cup sugar
4 tablespoons amaretto
½ cup slivered almonds, toasted

Combine macaroons, almond extract, ice cream and 6 tablespoons amaretto in a bowl. Fold in whipped cream. Pour mixture into a Bundt pan and freeze. Combine raspberries, sugar and 4 tablespoons amaretto in a saucepan. Bring to a boil and cook 3 minutes. Pour raspberry sauce through a wire mesh strainer and discard seeds.

To serve, set Bundt pan briefly in cold water to soften. Unmold onto a platter. Spoon raspberry sauce onto individual dessert plates. Top with a slice of cake and drizzle with more sauce. Sprinkle almonds on top.

Serve immediately.

Yield: 10 to 12 servings

Frozen Toffee Dessert

12 ladyfingers, split

2 tablespoons powdered instant coffee

1 tablespoon boiling water

1 quart vanilla ice cream, softened

4 (1.4 ounce) chocolate-covered
toffee bars, frozen and crushed

1 cup heavy cream

3 tablespoons white crème de cacao
liqueur

2 (1.4 ounce) chocolate-covered
toffee bars, frozen and crushed

Use ladyfingers to line the bottom and 2 inches up the sides of a 9 inch springform pan. Dissolve coffee in boiling water; cool. Stir together coffee, ice cream and 4 crushed toffee bars. Spoon mixture into pan. Cover and freeze until firm. When ready to serve, whip cream and liqueur until soft peaks form. Spread whipped cream over frozen ice cream layer. Garnish with 2 crushed toffee bars.

Yield: 10 to 12 servings

Soften hard ice cream by microwaving at 30% power. One pint will take 15 to 30 seconds; one quart, 30 to 45 seconds; and one half gallon, 40 to 60 seconds.

Divinity

This candy recipe can only be made on sunny days. It does not work when it rains!

3 cups sugar

½ cup corn syrup

⅔ cup water

⅛ teaspoon salt

2 egg whites, room temperature

1 teaspoon vanilla

1 cup nuts, chopped (optional)

In a heavy saucepan, cook sugar, corn syrup, water and salt until mixture spins a thread or forms a soft ball that holds its shape when dropped into cold water, or when a candy thermometer reaches 240 degrees. Beat egg whites until stiff. Fold in syrup mixture slowly. Beat 20 minutes or until mixture has a dull finish. Add vanilla and nuts and beat 5 to 8 minutes. Drop by rounded teaspoonfuls onto wax paper. Swirl spoon up after dropping onto paper. Cool completely.

Yield: 6 dozen

My Christmas is not complete without a taste of Grandmother's divinity.

There are many hot fudge sauce recipes, but this one is truly angelic.

Heavenly Hot Fudge Sauce

2 cups sifted powdered sugar

1 (6 ounce) package semi-sweet chocolate chips

1 stick butter

1 (12 ounce) can evaporated milk

¼ teaspoon salt

¾ teaspoon vanilla

Combine sugar, chocolate chips, butter, milk and salt in a medium saucepan. Cook over medium heat, stirring frequently, for 15 to 20 minutes or until mixture comes to a boil. Boil 1 minute, stirring constantly. Remove from heat and stir in vanilla. Cool.

Yield: 3 cups

This recipe was handed down to me from the days of my church's Plum Pudding Festival held during the holiday season.

Royal Plum Supreme

1 (16 ounce) can purple plums

1 (1 pound) package gingerbread mix

½ teaspoon salt

1 cup raisins

½ cup chopped walnuts

5 tablespoons butter, melted

1½ cups powdered sugar

1 teaspoon vanilla

1 cup heavy cream, whipped

Drain plums, remove pits and cut into quarters. Mix gingerbread as directed on box. Stir plums, salt, raisins and walnuts into batter. Grease a Bundt pan with solid shortening and flour. Pour batter into a pan. Bake, uncovered, at 375 degrees for 40 to 45 minutes. Loosen edges and let stand 5 minutes before removing from pan.

For a topping, combine butter, sugar and vanilla. Fold in cream and refrigerate until ready to serve.

Yield: 10 to 12 servings

Bread Pudding with Anglaise

Bread Pudding

1 loaf cinnamon raisin bread, cut into 1 inch squares

1 stick butter, melted

6 eggs

4 cups milk

1 cup sugar

½ cup raisins

1 teaspoon vanilla

1½ teaspoons cinnamon

Crème Anglaise Sauce

1 cup heavy cream

¼ cup sugar

2 egg yolks

1½ teaspoons all-purpose flour

⅛ teaspoon salt

1 medium scoop vanilla ice cream

3 tablespoons bourbon or brandy

Bread Pudding

Spread bread squares on a baking sheet and toast at 375 degrees for 8 minutes or until brown. Pack bread into eight 1 cup ramekins or a 9x13 inch glass baking dish. Drizzle with melted butter. In a medium bowl, whisk together eggs, milk and sugar until dissolved. Add raisins, vanilla and cinnamon. Pour mixture over bread and let stand 10 minutes. Reduce oven temperature to 350 degrees. Bake at 350 degrees for 45 minutes or until pudding is slightly puffed and firm. Cool slightly and serve with warm sauce.

Crème Anglaise Sauce

Combine cream and sugar in a small saucepan. Bring to a boil and stir until sugar is dissolved. In a small bowl, whisk together egg yolks, flour and salt until smooth. Pour a small amount of hot cream into yolk mixture and whisk until smooth. Pour yolk mixture back into cream. Cook over low heat without boiling, stirring constantly until sauce coats a wooden spoon and holds when you run your finger across the back of the spoon. Remove from heat. Add ice cream and stir until melted. Strain sauce through a fine sieve. Add bourbon and serve warm.

Yield: 8 servings

To ripen bananas quickly, peel and place in a 350 degree oven for 10 minutes.

Bananas Foster Ice Cream

This ice cream wins high praise with my family and friends.

Ice Cream Base

1 quart half-and-half

1 pint heavy cream

2 (14 ounce) cans sweetened condensed milk

Banana Mixture

Banana Mixture

4 ripe bananas, peeled

4 tablespoons butter

½ cup packed light brown sugar

4 dashes cinnamon or to taste

¼ cup banana liqueur

½ cup light rum

Ice Cream Base

Combine half-and-half, cream, milk and banana mixture in an ice cream maker and prepare according to manufacturer's directions. Freeze for about half the freezing process or until ice cream starts to get mushy. Stir in banana mixture. Continue with freezing process until frozen.

Banana Mixture

Slice bananas lengthwise, then slice crosswise into chunks. Melt butter with sugar in a shallow skillet. Add banana chunks and sauté briefly over high heat. Sprinkle with cinnamon. Pour in liqueur and rum and baste bananas. Ignite mixture and continue to baste until flame burns out. Cool before adding to ice cream base.

Yield: 1 gallon

The Best Coconut Ice Cream

1 pint heavy cream

1 quart half-and-half

2 (14 ounce) cans sweetened condensed milk

1 (1 ounce) bottle coconut extract

1½ to 2 cups fresh or frozen flaked coconut

Combine cream, half-and-half, condensed milk and extract in an ice cream maker and prepare according to manufacturer's directions. Freeze until mixture starts to get mushy. Stop freezing process and mix in coconut. Continue freezing until hardened.

Yield: 1 gallon

Toast coconut before adding to ice cream base for a different flavor. To toast coconut in the microwave, Spread ½ cup coconut in a pie plate and cook for 3 to 4 minutes, stirring every 30 seconds after 2 minutes. Watch closely as it will over brown too quickly.

I entered my husband's recipe for this ice cream in the Mid-South Fair. It won three years in a row. He used both the regular and toasted coconut and received blue ribbons for each. Because this ice cream does not use eggs or sugar, it is never icy, but very, very smooth. You won't believe how good it tastes.

Praline Pecan Ice Cream Sauce

1½ cups chopped pecans

4 tablespoons butter

1½ cups packed light brown sugar

¾ cup light corn syrup

¼ cup all-purpose flour

1 (5⅓ ounce) can evaporated milk

Spread pecans on a baking sheet. Bake at 300 degrees for 15 minutes; set aside. Melt butter in a saucepan. Add sugar, corn syrup and flour and stir well. Bring to a boil. Reduce heat and simmer 5 minutes, stirring constantly. Remove from heat and cool to lukewarm. Gradually stir in milk and pecans. Serve warm over vanilla ice cream.

Yield: 3 cups

Fresh Out of Buttermilk

1 cup buttermilk =
1 tablespoon vinegar
or lemon juice plus
enough milk to make
1 cup. Let stand
5 minutes to thicken.
Or use 1 cup plain
yogurt.

Lemon Sorbet

2 cups sugar

½ cup fresh lemon juice

4 cups buttermilk

2½ tablespoons lemon zest

Combine sugar and lemon juice in a bowl. Whisk in buttermilk and zest. Pour into an ice cream maker and freeze for 15 minutes. Transfer ice cream to an airtight container and freeze at least 3 hours.

Yield: 8 to 10 servings

Orange Sherbet

6 (12 ounce) cans orange soft drink

1 (14 ounce) can sweetened
    condensed milk

1 (8 ounce) can crushed pineapple

Combine orange soft drink, milk and pineapple in a 1 gallon ice cream maker. Prepare ice cream according to manufacturer's directions, freezing until hard.

Yield: 1 gallon

Hot Banana Topping

¼ cup pecans, toasted

⅓ cup packed light brown sugar

¼ cup fresh lemon juice

1 tablespoon margarine or butter, melted

¼ teaspoon cinnamon

4 large ripe and firm bananas, peeled

To toast pecans, bake on a baking sheet at 350 degrees for 12 to 15 minutes, stirring occasionally and watching closely. In a small bowl, combine sugar, lemon juice, margarine and cinnamon. Line a jelly roll pan with foil and spray lightly with cooking spray. Cut bananas in half lengthwise and place cut-side up on jelly roll pan. Bake at 425 degrees for 4 minutes. Drizzle sugar sauce evenly over bananas, reserving any leftover sauce for later. Sprinkle with pecans. Bake 3 minutes longer or until lightly browned. Cut each banana half crosswise into thirds. Serve with vanilla ice cream and drizzle remaining sauce on top.

Yield: 2 cups

Raspberry Sauce

1 (16 ounce) package frozen raspberries, thawed

¼ cup White Zinfandel wine

¼ cup powdered sugar

Puree raspberries and strain. Combine stained raspberries with wine and sugar.

Yield: 2 cups

Celebration Stars

2 sticks butter, softened
½ cup sugar
1 egg, beaten
½ teaspoon almond extract
1 tablespoon orange zest

2 teaspoons fresh orange juice
3 cups all-purpose flour
½ teaspoon baking powder
½ teaspoon salt
3 ounces semi-sweet chocolate, melted

Cream butter and sugar until fluffy. Add egg, extract, orange zest and juice. In a separate bowl, sift together flour, baking powder and salt. Stir dry ingredients gradually into creamed mixture. Refrigerate dough 1 hour. Roll out dough to ¼ inch thickness and cut with a star-shaped cookie cutter. Bake on an ungreased baking sheet at 350 degrees for 10 minutes. Cool and drizzle with melted chocolate.

Yield: 48 stars

Espresso Brownies

Brownie Layer

8 ounces semi-sweet chocolate, chopped

1½ sticks butter

¼ cup water

2 tablespoons espresso powder

1½ cups sugar

4 eggs

1 cup all-purpose flour

¼ teaspoon salt

1 cup chopped nuts (optional)

Cream Cheese Layer

2 (8 ounce) packages cream cheese, softened

6 tablespoons butter, softened

1½ cups powdered sugar

2 teaspoons cinnamon

1 teaspoon vanilla

Glaze

12 ounces semi-sweet chocolate

4 tablespoons butter

½ cup heavy cream or half-and-half

Brownie Layer

Combine chocolate, butter, water and espresso powder in a medium saucepan. Cook until melted and smooth; cool. When cool, whisk in sugar. Add eggs, one at a time, mixing well after each addition. Mix in flour, salt and nuts. Pour batter into a greased 9x13 inch pan. Bake at 350 degrees for 20 minutes; cool.

Cream Cheese Layer

Beat cream cheese and butter until smooth. Add powdered sugar, cinnamon and vanilla. Spread over brownie layer and chill 2 hours.

Glaze

Heat and stir chocolate, butter and cream in a saucepan until smooth. Cool 15 minutes or until lukewarm. Pour glaze over cream cheese layer. Refrigerate until glaze is set. Cut into squares.

Yield: 10 to 12 brownies

If short on time, use a brownie mix for the brownie layer, adding espresso powder to mix.

Southern Praline Cookies

Cookies

4 sticks butter, softened

2 cups sifted powdered sugar

4 cups sifted all-purpose flour

2 cups finely chopped pecans

2 tablespoons vanilla

Praline Sauce

1 stick butter

1 cup packed light brown sugar

Dash of salt

½ cup evaporated milk

2 cups sifted powdered sugar

½ teaspoon vanilla

Cookies

Cream butter. Gradually beat in sugar. Add flour, mixing well. Stir in pecans and vanilla. Shape dough into 1 inch balls and place on an ungreased baking sheet. Use a finger to make an indentation in each dough ball. Bake at 375 degrees for 12 to 14 minutes. Cool on wire racks. Spoon a small amount of Praline Sauce onto cookies.

Praline Sauce

Melt butter in a medium saucepan. Add brown sugar and salt and bring to a boil. Boil, stirring constantly, for 2 minutes. Remove from heat and stir in milk. Bring to a boil and cook 2 minutes. Remove from heat and cool to lukewarm. Stir in sugar and vanilla and beat with a wooden spoon until mixture is smooth. If sauce hardens while spooning over cookies, heat 15 to 20 seconds in microwave to soften. Store leftover sauce in refrigerator.

Yield: 6 dozen cookies

For years we hosted cookie swaps for each of our children's school classes. Guests were asked to bring 3 dozen cookies and an unwrapped toy for a needy child. During the party the children made a craft and the "helper" Moms preferred these cookies.

The unwrapped toys were donated to the Bunny Room at Le Bonheur.

Prize-Winning Gingersnaps

¾ cup vegetable shortening

1 cup sugar

1 egg

¼ cup molasses

2½ cups all-purpose flour

2 teaspoons baking soda

1 teaspoon salt

1 teaspoon ground ginger

½ teaspoon cinnamon

¼ teaspoon ground cloves

1½ cups raisins

3 tablespoons sugar

Beat shortening in a large bowl with an electric mixer until creamy. Gradually beat in 1 cup sugar until light and fluffy. Add egg and beat until blended. Scrape down sides of bowl and beaters. Blend in molasses with mixer at medium speed. In a separate bowl, sift together flour, baking soda, salt, ginger, cinnamon and cloves. At low speed, beat dry ingredients into creamed mixture. Stir in raisins. Turn dough onto a sheet of foil. Wrap and refrigerate 1 to 2 hours. Shape dough into 2 inch balls. Place 3 tablespoons sugar in a shallow dish. Roll dough balls in sugar and place on a greased baking sheet. Bake at 375 degrees for 10 to 12 minutes or until surface is cracked. Cool 2 minutes before removing from baking sheet. Cool completely on wire racks.

Yield: about 3 dozen gingersnaps

For a fancy dessert, try serving these with a lemon curd sauce.

This recipe has been in my family for years and has won First Place Ribbons for several generations at the East Tennessee State Fair.

Lacy Cookies

Do not make these cookies when your husband, children or grandchildren are home! They will keep stealing the batter and /or the cookies and your numbers will dwindle. They are a big hit with everyone.

1 stick margarine or butter
1½ cups dry quick oats
1 cup sugar
1 tablespoon all-purpose flour

1 teaspoon baking powder
1 egg, slightly beaten
1 teaspoon vanilla
Powdered sugar (optional)

Melt margarine in a saucepan. Stir in oats. Sift together sugar, flour and baking powder and stir into saucepan. Stir in egg, then vanilla. Line a 14x16 inch baking sheet with heavy duty foil, dull-side up. Drop batter by slightly rounded half teaspoonfuls onto foil about 2 inches apart. Cookies will spread while baking. Bake at 350 degrees on middle rack of oven for 9 to 10 minutes or until bubbling stops and cookies are slightly browned. Remove foil with cookies still on from baking sheet. Cool completely before gently peeling cookies off foil. Sprinkle with powdered sugar.

Yield: 8 dozen cookies

Chocolate Crinkle Cookies

½ cup vegetable oil
4 (1 ounce) squares unsweetened
    chocolate, melted, or ¾ cup
    cocoa plus 4 teaspoons oil
2 cups sugar
4 eggs

2 teaspoons vanilla
2 cups all-purpose flour
2 teaspoons baking powder
½ teaspoon salt
Powdered sugar for coating

Combine oil, chocolate, sugar, eggs and vanilla in a large bowl. Blend well. Slowly mix in flour, baking powder and salt. Cover and chill dough overnight. Place powdered sugar in a shallow dish. Roll dough into quarter-size balls. Roll balls in powdered sugar, patting sugar onto balls. Place on a greased baking sheet. Bake at 350 degrees for 8 to 10 minutes.

Yield: 3 dozen cookies

Shortbread Cookies

Cookies

2 sticks butter, softened
½ cup powdered sugar

2¼ cups all-purpose flour

Icing

½ cup powdered sugar
½ tablespoon butter, softened

Milk

Cookies

Cream butter, sugar and flour together. Roll dough into balls. Place on a baking sheet and flatten with a fork. Bake at 350 degrees for 8 to 12 minutes. Frost with icing when cooled.

Icing

Cream sugar and butter together. Gradually add milk to desired consistency.

Yield: 3 dozen cookies

For special occasions and holidays, add food coloring to icing. A small amount of almond extract can also be added.

Key Notes

Molasses Cookies

I tested this recipe for the cookbook. My husband tasted the cookies and declared them to be like his Grandmother's cookies when he was a young boy. He ate so many cookies, I had to make another batch for the tasting party.

2 sticks butter, softened
1½ cups granulated sugar
1 egg
2 tablespoons molasses
3 cups all-purpose flour
1 teaspoon baking soda

2 teaspoons cinnamon
2 teaspoons ground ginger
2 teaspoons ground cloves
1 egg white
1½ cups powdered sugar

Cream butter and granulated sugar until light and fluffy. Blend in egg and molasses. Add flour, baking soda, cinnamon, ginger and cloves. Mix well. Chill dough 4 hours or overnight. Roll out dough on a floured surface to ⅛ inch thickness. Cut with a cookie cutter and place on ungreased baking sheets. Bake at 400 degrees for 6 to 8 minutes. Cool slightly before removing from baking sheets.

For icing, beat egg white with powdered sugar until smooth. Dip top of cookies into icing or spread icing over cookies.

Yield: 4½ dozen cookies

White Chocolate Macadamia Nut Cookies

2 cups all-purpose flour
1 teaspoon baking soda
1½ teaspoons salt
1 stick butter, softened
1 cup packed brown sugar

2 eggs
1 teaspoon vanilla
½ cup chopped macadamia nuts
9 ounces good quality white
    chocolate chips

Combine flour, baking soda and salt in a bowl; set aside. Cream butter and sugar in a separate bowl. Beat in eggs and vanilla. Gradually blend in dry ingredients. Stir in nuts and chocolate chips. Spoon by teaspoonfuls onto baking sheets. Bake at 350 degrees for 10 minutes.

Yield: 3 dozen cookies

A combination of white and semi-sweet chocolate chips could be used.

Raspberry Bars

Crust

1 stick butter, softened
1¼ cups all-purpose flour

⅓ cup packed light brown sugar

Topping

1 cup raspberry preserves
¾ cup all-purpose flour
½ cup packed light brown sugar

4 tablespoons butter, softened
⅛ teaspoon salt
½ teaspoon almond or vanilla extract

Icing

¾ cup powdered sugar

1 tablespoon milk

Crust

Using an electric mixer, blend butter, flour and sugar. Pat into a greased 9x13 inch baking pan. Bake at 350 degrees for 10 to 15 minutes.

Topping

Spread preserves over baked crust. Mix flour, sugar, butter, salt and extract together and crumble over preserves. Bake at 350 degrees for 20 to 25 minutes.

Icing

Combine sugar and milk. Drizzle over cooled bars. Cut into squares.

Yield: 8 to 10 servings

For a different flavor, mix raspberry preserves with 1 cup flaked coconut.

Triple Layered Lemon Bars

Generously submitted to us from Mrs. Debbie Fields

Crust

1 stick butter, softened

¼ cup powdered sugar

1 teaspoon vanilla

1 cup all-purpose flour

Cream Cheese Filling

1 (8 ounce) package cream cheese, softened

1½ cups powdered sugar

1 egg

1 teaspoon lemon extract

Lemon Curd

4 egg yolks

1 tablespoon cornstarch

¾ cup granulated sugar

¾ cup water

¼ cup fresh lemon juice

2 teaspoons lemon zest

2 tablespoons butter, softened

Topping

2 tablespoons powdered sugar

Crust

Cream butter and sugar in a medium bowl with an electric mixer on high speed. Add vanilla and mix until combined. Add flour and mix at low speed until fully incorporated. Press dough evenly into an 8 inch square baking pan. Refrigerate 30 minutes or until firm. Prick crust with a fork. Bake at 325 degrees for 30 minutes or until crust turns golden brown. Cool on a wire rack to room temperature.

Cream Cheese Filling

Beat cream cheese and sugar until smooth in a medium bowl with an electric mixer on high speed. Add egg and lemon extract and beat on medium speed until light and smooth. Cover bowl tightly and refrigerate until chilled.

Lemon Curd

Blend egg yolks with cornstarch and sugar in a medium non-aluminum saucepan. Place over low heat and slowly whisk in water and lemon juice. Increase heat to medium-low and cook, stirring constantly, until mixture thickens enough to coat the back of a spoon. Remove from heat and stir in lemon zest and butter. Cool 10 minutes.

Assembly and Topping

To assemble bars, spread chilled cream cheese filling evenly over cooled crust with a spatula. Spread lemon curd evenly over cream cheese filling. Bake at 325 degrees on center rack of oven for 30 to 40 minutes or until edges begin to turn light golden brown. Cool to room temperature on a rack. Chill in refrigerator for 1 hour before cutting into bars. Dust top of bars with powdered sugar.

Yield: 12 bars

Pat Klinke's Rum Cake

Cake

1 (18 ounce) package yellow butter
   cake mix

½ (3½ ounce) package instant
   vanilla pudding mix

½ cup white rum

½ cup water

½ cup vegetable oil

4 eggs, room temperature

½ cup chopped pecans

Glaze

1 stick butter

1 cup sugar

¼ cup water

¼ cup rum

Cake

In the bowl of an electric mixer, combine cake mix, pudding mix, rum, water and oil and beat until blended. Add eggs, one at a time while beating on medium speed. Continue to beat for 2 minutes. Stir in pecans. Pour batter into a greased and floured 12 cup Bundt pan. Bake at 350 degrees for 35 to 45 minutes or until a tester comes out clean. Leave cake in pan and pierce with a fork. Pour some of glaze over top of hot cake. Cool 30 to 40 minutes. Loosen sides of cake with a spatula and invert onto a serving plate. Drizzle with remaining glaze.

Glaze

Melt butter in a saucepan. Stir in sugar. Add water and bring to a boil. Add rum and continue to boil for 2 minutes.

Yield: 16 to 18 servings

Pat Klinke

The key to any volunteer group's success is the dedication of its members. Le Bonheur Club has been fortunate to have members who genuinely love children and have a great concern for their welfare in our community. One of the most outstanding members of the Le Bonheur Club is Patricia Gardner Klinke, whose dedication to the Club and the Le Bonheur Children's Medical Center is an inspiration to all of us.

Pat joined the Le Bonheur Club in 1970. In those early years, Club members performed many services at the hospital, sewing the children's gowns, making the toys for the Bunny Room and visiting young patients in the hospital. Pat spent thousands of hours happily performing these tasks. Even today, Pat and her son can be found at the hospital on Christmas Day passing out coffee and doughnuts to many grateful parents who find themselves spending their holiday away from home, family and friends.

Pat has always been an active participant in Le Bonheur Club projects, serving as chair on numerous committees. Pat was President of the Club in 1982-1983. During that year, she hand-delivered Gold Tags and Memphis Tags to everyone from President Ronald Reagan to Governor Lamar Alexander in her efforts to increase awareness of our special children's hospital.

One of Pat's many talents is her ability to raise funds for Le Bonheur. Her first year as a Club member, she was named the Club's top fundraiser for the Children's Fund Drive (Gold Tag), the Club's campaign to raise money for the Le Bonheur Children's Medical Center. Over the years, Pat has raised over $500,000 for the hospital and she is still going strong. Many believe that Pat's famous homemade rum cake she takes with her on fundraising calls may help business executives bring out their checkbooks. We do know that many CEO's look forward to Pat's visits, not only for her wonderful stories about Le Bonheur, but also for a slice of cake.

In 1998, the Le Bonheur Club established the Pat Klinke Award to honor her outstanding service to the Club and hospital. Pat was the first recipient of this award. Other outstanding Club volunteers will be added each year. The Pat Klinke Award plaque is displayed in the lobby of the hospital she loves so much. It is a fitting tribute to a very special lady.

Kids

The History of the Red Wagon and Margaret

When most people familiar with Le Bonheur Children's Medical Center think of the hospital, two things come to mind - little red wagons and a cute cartoon character named "Margaret." Little wagons with wooden sides can be seen everywhere at Le Bonheur, from the halls near the patient rooms to the lobby of the hospital. Each of these wagons carries very precious cargo, the littlest patients at Le Bonheur. Since wheelchairs for these young children are not the best or safest way to move these smallest patients, the idea of using little red wagons was born. As a result, parents are able to take their children in comfort and safety throughout the hospital. The patients love the ride as well!

"Margaret," the cute little girl with curly, blonde hair was created in 1984 to represent all the children who come through Le Bonheur's doors. Margaret has been a very popular young lady. Her picture can be found on numerous Le Bonheur brochures, signs pointing the way through the hospital and on coloring pages for the children. For a brief time, the Le Bonheur Club honored Margaret by sewing Margaret dolls for the Bunny Room and selling Margaret candy. Margaret is so well known in the community that she has become one of the most famous "little girls" in town.

Circus Cake

1 cup unpopped popcorn, or
    1 (3½ ounce) bag microwave
    popcorn
1 (16 ounce) package plain candy
    coated chocolate pieces

1 (16 ounce) package candy coated
    chocolate pieces with peanuts
1 (16 ounce) jar dry roasted peanuts
1 (10 ounce) package jumbo
    marshmallows
4 tablespoons margarine

Pop popcorn, cool and remove all unpopped kernels. Combine popped popcorn, candy and peanuts in a large bowl. Melt marshmallows with margarine and stir until smooth. Pour marshmallow mixture over popcorn mixture and mix well. Press mixture firmly into a greased Bundt pan. Let stand for several hours or overnight. Loosen cake from edge of pan with a knife before removing. Use an electric knife to slice for best results.

Yield: 10 to 12 servings

For an innovative Christmas gift, wrap this cake in green cellophane and red ribbon to give to your friends. You can substitute raisins for the peanuts.

Because my sweet neighbor's grandchildren lived far away, she indulged my children with this cake. It has become a family "favorite."

Everybody's Favorite Chocolate Chip Cake

1 (18 ounce) package yellow butter cake mix

1 (3 ounce) package instant vanilla pudding

1 cup vegetable oil

1 cup milk

4 eggs

1 (6 ounce) package chocolate chips

1 (4 ounce) bar German chocolate, finely grated

Beat together cake mix, pudding, oil and milk with an electric mixer. Add eggs, one at a time, beating after each addition. Use a spoon to stir in chocolate chips and grated chocolate. Pour batter into a greased and floured Bundt pan. Bake at 350 degrees for 1 hour. Cool 10 minutes in pan before inverting onto a serving plate.

Yield: 10 to 12 servings

I made this strawberry ice cream pie with strawberry sauce for my daughter's Barbie party. As a teenager, she created a mint chocolate chip pie with hot fudge sauce and crushed Oreos for her girlfriends who came for a slumber party. This pie can be adapted to any taste and will put a smile on anyone's face.

Design Your Own Pie

22 chocolate sandwich cookies, broken into pieces

4 tablespoons unsalted butter, melted

1 quart ice cream, flavor of your choice, slightly softened

1 cup sundae topping, flavor of your choice

Combine cookie pieces and melted butter in a food processor. Process until crumbs are ground fine and mixture forms moist clumps. Press mixture into a 9 inch metal pie plate. Freeze 15 minutes. Spoon ice cream into crust, mounding the center. Freeze 30 minutes or until ice cream is firm. Spread topping over ice cream, covering completely. Freeze 30 minutes or until topping is firm. Pie can be prepared, covered and frozen up to 2 days ahead. When ready to serve, let stand 5 to 10 minutes at room temperature to make cutting easier.

Yield: 8 to 10 servings

Chocolate Chip
and Peanut Butter Pie

Crust

1½ cups chocolate graham cracker
  crumbs

½ cup sugar

4 tablespoons butter, melted

Filling

½ cup heavy cream

8 ounces semi-sweet chocolate
  squares, cut up

1 (8 ounce) package cream cheese,
  softened

1 cup powdered sugar

¾ cup creamy peanut butter

1 cup heavy cream

1 cup semi-sweet mini chocolate
  chips

Crust

Combine cracker crumbs, sugar and butter and press firmly into the bottom and up the sides of a 9 inch springform pan. Freeze while preparing filling.

Filling

Combine ½ cup heavy cream and chocolate squares in a small glass bowl. Microwave 1 to 1½ minutes or until chocolate melts and mixture is smooth; cool. Spread half of chocolate mixture over crust. Freeze until set.

Meanwhile, beat cream cheese, powdered sugar and peanut butter in a medium bowl for 1 to 1½ minutes or until blended and fluffy. Whip 1 cup heavy cream until stiff. Add half of whipped cream to peanut butter mixture and beat until well mixed. Fold in remaining whipped cream and mini chocolate chips. Spread filling evenly over frozen mixture. Freeze 30 minutes. Top with remaining chocolate mixture, cover and freeze 6 hours or until frozen.

Yield: 8 to 10 servings

To engage your children, approach food with enthusiasm and interest. Never say, "you won't like it." Discuss the flavor and texture to give kids a more conscious experience of eating.

Scalded Milk

To scald milk, cook
1 cup for 2 to
2½ minutes, stirring
one time each
minute.

Rolled Cinnamon Bread

1 (¼ ounce) package active dry yeast

¼ cup warm water
   (115 to 120 degrees)

½ cup sugar

6 tablespoons butter, softened

½ teaspoon salt

1 cup milk

2 cups all-purpose flour

1 egg

3 cups all-purpose flour

Softened butter to spread on dough

1 tablespoon cinnamon

1 cup sugar

2 tablespoons butter, melted

Mix yeast and warm water; set aside. Combine ½ cup sugar, 6 tablespoons butter and salt. Scald milk by bringing just to a boil, then pour over sugar mixture. Cool to lukewarm. Add 2 cups flour, egg and yeast mixture. Incorporate 3 cups flour until dough pulls from sides of bowl. Turn dough out onto a floured surface and cover with a bowl. Let dough rest 10 minutes. Knead dough until smooth and elastic. Let rise 1 to 2 hours or until doubled. Punch down dough and divide in half. Roll out each half into a 12x7 inch, ¼ inch thick rectangle. Spread butter over dough. Combine cinnamon and 1 cup sugar and sprinkle over rectangles. Roll up rectangles jelly roll fashion to make 2 loaves. Carefully place loaves on a greased baking sheet, keeping loaves level during transfer so cinnamon sugar does not spill out. Let rise for about 30 minutes. Brush top of loaves with 2 tablespoons melted butter. Bake at 375 degrees for 20 to 25 minutes.

Yield: 2 loaves

Sunshine Muffins

1 (18 ounce) package lemon
    supreme cake mix
1 (3¾ ounce) package lemon instant
    pudding
½ cup vegetable oil

1 cup buttermilk
4 eggs
1¼ cups powdered sugar, sifted
¾ teaspoon vanilla
5 tablespoons orange juice

Combine cake mix, pudding, oil, buttermilk and eggs and mix well. Pour batter into greased mini muffin cups, filling two-thirds full. Bake at 350 degrees for 10 minutes. Cool slightly. Meanwhile, make a glaze by blending powdered sugar, vanilla and orange juice. Dip warm muffins into glaze. Cool completely before serving.

Yield: 36 mini muffins

These are perfect for a Sunday morning breakfast or little girls' tea party. Garnish platter with pansy petals.

E. T. Bars

1 (13½ ounce) package graham
    crackers, finely crushed
1 (16 ounce) package powdered
    sugar

3 cups creamy peanut butter
    (28 ounces)
1½ sticks margarine, melted
1 (12 ounce) package chocolate chips,
    melted

Combine cracker crumbs and sugar in a large bowl. Add peanut butter and mix well. Stir in melted margarine. Press mixture into a 10x15 inch baking sheet. Spread melted chocolate over cracker crust. Refrigerate until set. Let stand at room temperature for a while before cutting into squares; cutting bars cold may cause them to crack. Cut bars can be frozen.

Yield: 15 to 20 servings

Easy-Treat Bars

My son "phones home" to be sure that these are ready when he arrives from college.

Involve children as much as possible in the cooking process. If they are involved in the preparation, they will be more likely to eat the dish. Children are learning, while having fun!

Sweet Monkey Bread

My mother made this for my slumber parties and now I am making it for my children's slumber parties.

Bread

½ cup granulated sugar

⅓ cup packed light brown sugar

1 tablespoon cinnamon

4 (10 ounce) cans country or buttermilk style refrigerated biscuits

Sauce

1½ sticks butter

½ cup granulated sugar

½ cup packed light brown sugar

Bread

Combine sugars and cinnamon in a plastic bag. Cut each biscuit into quarters. Working in batches of ten to twelve at a time, drop biscuit pieces into plastic bag and shake to coat. Place coated pieces in a greased tube or Bundt pan.

Sauce

Melt butter in a small saucepan. Stir in sugars and cook over medium heat for 5 to 10 minutes or until syrupy. Pour sauce over biscuits. Bake at 350 degrees for 30 minutes or until top is browned.

Yield: 8 to 10 servings

Choco-Scotch Surprises

1 (6 ounce) package semi-sweet chocolate chips

1 (6 ounce) package butterscotch chips

2 tablespoons creamy peanut butter

1 cup cocktail peanuts

1½ cups chow mein noodles, broken into ½ inch pieces

Melt chocolate and butterscotch chips in the top of a double boiler. Stir in peanut butter. Add peanuts and noodles and mix. Cool slightly in refrigerator, but not too long. Drop mixture by teaspoonfuls onto an ungreased baking sheet. Refrigerate until firm.

Yield: 36 surprises

Bernard's Big Cookie

2 sticks butter, softened

¾ cup creamy peanut butter

1 cup granulated sugar

1 cup packed brown sugar

2 eggs

1½ cups all-purpose flour

1 teaspoon baking soda

¾ teaspoon salt

1½ cups dry quick oats

¾ cup chocolate chips

¼ cup plain candy coated chocolate pieces

½ cup plain candy coated chocolate pieces

Cream butter, peanut butter and sugars until light and fluffy. Beat in eggs. In a separate bowl, mix together flour, baking soda and salt. Add flour mixture to creamed mixture and blend well. Stir in oats, chocolate chips and ¼ cup candy pieces. Divide dough in half. Spread each half onto a foil-lined and lightly greased 12 inch pizza pan. Spread dough to within an inch of the edge of pan. Sprinkle each cookie with ¼ cup candy pieces. Bake at 325 degrees for 20 to 22 minutes or until lightly golden brown. Cool 10 minutes in pans. Gently remove each cookie with foil liner to a wire rack. Cool completely and remove foil.

Yield: 2 giant cookies

Bernard has been a patient at Le Bonheur Children's Medical Center since March 18, 1991. During that time, Bernard has been diagnosed with several of the diseases from which many of his young fellow patients also suffer. For example, he has a heart defect, cystic fibrosis, sickle cell, asthma, epilepsy, diabetes, and kidney disease. And, of course, at first glance one can see that he suffers from a rare skin disease, which has turned his skin green. And, it is evident that he has an even rarer age disordering disease called the "Peter Pan Syndrome." It seems that every year Bernard continues to turn four years old. Indeed, Bernard is a unique, one-of-a-kind patient, friend and comforter to each child (and parent) he meets.

This is a perfect edible activity for Easter. Carry them home in a hand decorated basket.

Chocolate Dipped Easter Edibles

1 stick butter, softened
1 teaspoon vanilla
1 teaspoon salt

⅔ cup sweetened condensed milk
6 cups sifted powdered sugar
2 cups shaved bark chocolate coating

Cream butter, vanilla and salt in a medium bowl. Blend in milk until smooth. Gradually add sugar, blending after each addition, and adding until mixture becomes very thick. Turn mixture onto a clean surface and carefully knead in any remaining sugar. Continue to knead until mixture is smooth and no longer sticky. Mold mixture into walnut-sized egg shapes. Place egg shapes on a wax paper-lined baking sheet. Refrigerate several hours. Melt chocolate in the top of a double boiler, stirring with a whisk until blended. Remove from heat. Dip egg shapes into chocolate using a double pronged kitchen fork. Let excess chocolate drip off and return eggs to wax paper. Let chocolate harden before adding decorations.

Yield: 40 decorated eggs suitable for eating

Buckeyes

1 stick butter, softened
1 (16 ounce) package powdered
    sugar
1 teaspoon vanilla

1 (12 ounce) jar creamy peanut
    butter
1 (12 ounce) bag semi-sweet
    chocolate chips

Cream butter and sugar in a large bowl. Add vanilla and peanut butter and mix until well blended. Roll mixture into 1 inch balls and place on a wax paper-lined baking sheet. Refrigerate at least 30 minutes. Melt chocolate in the top of a double boiler. Using a toothpick, dip each ball into chocolate, leaving a small area around toothpick without chocolate so to resemble a buckeye. Return balls to wax paper and close hole left by the toothpick. Refrigerate until chocolate sets. Store in a covered container in the refrigerator or freezer.

Yield: 60 buckeyes

Fun Fruit Freezes

1 cup plain yogurt

½ cup chopped fruit, such as apples, bananas, blueberries, peaches, pineapple, plums or pears

Combine yogurt and fruit of choice in a blender. Whip 1 minute. Pour mixture into freezer pop molds, paper cups or ice cube trays. Insert a stick and freeze at least 4 hours.

Yield: 3 servings

Peanut Butter Play Dough

1 cup peanut butter

1 cup white corn syrup or honey

1¼ cups powdered milk

1¼ cups powdered sugar

Combine peanut butter, corn syrup, milk and sugar together until blended. Form into a ball. After playing with it, the dough can be eaten.

Yield: One play dough ball suitable for eating

"No Bake" Chocolate Oatmeal Cookies

1½ sticks butter

1 tablespoon cocoa

2 cups sugar

½ cup evaporated milk

½ cup creamy peanut butter

3 cups dry old-fashioned oats

1 teaspoon vanilla

Combine butter, cocoa, sugar and milk in a saucepan. Bring to a boil. Add peanut butter, oats and vanilla. Mix well and remove from heat. Drop by spoonfuls onto greased wax paper; cool.

Yield: 48 cookies

Take your kids to the farmer's market to buy fresh fruit. Before you go, make a list of as many colors as they can come up with. At the market, search for fruit or vegetables that match the colors. Keep track of the colors from season to season.

Blonde Rocky Road Candy

1 pound vanilla flavored candy coating
½ cup creamy peanut butter

1½ cups mini marshmallows
1½ cups unsalted peanuts
1½ cups crispy rice cereal

Melt candy coating in the top of a double boiler. Add peanut butter and stir until smooth. Remove from heat. Add marshmallows, peanuts and cereal and stir until coated. Drop by teaspoonfuls onto wax paper. Cool.

Yield: about 50 pieces

Space Invaders

These are guaranteed to provide energy for any space attack!

Maraschino cherries
Grape juice
Ginger ale

Orange slices
Pineapple chunks
Empty ice cube trays

Place a maraschino cherry in each section of an empty ice cube tray. Fill each section with grape juice, covering the cherry. Freeze about 2 hours to make a space cube. Fill a tall glass with space cubes. Pour ginger ale (space juice) over cubes. Real space juice should bubble and fizz. Spear a toothpick through an orange slice, a cherry and a pineapple chunk, making a saber. Float the saber on top of the space invader and serve.

Yield: varies

Barbi-Qute Cups

1 pound ground beef
½ cup barbecue sauce
1 tablespoon onion, minced
1 (10 count) can refrigerated biscuits

10 thin onion slices
10 thin tomato slices
½ cup Cheddar cheese, shredded

This is a great make ahead alternative to pizza or hot dogs for your daughter's Barbie birthday party.

Brown beef in a skillet; drain. Add barbecue sauce and onions. Cover and simmer 5 minutes. Separate biscuits and press into bottom and up sides of lightly greased muffin tins. Place an onion slice and a tomato slice in the bottom of each cup. Spoon in meat mixture to fill cups. Sprinkle with cheese. Bake at 400 degrees for 10 to 12 minutes.

Yield: 10 cups

Homemade biscuits work even better.

Sparkling Cranberry Punch

1 cup cranberry juice
1 (3 ounce) package raspberry
  gelatin
2 cups cranberry juice

1 (6 ounce) can frozen lemonade
  concentrate, thawed
1 (2 liter) bottle lemon-lime soda,
  well chilled

Heat 1 cup cranberry juice until almost boiling. Add gelatin and stir until dissolved. Add 2 cups cranberry juice and lemonade concentrate. Stir very well. Just before serving, stir in soda. Serve over ice.

Yield: 20 to 25 servings

Key Elements

Ingredient Equivalents

Apples 1 pound = 3 medium or 3 cups sliced

Bananas 1 pound = 3 medium or 1½ cups mashed

Beans 1 cup dry = 2 to 2½ cups cooked

Blueberries 1 pint = 3 cups

Bread crumbs ½ cup fresh = 1 slice bread with crust

Buttermilk 1 cup = 1 tablespoon vinegar or lemon juice, plus enough milk to equal 1 cup. Let stand 5 minutes to thicken or use 1 cup plain yogurt.

Celery 1 medium-size bunch = 4 cups chopped

Cheese 4 ounces = 1 cup shredded

Chicken 2½ to 3 pounds = 2½ cups diced cooked meat

Chocolate chips 6 ounce package = 1 cup

Cocoa 8 ounce can unsweetened = 2 cups

Cornmeal 1 cup raw = 4 cups cooked

Couscous 1 cup raw = 2½ cups cooked

Cranberries 12 ounce bag = 3 cups

Cream 1 cup heavy = 2 cups whipped

Cream cheese 8 ounce package = 1 cup

Egg whites 1 large = 2 tablespoons

Egg yolks 1 large = 1½ tablespoons

Flour 1 pound all-purpose = 3½ cups

Gingersnaps 15 cookies = 1 cup crumbs

Graham crackers 7 whole crackers = 1 cup crumbs

Hominy grits 1 cup = 4½ cups cooked

Lemon 1 medium = 3 tablespoons juice and 1 tablespoon zest

Lentils 1 cup = 2½ cups cooked

Macaroni, elbow 1 cup = 2 cups cooked

Milk, condensed 14 ounce can = 1¼ cups

Milk, evaporated 5 ounce can = ⅔ cup

Noodles 8 ounce uncooked medium = 4 cups cooked

Nuts 1 cup chopped = 3 to 4 ounces

Oats 1 cup quick raw = 2 cups cooked

Onion 1 large = 1 cup chopped

Orange 1 medium = ⅓ to ½ cup juice and 2 tablespoons zest

Peaches 1 pound = 3 medium or 2½ cups sliced

Pears 1 pound = 3 medium or 2¼ cups sliced

Peppers 1 large bell = about 1 cup chopped

Pineapple 1 large = about 4 cups cubed

Popcorn ¼ cup unpopped = about 4 cups popped

Potatoes 1 pound all-purpose = about 3 cups medium or 3 cups sliced or 2 cups mashed

Rice 1 cup uncooked regular = about 3 cups cooked; 1 cup uncooked instant = 2 cups cooked

Saltine crackers 28 squares = 1 cup crumbs

Shortening 1 pound = 2½ cups

Spaghetti 8 ounces uncooked = 4 cups cooked

Strawberries 1 pint = 3¼ cups whole or 2¼ cups sliced

Sugar 1 pound confectioners' = 3¾ cups; 1 pound granulated = 2½ cups; 1 pound brown = 2¼ cups packed

Tomatoes 1 pound = 3 medium

Vanilla wafers 22 cookies = 1 cup crumbs

Yeast 1 package active dry = 2½ teaspoons

Estimating Food For A Crowd

When you serve twelve guests, you want to get the right amount of food. Amounts allow for two modest servings each and can be halved for six guests.

FOOD	TOTAL AMOUNT NEEDED
BEEF	
London Broil	10 pounds
Rib-Eye roast, boneless	6 pounds
Tenderloin or filet mignon steaks	6 pounds
CHICKEN	
Breasts, bone-in	24 medium breasts
Breasts, boneless	6 pounds
Whole	Six 3 pound broilers
LAMB	
Leg of Lamb, bone-in	2 legs, 6 pounds each
Rack of Lamb	6 racks
PORK	
Center-cut loin or chops, boneless	6 pounds
Half-ham, bone-in	8 pounds
Ham, boneless	6 pounds
Spare ribs	24 pounds
Tenderloin	6 pounds
SEAFOOD	
Clams, mussels, oysters or shrimp, fresh	144 to 180 pieces
Fish, fresh filets or steaks	4 to 6 pounds
Fish, fresh whole	9 to 12 pounds
Scallops, raw	3 to 5 pounds
Shrimp, crabmeat or lobster meat, cooked	3 to 5 pounds
TURKEY	
Whole	18 to 20 pounds

Cooking Fish

Thin fillets are no more than ½ inch thick. These include sole, haddock, snapper, catfish and flounder.

Thick fillets average about 1½ inch thick. Cod, center cuts of salmon, orange roughy and grouper are thick fillets.

Steaks are usually 1 inch thick and include swordfish, tuna, mahi mahi and salmon.

	THIN FILLETS	THICK FILLETS	STEAKS
Broil	2 to 6 minutes; place 4 to 6 inches from broiler	10 minutes per 1 inch; place 4 to 6 inches from broiler	10 minutes per 1 inch; place very close to broiler
Grill	3 to 5 minutes; Medium-hot fire	5 to 7 minutes; medium-hot fire	5 to 7 minutes; hot fire
Roast	About 6 minutes; 450 degrees	10 minutes per 1 inch; 450 degrees	10 minutes per 1 inch; 450 degrees
Sauté/Sear	4 to 5 minutes; Medium-high heat	8 to 10 minutes; medium-high heat	8 to 10 minutes; high heat

Special Thanks

The Le Bonheur Club Cookbook Committee appreciates the families who contributed their child's compelling patient stories about their stay at Le Bonheur Children's Medical Center. By utilizing their stories, we hope to illustrate the "miracles" that occur in the hospital and provide public awareness of the widespread services that are available. We are fortunate to have a children's hospital of this caliber in our area.

The Le Bonheur Club Cookbook Committee thanks Kavanaugh Casey, Volunteer Manager of Development with the hospital, for providing us with the wonderful patient stories.

Recipe Contributors and Testers

Key Ingredients gratefully acknowledges the following individuals who shared their time-tested recipes, new classics, most dearly held secrets and food memories with us. Our sincere gratitude to the individuals and their families who spent countless hours and dollars testing and evaluating the recipes for *Key Ingredients*, ensuring that our recipes are fabulous. Many thanks to those who opened their homes for testing parties. We hope that we have not inadvertently overlooked any contributors.

Patti Adams	Jackie Smith Betz	Beverly Carrick	J.J. Doughtie
Allison Amick	Lynda Biggs	Betty Cartwright	Lana Dowdy
Gloria Andereck	Barbara Billions	Shari Caruthers	Susan Duke
Kay Anderson	Marilyn Blackmon	Kavanaugh Casey	Debbie Edmundson
Marilynn Andrews	Julian Boyd	Carol Clark	Claudia Efird
Pat Anthony	Marilyn Boyd	Sue Clark	June Elliott
Shelley Arthur	Linda Brawner	Linda Coleman	Anne Farst
Ann Bailey	Betty Brendel	Debbie Compton	Becky Fiedler
Debbie Baker	Paula Brown	Dinny Costen	Debbie Fields
Gauger Barb	Betty Buchanan	Sammy Crawford	Debra Flanary
Ellen Barkley	Lindley Buchas	Jill Crocker	Mary Lawrence Flinn
Nancy Barnett	Mary Buchas	Malise Culpepper	Donna Flinn
Caroline Bartusch	Anita Burkett	Lucy Cummings	Debbie Florendo
Vici Bates	Judy Burkett	Jennifer Davenport	Mary Ann Ford
Krista Beaver	Paula Buttross	Buddy Dearman	Ann Fordice
Joey Beckford	Pattie Cabrera	Laura Dearman	Debbi Freeburg
Sarah Belenchia	Janet Canale	Sue Dewald	Gail French
Laurie Benton	Beth Carr	Sue Dodd	Missy Fuehrer

Lea Fyfe
Cindy Gambrell
Anne Leigh Garrett
Kim Gibson
Jeanne Good
Jean Gorham
Janine Gorline
Susan Graf
Kathy Greene
Betty Griffin
Sylvia Griffin
Carolyn Grizzard
Richard Gruenewald
Ansley Guenther
Ann Gusmus
Donna Guthrie
Helen Hanks
Anita Harris
Ann Clark Harris
Leigh Harwell
Diane Hawkins
Lauren Hendrix
Denise Henning
Suzanne Hieserman
Joanna Higdon
Roger Hill
Mary Hines
Cheryl Hobbs
Jane Hobson
Jane Holmgrain
Clara Dean Hope
Kathy Horner
Sherry Hudson
Brenda Hughes
Marcia Hughes
Jan Hume
Julie Isaacson
Margaret Jabbour
Mary Jackson
Ila Johnson
Jane D. Jones
Reba Jones

Sirella Joyner
Lauren Keel
Nancy Kelley
Louise Kelley
Eileen Keogh
Pat Klinke
Fini Koerner
Anne Krieg
Jennifer Kruchten
Lisa Lendermon
Susan Liddon
Tina Liollio
Bernice Lutterow
Kim MacQueen
Nancy Malmo
Mary Marconi
Carol Martin
Eloise Mays
Helen McCaskill
Judy McCullough
Margaret McDaniel
Michele McDonagh
Jamie McDonnell
Cynthia McElhaney
Anne McGaha
Tina McKelvy
Penne McWaters
Elizabeth Mednikow
Barbie Meloni
Sarah Menkel
Kerry Miller
Sandra Miller
Lala Miller
Shawn Miller
Laurie Monypeny
Sandi Morris
Nancy Morris
Kate Morrison
Donna Mulhern
Christy Muller
Courtney Murray
Jerra Myers

Linda Mynatt
Jane Nall
Vicki Nelson
Kathleen Norfleet
Kathy Owens
Kathy Page
Kerry Palmtree
Julie Pashcall
Barbara Pera
Phil Phalinsky
Janet Pinkley Phillips
Bebe Pinkley
Kim Pitts
Donna Platt
Martha Podesta
Suzanne Preston
Leslie Pretsch
Susan Price
Beth Price
Debbie Pryor
Anna Grace Quinn
Joan Ramier
Brett Ray
Juloy Raymer
Susan Razzouk
Donna Rhodes
Barbara Rideout
Vicki Riggs
Annie Robbins
Margaret Roberts
Lindy Ruffin
Suellyn Ruffin
Melinda Russell
Rita Rutherford
Julia Rutland
Jennie Sampson
Camille Schaeffer
Quinn Scott
Evelyn Scott
Jill Seabrook
Joyce Sellers
Rosemary Shaw

Susan Simpson
Maida Pearson Smith
Judy Sossaman
Beth Sousoulas
Sophie Sousoulas
Hollye Spiotta
Dusty Stem
Kitty Stimson
Missy Stockstill
Lucy Strong
Carol Strong
Whitney Strong
Meg Sutherland
Julie Szovati
Nancy Tashie
Margaret Anne Taylor
Camille Thompson
Jan Thompson
Ann Marie Thrasher
Jane Tribble
Jean Tuggle
Lida Utkov
Beth Vick
Sharon Voehringer
Arlene Wade
Carol Wade
Gaye S. Wagner
Alyce Waller
Christy Watridge
Karen Watson
Kate Weathersby
Marion Weaver
Mike Webster
Beth Whitsitt
Linda Wilson
Susan Wilson
Darcy Winters
Martha Witherspoon
Mary Lou Woods
Jane Work
Jennifer Wunderlich
Carol Ann Zelley

Index

𝒟

E

F

G

O

P

V

VEAL

Z

ZUCCHINI (*also see Squash*)

Key Ingredients

OPENING DOORS TO HOURS OF HAPPINESS

 **Le Bonheur** Children's Medical Center

Le Bonheur Club, Inc.
1047 Cresthaven
Memphis, Tennessee 38119
(901) 682-9905
www.lebonheurclub.org

Please send me:

Key Ingredients Cookbook   @ $23.95 each   Quantity _____ $ _____

Postage & Handling for first book   @ $ 5.00 $ _____

Each additional book to same address   @ $ 2.00 $ _____

                                                               Total Enclosed $ _____

Ship to:

Name _____ Address _____

City _____ State _____ Zip Code _____

Telephone _____ e-mail _____

Make checks payable to Le Bonheur Club Cookbook

Charge to   ❏ VISA   ❏ MasterCard   Signature _____

Account Number _____ Expiration Date _____

Proceeds from *Key Ingredients* will benefit the Le Bonheur Children's Medical Center.
Thank you for your order.

- -

Key Ingredients

OPENING DOORS TO HOURS OF HAPPINESS

Le Bonheur Children's Medical Center

Le Bonheur Club, Inc.
1047 Cresthaven
Memphis, Tennessee 38119
(901) 682-9905
www.lebonheurclub.org

Please send me:

Key Ingredients Cookbook   @ $23.95 each   Quantity _____ $ _____

Postage & Handling for first book   @ $ 5.00 $ _____

Each additional book to same address   @ $ 2.00 $ _____

                                                               Total Enclosed $ _____

Ship to:

Name _____ Address _____

City _____ State _____ Zip Code _____

Telephone _____ e-mail _____

Make checks payable to Le Bonheur Club Cookbook

Charge to   ❏ VISA   ❏ MasterCard   Signature _____

Account Number _____ Expiration Date _____

Proceeds from *Key Ingredients* will benefit the Le Bonheur Children's Medical Center.
Thank you for your order.